D1188125

*The Teacher
and Administrative Relationships
in School Systems*

James E. Heald
Samuel A. Moore, II

Michigan State University

The *TEACHER* and *ADMINISTRATIVE* *RELATIONSHIPS* in *SCHOOL SYSTEMS*

THE MACMILLAN COMPANY, *New York*
COLLIER-MACMILLAN LIMITED, *London*

Library of Congress catalog card number: 68–10461

THE MACMILLAN COMPANY, NEW YORK
COLLIER-MACMILLAN CANADA, LTD., TORONTO, ONTARIO

PRINTED IN THE UNITED STATES OF AMERICA

Contents

Introduction

The study of the administration of American public
school systems is normally a function of graduate schools. Many
persons enter the teaching profession with only a little understanding of how the system of their employment is administered.
Teacher preparation programs which deny teachers even cursory
understanding of the relationship between administrative responsibilities and teaching responsibilities do an injustice to teachers.
A lack of understanding of the ways in which all components—
teachers, administrators, and boards of education—contribute to
the effectiveness of public school systems drives divisive wedges
between these various groups.

The Teacher and Administrative Relationships in School Systems
was designed primarily for the teacher and the inexperienced administrator. Foreign students and others not familiar with the
manner in which American public schools are controlled, governed,
and administered should also find the approach taken in the text
appropriate to understanding school systems operations. Although
many books exist for the professional administrator, very few have
been written *about* administration for teachers and those who are
not experienced in administering schools or school systems. This
book deals with the following questions: "How are school systems
run?"; "Where do I as a teaching component fit in the total operation?"; "What kind of interactions should I expect?"; and "How
can I participate in changing the system?" These questions require
an approach different from that normally taken in texts for administrators.

To help teachers understand how public schools are administered,
the authors have used a systems analysis technique which requires
that attention be given to the components of educational systems,
the nature of their goal-directed interactions, and the environments

of the interactions. The discussion therefore focuses upon boards of education, administrators, teachers, and students as the components comprising the system; upon the interactions which take place in personnel processes, supervision, curriculum development, policy formulations, budget preparations, school-building programs, and negotiations processes; and upon the social, legal, economic, and political environments of the interactions. Throughout the text the focus has remained upon how the goals of American public school systems serve as the principal determinants of organizational directions and how these goals contribute to the shaping of human interactions.

Systems Analysis

The tremendous complex of ideas, organizations, and purposes which characterizes American schools appears to be almost imponderable. What can we learn from their similarities? How can we grapple with their diversity? How can the imponderable be reduced to a size small enough to study?

Systems analysis techniques offer a particular method of study which holds promise for helping teachers understand the administrative structure and understand their own role in promoting the ends of educational organizations.

DEFINITIONS

Thousands of times in his professional life a teacher will make reference to his "school system." Seldom, however, does he pause to develop an image of the term *system*. A system is defined by Webster as "a regularly interacting or interdependent group of items forming a unified whole." While Webster's definition is helpful in portraying an image of a system, it is not particularly useful to the student seeking a construct for his study of teacher-administrative relationships.

Better definitions, capable of directing an inquiry, come from the fields of biology and engineering. To people from both of the disciplines, a system is *a series of essential components whose functions are coordinated for the purpose of achieving the goals of the organismic whole*. Such a definition adds purpose to the functioning of component parts and supplies the student with the opportunity to view the system as a whole in terms of its operating parts.

"Systems analysis" as a concept began with industrial engineers concerned with systems composed of men and machines. Charged with making industrial production as efficient as possible, the engineer established a method of study designed to provide knowledge about the interaction of man and machine—the components. His purpose was to redesign the relationships between man and man, between man and machine, or between machine and machine, so that efficient production could be facilitated. In its simplest form, when the system's components were men and machines, manufacturing was the interaction, and profitable production was the goal of the company—the organismic whole. The engineer thus found himself analyzing the goal contribution of components whose interaction required coordination; hence, the term *systems analysis* was born.

MODEL SYSTEMS

To understand more completely the requirements of systems analysis techniques and of the general nature of systems, it seems appropriate to review two familiar systems.

The first model—the circulatory system—is drawn from the field of biology. In relationship to our definition, the circulatory system would seem to qualify in the following ways: The circulatory system is composed of essential components—heart, arteries, veins, and capillaries—and the components are coordinated to accomplish the goals of the organismic whole: to provide oxygen, nutrients, and other substances and to remove waste materials from each body cell.

The second model—the ignition system—is drawn from electrical engineering. Here too we find a system composed of component parts—battery, coil, spark plugs, generator, distributor, and connecting wire—with each of the elements coordinated to accomplish the goal for which the system was designed: to provide an electrical spark at the appropriate moment to ignite vaporized gasoline within the individual cylinders.

To the physician charged with correcting a malfunctioning circulatory system and the electrical engineer trying to improve the ignition system, the task is viewed in a somewhat similar manner. Systems analysis techniques require that the analyst carefully study and understand the *nature* and *function* of each component, that he understand the contribution of each component to *goal* accomplishment, and that he understand the manner in which the components have been *coordinated*.

How much is enough? To what depth must we study? In each of the model systems, varying degrees of analytical competence are possible. The nurse or the first-year medical student is not likely to be as competent as the cardiologist or hematologist in analyzing the circulatory system. Likewise, the garage mechanic and the electrical engineer represent degrees of competence in understanding the ignition system. As students of *American school systems*, should we stop at knowing the names of the four cavities of the heart or should we continue our study to the point of understanding the histology of the minutest capillary tissue? Should we stop at knowing the name of the spark plug or must we understand the chemical relationship between lead and sulfuric acid in our storage batteries?

As social systems, public school systems are exceedingly complex, and they permit each student the opportunity to delve in as much depth as he desires. To the teacher who serves time in a job within the system while awaiting the ship of his first love to arrive, practically no study is undertaken or required. To those seeking professional status, the study of school systems will be a lifelong pursuit in which the educator seeks to understand and improve the coordinated relationships which must exist between the components of the system.

Improved understanding should lead to improved practice; improved practice should include improved coordination; and improved coordination holds promise for mobilizing component strength toward the accomplishment of educational goals.

*The Teacher
and Administrative Relationships
in School Systems*

part I

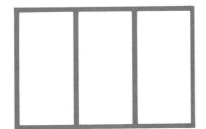

American School Systems

chapter 1

◼ *Studying American Public School Systems*

The teacher, new or old, embarking upon the study of teacher-administrative relationships soon comes to realize that he is only partially equipped for the undertaking. Teacher education and teaching experience touch the area of administration in only the most tangential ways. To understand the administrator and his role requires that the teacher enter more fully into his discipline to partake, at least in part, of his joys and his disappointments, his duties and his responsibilities, his values and his ethics.

Understanding, however, is not the sole justification for the study of administration by the nonadministrator. While administrators might welcome sympathy and empathy which can arise from understanding, what they more desperately need are faculties committed to the goals of education. Out of commitment arise new teacher-administrative relationships more capable of furthering higher goal accomplishment.

To launch a study of *what is* and to induce *what might be* in the relationships between teachers and administrators, it is appropriate to revisit the arena where the teamwork, and sometimes the antagonism, takes place—the public schools of America. How teachers and the administrators, the two major elements for consideration, ultimately choose to relate within the systems will in large measure determine the course of public education.

Characteristics of American Public Schools

DIVERSITY

Unlike countries possessing central ministries of education, the public schools of the United States exhibit great differences one from another. As an example, consider the organizational patterns of various school districts. In terms of grade-level organizations, districts advertise K–12, 6–3–3, K–8, 9–12, K–6–6, and so on as their pattern of organization.

The grouping of grade levels for administrative purposes takes even more unusual turns in such districts as Novi and Melbourne, Fla. The Novi district will ultimately be developed to include educational programs from kindergarten through college degrees at the graduate level. On the other hand, the high school at Melbourne is proud of the fact that it has *no* grade levels for students to methodically pass through.

Organizational patterns based on geography are just as diverse. Throughout the land, the political unit of educational authority varies with the organizing authority. In Delaware, the state is the unit of organization; in Utah, the county-wide district is common; in Illinois, the township is still the unit for many high school districts; city boundaries are the units in the metropolitan areas of many states; and throughout the country, urban and rural districts have boundary lines to delight the gerrymanderer.

Another area which prevents the development of a single discussion to cover American public schools is the difference in purposes between and among schools and school districts. There are American public schools devoted to training young people to enter various trades; others are concerned with preparing young persons for college and university experiences; and still others accept a terminal, general education as their fundamental *raison d'être*. Even the so-called comprehensive high schools will admit that because a large segment of its population is headed in a single direction its purpose becomes more narrow and provincial than the term "comprehensive" would imply.

Diversity is also present in the manner in which schools are financially supported. In some states, large proportions of local educational costs are borne by the state treasury through their allocations to local districts. At the other extreme are local districts in some states which receive little if any support from the state level.

The money which the states have to distribute may come from income taxes, sales taxes, personal property taxes, excise taxes, nuisance taxes, or other statewide tax sources. In some states, local need as measured by enrollments is the basis for distribution; in others, financial ability, as measured by taxable wealth, is the distributional basis; in still other states, effort, as measured by the degree of local taxation, is a basis for distribution. The weight assigned to various distributional factors varies in fifty ways among the fifty states.

Certainly no uniformity exists among schools with regard to the student bodies being served. The students in a reservation school are different from those in a large city slum area. The student population of a school in the rural south bears little similarity to that of a posh, eastern suburban district. Likewise, a midwestern farm community has a student body which differs significantly from that found in a western city.

American schools are also different in terms of community expectation. The communities just mentioned exhibit expectations which vary according to community educational, social, and economic level. Within even similar kinds of communities, there is variance in parental aspiration and in the reality of expectations which parents hold for their schools.

SIMILARITY

The study of schools within this country is not entirely thwarted by unending diversity. American public schools do have some degrees of similarity which are worthy of note.

To varying extents, all public schools of the United States commit themselves to a program of free public education. Freedom from tuition costs through the twelfth grade is the pattern in every state, with the trend, led by California, in the direction of providing free education beyond the senior high school level. It is of course true that education, at any level, is not purely "free." Nevertheless, the obligation of all citizens to finance the education of all students is a clearly defined doctrine stemming from the belief that all of society profits from an educated populace. To the extent that schools must resort to fee systems to finance desired programs, society pays the price of lost education for some of its membership.

For similar reasons, American public schools have established clearly defined expectations for school attendance. All states have established minimum attendance laws requiring that every person between specified ages attend school. Likewise, the states have further stipulated that the years of attendance shall be of certain minimum lengths.

All of the public schools operate under a national concept of legal authority. In every case, the ultimate authority for the establishment and operation of public schools resides with the state. The various states have developed diverse school systems because of this freedom, but the state-level responsibility is similar.

Another legal aspect, currently undergoing a great deal of testing, in which all schools are similar is that their operation must not conflict with existing state or national law. Although the state laws may vary, the United States Constitution is common to all states, and constitutional decisions arising from the United States

Supreme Court are binding upon all districts. Recent rulings on school prayers and *de facto* segregation exemplify the uniform application of federal law to all school districts.

The concept of the school as a nonsectarian institution is almost universally accepted. While the issue of religion in the public schools has not been fully satisfied (either philosophically or legally), no community, excepting the most parochial, would claim that the schools should serve a sectarian function. Communities with a broad religious base find the use of the schools for sectarian purposes so distasteful that the issue rarely arises.

From a financial standpoint, almost all public schools are heavily financed from revenues collected from local citizens. Undoubtedly, the most common single source of revenue is the local property tax. Such a tax is normally levied against the property owner, with his consent to be taxed determined by a local referendum.

From a political standpoint, schools are similar in that a representative body governs their educational affairs. Throughout the country, boards of education or their counterparts serve communities as the developers of operational policies. Those same boards hire executive officers to carry forward the educational implications of policy. In the process of electing boards of education, states and local communities have gone to extreme lengths to protect their children from the dangers of partisan political influence and control. School elections are often held at times other than partisan state and national elections. Furthermore, the vast majority of states and districts require school board elections to be held using nonpartisan ballots.

One area, open to dispute, in which many schools are similar is curriculum. Before casting the uniform curriculum aside as ridiculous, one must consider that only a small, limited number of publishing companies supply curricular materials. Beyond the limitation of choice presented to the consuming profession, there is the factor of acceptance. A few materials, through multiple state adoptions, far outdistance the others in their use. Unfortunately, the published text is the backbone of the actual experiences which students undergo. The adoption of a reading series by several states as the authorized text almost guarantees that students in those states will be exposed to not only the same material but also the same method.

Schools are certainly bound together by the common dilemma of treading the fine educational line between providing for local, state, or national stability while making possible local, state, and national progress. With stability and progress very nearly antithetical, the task is doubly difficult. The dilemma of leading or reflecting society will undoubtedly be one of crucial dimensions in coming decades.

Providing compulsory services to a particular group during their formative years has made the schools especially attractive to groups seeking to satisfy specific desires. As a result *all* schools find themselves engaged in educationally marginal activities ranging from health services to law enforcement. Examples of such activities are the enforcement of compulsory inoculation legislation and the administration of eye and dental examinations.

American public schools are similar in at least one other way: They express similar professional needs. The need for additional professional staff, the requests for new and better materials, and the search for more effective educational methods are indicative of the desires of teachers and administrators to upgrade their professional stature and to improve the professional posture of their schools.

UNIQUE POWER

The various states, in delegating much authority to the boards of education of local school districts, instituted a concept of education which has proven to have a unique power. The variation and divergence in local operation and in local control has created variation and divergence among local school systems. Out of local systems, which are always parochial and provincial to some degree, has come an educational product which also reflects variance and divergence according to the source.

While adherence to a "party line" is necessary in a dictatorial or authoritarian culture (hence reliance upon centralized systems which can be "party-controlled"), adherence to a single *right way* to educate would be catastrophic to a democratic culture which values the right and privilege of an individual to achieve his potential without undue regard to "party needs." One of America's greatest strengths is the egalitarian benefits received from the intermix of cultures. In a similar and related way, the intermix of products of differing educational systems with their differing biases has allowed us to compare one system with another. It is the process of comparison that emancipates man from the ignorance that arises from an acceptance that is due to lack of alternatives.

Along with the mass migrations of recent decades, the subsequent interaction of the products of diverse educational programs has stimulated the creation of a more eclectic educational enterprise. New opportunities for the comparison of educational institutions have arisen. The values of the several are reflected in changing patterns, and the shortcomings of each are more often being subjected to the light of self-criticism. Such criticism by student, patron, or professional bodes well for future improvements within the educational community.

In spite of problems created, the increasingly mobile population is helping to reduce local provincialism. The newer members of communities are proving less and less satisfied with local conservatism which the community has relied upon to protect its particular culture from external onslaughts. In addition, the provincials are representing smaller and smaller proportions of mobile, expanding communities. As a result there will be educational turmoil and ferment in decades to come, but the enterprise will continue to improve and to be motivated by the sparks of the conflict.

DANGER OF PAROCHIALISM

The preceding paragraphs have been quite optimistic in supposing that the power inherent in a system of local control will be utilized by the profession and concerned citizens to remold a continually improving educational system. Such a direction can actually be predicted. However, local control also carries an inherent potential danger—a danger that the local community will embark upon programs of indoctrination designed to coincide with a perverted, prejudiced, parochial view of what constitutes *truth*.

Out of parochialism comes a demand for indoctrination. Those who look in and never out, those who seek the static rather than the dynamic, those who are satisfied with the *status quo* find in indoctrination a tool for self preservation. Education is a process of emancipation, and to become emancipated requires that ignorance be cast aside. Emancipation is antithetical to indoctrination. Because knowledge of alternatives reduces ignorance and increases degrees of freedom, the parochial loses his power in a system of academic freedom.

If his school system can indoctrinate, alternatives remain disguised and the learner, now unwillingly and unwittingly shackled, is doomed to remaining a pawn of the society that crippled him. Modern American society cannot withstand a population of pawns. Local communities who elect to abuse the privilege of educating granted by the state can indeed prove dangerous.

Public School Systems

In using systems analysis techniques for the study of public schools, we must investigate the *components* of the school system, the *goals* of the system, and the *interaction* of the components as goal accomplishment is sought, and the *environmental* factors.

In the structure of this text, the dimension of interaction was deliberately placed in the final portion so that students might freely induce principles of desirable relationships from their study of the other dimensions.

GOALS

The ends toward which the organismic whole of public education is moving are usually referred to as its goals. Most normally goals are expressed in terms designed to expose *what we would like to become*. Sometimes they refer to education as an organization, sometimes they express professional desires, and they often attempt to describe the most desirable characteristics of the students whose behaviors we seek to change through educative processes.

Goals are not to be confused with objectives although the terms are too often used synonymously. Goals express what we wish to become; objectives describe *how we hope to become*. Objectives are generally small enough and specific enough to lend themselves to ready evaluation. We may, for example, set a goal for students couched in such general terms as "civic responsibility," implying that we want students *to become* responsible citizens. Such a goal has no clearly defined limits such that we can say, at a given instant, "that student is now a responsible citizen." To meet the goal of civic responsibility, we might decide that the study of civics in our social studies program should receive more attention at grades three, eight, and eleven. The latter decision would result in the formation of objectives so specific that we would know whether they had been accomplished.

We should not assume that goals cannot be evaluated. However, it should be recognized that to do so requires a great amount of patience, a good deal of ingenuity, a variety of tools and techniques, and a personality which can find pleasure in the minutest of gains. Chapter two outlines goals which have, at various times, been proposed as appropriate guides for the development and conduct of public school systems.

SYSTEMIC ENVIRONMENTS

In considering schools as social systems, it might be expected that the environment of most concern would be the social one. While such might be the case, we must also consider other kinds of environments—legal, economic, and political. Chapters 3 through 6 deal with the four characteristic environments.

Why study the environments of the public school systems? In the first place, a study of the factors surrounding and permeating the public schools should aid understanding of the reasons for diversity between and among systems. Even when systems operate in similar environments they seem to exhibit differing characteristics. This phenomenon may be due to the differences in perceptions of those who develop educational systems about the relative power of the components of the system. These differences in perception lead to dissimilar behaviors within the respective systems. Perhaps the occurrence of different characteristics within similar environments is analogous to differences which develop between children raised in the same family.

Secondly, man will undoubtedly continue to be force-directed and force-directing. If we assume that the four kinds of environments are force-filled, we must assume that public school systems will remain dynamic systems undergoing constant change. If the changes are to be planned rather than random, educators need to be prepared to channel forces into fruitful directions. With no knowledge of a dragon's anatomy, the knight is ill prepared to do battle! As a corollary, the students in the school systems live in and later more fully enter into the environments. Our knowledge of environments should aid us in developing dynamic goals for our system which will bear greater relevance for student preparation.

Another reason for studying environments is that understanding is requisite to sorting *what must be* from *what should be*. Elements from the legal environment, for example, are often very specific about what a school system must do. Political, economic, and social environments make similar strong demands. Wisdom will reside in developing dynamic systems of high value within the limitations of the environments. Simultaneously, knowledge of limitations must precede constructive action to reduce them. That same knowledge can permit purposeful professional activity which can override passivity.

ESSENTIAL COMPONENTS

The designation of components comprising the public schools is not a simple task. Part II of this text, comprised of Chapters 7 through 10, discusses what the authors view as the four components essential to the operation of public school systems—boards of education, administrators, teachers, and students.

Other possibilities were given consideration but were finally rejected as not absolutely essential to the conduct of the system. Among the most difficult groups to omit were parents and the community in general. However, the decision was ultimately made to consider parental and community elements as environmental factors which contribute to the determination of systemic direction.

In studying the various components of the public school system, it should be borne in mind that it is through the components that goals are ultimately achieved. Ill-chosen components, malfunctioning components, poorly coordinated components, have little chance to achieve the goals for which the system was supposedly designed.

In terms of the established goals and in light of the environment in which the systems operate, we might ask: (1) Why are the components like they are? (2) How do they contribute to goal accomplishment? (3) How can their individual functions be improved? (4) In view of their purpose, what would be the impact of altering the component roles? (5) What impact will changing environments have on the manner of component functioning? and (6) What responsibilities do the components have for improving the system?

Board of Education

To the experienced teacher, studying boards of education may seem to be an exercise in futility. Somehow the feeling that you cannot really do anything about boards of education prevails among members of the teaching profession. However, a new era is upon us in which teachers and boards of education will increasingly find themselves in face to face situations. To understand the character, the responsibility, the legal status, and the *modus operandi* of boards of education should permit the development of more efficient relationships. To accept boards of education only as they are now constituted is to restrict the dynamic potential inherent in professional interaction.

Administrators

Why study administrators? There is an implication in the authors' approach that the successful operation and the continual improvement of public school systems is a cooperative venture requiring thoughtful coordination. Such an implication, drawn from emphasis upon interacting components, is indeed intended. Teachers who seek to understand and improve their school systems would be well advised to understand the role of other components. Misunderstandings about the superintendent's and principal's roles and responsibilities and inadequate communication is dangerous to the efficient functioning of these two components. On the other hand, understanding the systemic purposes served by superintendents, principals, business managers, and curriculum supervisors should facilitate improved interaction between administrators and the teaching faculty.

Teachers

Teachers must study teachers in a manner not common to undergraduate education courses if teacher-administrative relationships are to be improved. The preparation of a teacher is a long and particularly difficult task. Even the most effective preparatory techniques seem to consume more than the amount of time available. The typical four-year preparation program must be concerned with teacher-pupil reationlships so complex and so crucial that little time remains for adequate examination of the relationships between teachers and administrators, which the new teacher will encounter in his first position.

The effective teacher is not detached from other elements of the school system, however, and although his primary responsibilities do lie with his student relationships, he is not a professional island unto himself. When his own responsibilities are juxtaposed with those of other systemic components, he should be better prepared to draw additional strength from others. Even the teacher in the most self-contained classroom soon comes to recognize that he must rely upon others. To the degree that he understands the unique contribution which he can make to the accomplishment of educational goals, he will be successful in coordinating his contributions with those of others.

The Student

The role students play within educational systems needs consideration if the system is to be better understood. The kinds of students coming to the system play a large role in determining the kind of system we wish to engineer. The kinds of students that we seek to create ultimately also are determining factors in our systems development activities. Their contributions to systemic success must not be underestimated. We should be vitally interested in the manner in which student characteristics are determinants of systems design.

Of great concern, because most of our goals are student oriented, should be the total relationship of the various components and their interaction with the ability of students to accomplish educational goals. In conducting systems analysis, in hypothesizing the results of systemic changes, in creating new opportunities for component interaction, we must make a continual check concerning potential impacts upon the students and their accomplishments.

COORDINATING INTERACTION

With goals determined, the environments studied, and components understood, there remains a most important task, the induction of the kinds of relationships which must exist within a successful system. Chapters 11 through 17 attempt to develop the kinds of relationships which hold greatest promise for goal achievement. The final chapters are devoted to those areas in which the professional paths of teachers and administrators cross.

Crucial relationships between teachers and administrators develop at the points of interaction: when school facilities are planned; when budgets are prepared; when salary programs are being discussed; when policies are developed, interpreted, or implemented; when curricula are developed; when instruction is supervised for either improvement or evaluation purposes; when teachers are recruited, employed, assigned, and utilized. A clear understanding of the ends toward which both professions are actively headed should aid in developing desirable and fruitful relationships in the areas of interaction. Discussions of *what is* and *what ought to be* should provide the basis for developing a personal and professional concept of working relationships between teachers and administrators.

Systems Development

School systems are here and operating. They are not static, however. In constantly changing and evolving systems, professional educators have the opportunity to passively allow society with its various environmental forces to shape the course of public education. However, if they become unhappy with the random and vacillating nature of externally enforced change, they may, as an alternative, elect to take the change elements out of the realm of the random and into the domain of the ordered and the planned.

To develop a better school system, professional educators will have to become systems engineers. In the engineering process, consideration should first be given to the general acceptability of the goals toward which the system is to be designed. If we then find that the goals are satisfactory but the accomplishment is less than we desire, the conditions are correct for systems development activities. But where do we begin in the redesign process?

Obviously we might look to the environment. Changes in the environment should be followed by changes in environmental forces. If we were wise enough, or powerful enough, to make the appropriate changes in the environmental conditions, we would indeed be confronted with forces which would help us mold a new system. It was an upset society, for instance, which initiated great pressures for revised science curricula following the advent of the first Russian satellite. Societal "upset" engineered by educators might indeed speed some changes which we might view as essential. Nevertheless, we educators have not been very good revolutionaries. We have been much more successful as evolutionaries and perhaps the radical environmental changes needed to stimulate educational changes are better influenced by educators than initiated by them.

The component parts represent the second place toward which we might turn to redesign our educational systems. We might be able to add components, to drop components, or to redefine the functions of the existing ones. Such action has been initiated to some degree in systems that add guidance counselors, curriculum coordinators, and business managers. Environmental factors limit the amount of manipulation that we can do with the components, and the systems redesign and redevelopment therefore seem to reside most logically in the realm of changing interaction patterns.

Systems engineering has normally been considered a function of the superintendent, and in many cases it has been a jealously guarded function. Changes in the administrative concept have been such that emerging theories give a far greater role to teachers. However, to expect teachers to be automatically ready to fulfill this new role seems to be somewhat naïve. It is therefore a major *purpose of this book to more adequately prepare teachers to become systemic change agents.*

The fundamental tenet accompanying the purpose is that the relationships which develop between teachers and administrators must be those which improve the capacity of the educational system to accomplish its intended purposes. To that end, teachers and administrators would do well to define for themselves the ends toward which their professional energies are to be directed and to design working relationships which will guarantee that the ends will, in fact, be furthered by the very nature of the interactions.

Problems and Issues

1. *To what degree should American public school teachers understand the system in which they are to spend their professional lives?* The individual performing subassemblies in a manufacturing process does not, in fact cannot, understand the nature of the corporation for which he works. Industries have attempted to improve employee understanding of those elements of the total manufacturing process in which they are personally involved. Understanding is actively sought on the premise that it will aid the morale of the worker and in some way increase his production.

On the other hand, the corporation president must have a broad and deep understanding of the manner in which the various segments of his enterprise contribute to the accomplishment of improved manufacturing, which is the corporation's primary goal. Intermediate administrative and supervisory personnel require narrow but deep understandings of the particular corporation aspects for which they are responsible. Intermediate personnel also require a good understanding of those corporation segments with which their segment must interact.

Teaching in a public school system is not a manufacturing process. Nevertheless, the teacher as a systemic component requires some degree of understanding about the total operation of the system—how much understanding—gained in what ways?—for what purpose?

2. *Under what conditions may internal components of a public school system legitimately undertake to change a system which "belongs" to an outside public?* Teachers, administrators, and pupils are internal components of public school systems. In later chapters, each component will be assigned specific roles which give meaning to his consideration as a basic systemic element. In a sense each of these components is present within the system at the will of the local public—a public which enjoys certain legal and cultural prerogatives in organizing a local system to serve its ends.

Local school systems are governed in a "representative" fashion. Their governing representatives are part-time personnel chosen for their capacity to develop and maintain a system capable of perpetuating and improving American life as sought by the constituent body. The board of education also is a "lay" body. Its lay membership carries no guarantee that educational expertise will reside within the body. It only guarantees that the wishes and desires of the local initiating society will be represented and, in fact, will play the predominant role in the governance of public school systems.

Occasionally, the wishes and desires of the various components and the society may be antagonistic toward each other. When one segment is demanding a change while another is resisting, who shall cast the deciding vote?—what role will the board of education play?—who shall determine when teachers shall participate in the change process?—by what process shall teacher participation be guaranteed?

3. *How can local systems, designed for the protection of parochial and provincial purposes, be opened to broader, more functional goals?* When a society specifically institutes a social organization such as a public school system to protect the local culture, ethics, and mores, it is understandable that the same society should be interested in retaining the public school system in any fashion which has proved successful in preserving the *status quo*. The cost of preservation, in many school districts, is the graduation of a student population ill-equipped to function in any society more broad in scope than the local one. If the system is to be opened, opened by whom?—under what conditions?—by what process?

Selected References

Blau, Peter, and W. Richard Scott. *Formal Organizations: A Comparative Approach.* San Francisco: Chandler Publishing Co., 1962.

Etzioni, Amitai. *Modern Organizations.* Englewood Cliffs, N.J.: Prentice-Hall, 1964.

Gross, Bertram. *The Managing of Organizations.* New York: Free Press, 1964.

March, James, ed. *Handbook of Organizations.* Chicago: Rand, McNally, 1965.

March, James, and Herbert Simon. *Organizations.* New York: John Wiley and Sons, 1963.

chapter 2

■ *Goals for the System*

Broadly Accepted Goals

Goals which are broadly accepted—whether they are goals for the American system of public schools or for any other system perceived as a social institution—tend to reflect the values of the society. These values are not necessarily related directly to how the members of the society behave. There is, in fact, a good likelihood that broadly accepted goals may be more obvious in the literature of the society than observable in the daily actions of its people.

These goals are really part of our heritage. Their being posited in our heritage has been a function of the tenets and precepts which have persisted through the years. They remain because people espouse them as desirable goals with the knowledge that they are *already* universally acceptable to other people. Controversial elements have been suppressed to the point where these broadly accepted goals have become traditional. Broadly accepted goals, then, are not usually *current* goals in the sense that they are the product of present needs and circumstances.

It is appropriate to mention some of the antecedents to present broadly accepted goals so that an understanding of their common and unique elements might better be grasped.

EDUCATION IN EARLY GREECE

A useful starting point might be an inspection of the ideals of an Athenian education. The Athenian youth was taught to become beautiful in figure, graceful in movement, and refined in behavior; he was taught to seek a balance in his life (both physical and intellectual) ; and he was to be educated for positive service to the

17

state. His duties to the state were seen as the highest interest in life; of second import among these four ideals was the development of good manners and morals.[1]

Projecting these goals to the present day one might suggest that beauty of figure is still supported through instruction in physical education and concern with physical fitness. Our diversified amateur sports program and national pride in accomplishments at Olympic games continue the notion that grace in movement has value. Only refinement in behavior might be difficult to defend as a persisting goal. But in this there has been cited a weakness in the Athenian ideal—no culture was provided for the masses.

Although the Athenian ideal of balance dictated the avoidance of specialization and professionalism, two elements which are very much demanded in our present culture, there is still value placed on the goal of balance. This becomes especially true when it is considered that young people are entering the work force at a later age than ever before and are leaving it sooner. The number of hours being worked during the week is decreasing for a large segment of our population. These very conditions predicate the continuing goal of the balanced man—the man who has avocational interests, who is able to use his increased leisure time productively. There is, too, a pragmatic consideration. Although this is the day of the specialist, the odds favor that even he will have to make several changes which require retraining and flexibility—or, a better balance in his education enabling adaptability.

There has been little lessening in the emphasis on the goal of service to the state from the Athenian day. As will be seen in the discussion of sociolegal goals for the system, there has been a reduction in the prescriptive indoctrination required for all youth; however, the goal of full attainment as a participating citizen in our American democracy is still highly valued. It is said that the Athenian ideal failed in attempts to make personal and universal that which was valued. Likewise today we are only on the periphery of reaching this goal. Such educative activities as the Peace Corps and Job Corps would seem to indicate efforts to invoke for all classes in many cultures the general goal of service to the state if these activities are viewed as opportunities for people to become active operants in their own systems—hopefully, productive participants in the future development of those systems.

Of the Athenian ideals for education, second in importance is the development of good manners and morals. Surely there is evidence

---

[1] Frederick Eby and Charles Arrowood, *The History and Philosophy of Education Ancient and Medieval* (Englewood Cliffs, N.J.: Prentice-Hall, 1940), pp. 228–233.

today that the system of public education is still disposed to inculcate in the young those manners and morals which will assure them of a reasonable acceptance in adult society. Although much is made of such things as individual differences, there would appear to continue to be a pervasive desire to educate the young for candidacy in today's society—to live by today's ethic. Education for the "other-directed" man has not gained wide support in the system of public education. Emphasis continues to be placed upon compliance and compromise. And this is hardly unreasonable when we remember that it is a public system. Thus it would be only reasonable to assume that the goals for the system include those which value its continuance.

COLONIAL AMERICAN EDUCATION

A further reference point in scanning the antecedents to present-day goals for the system of public education is the colonial period in this country. This particular period is important in that it reflected the goals for education which had emerged after the Renaissance in Europe and had then been brought to the New World. By this time the dominant churches of the day each claimed exclusive domain over truth. The goals of education were clearly those set by the church. Little reason or science was evident in those goals. In New England the theocracy of the day gave rise to laws which facilitated the emergence of schools with the avowed intent to enable man to read—read the scriptures—so that he would not fall into Satan's grasp. The middle colonies were a polyglot of nationalities and religions, hence the education provided was less uniform. Although education and its goals were parochial, there was evidence of poor children, Negro and white, being admitted to these schools. Southern colonies were strongly influenced by the Anglican church. However, proprietary interests dictated that plantation life be pointed toward economic prosperity more than the saving of souls through education. Often quoted is the statement of Virginia's Governor Berkeley in 1671 where he thanked God that there were no free schools in Virginia and hoped that there would be none for a hundred years. Berkeley said, "Learning has brought disobedience, and heresy, and sects into the world." One cannot help but parallel Berkeley's statement with the significant omission of any program for education of the masses in the Athenian ideals. Clearly education in colonial America supported the *status quo*. Where education was provided, the goal of the system was in no sense one of removing ignorance so that man might be free: rather it replaced ignorance with dicta which conscripted men to live by the ethic of the day.

EDUCATION IN THE MODERN ERA

The nineteenth century in the United States saw the common school, or the grade school, prosper. It also gave rise to what was to become a uniquely American element in public education—the high school. This second level of education was being extended to the masses. The National Education Association commissioned a Committee of Ten on Secondary School Studies to describe the function of the high school. The report of the committee in 1893 provided little vision for the secondary school. The doctrine of formal discipline was sustained. A more thorough study of the classics, formal history, literature, and grammar was suggested. Although the committee laid the groundwork for extending higher education to the masses, it did not come to grips with the fundamental problems of educating large numbers of youth in the high school.

The increasing number of non-college-bound youth in high school gave rise to the Seven Cardinal Principles of Education—principles which were formulated by an NEA commission in 1918. They were: (1) health; (2) command of fundamental processes; (3) worthy home membership; (4) vocational efficiency; (5) civic participation; (6) worthy uses of leisure time; and (7) ethical character. These principles were originally pointed for the secondary school but later came to be referred to as cardinal principles for education in general. Thus we come to broadly accepted goals of the present day.

Antecedents of present-day goals evidence a striking similarity with those currently in vogue. This analogue through the years may be the product of what really has been intended by providing education for people. Obviously, the sharpest differentiations are to be found in the objectives (how we hope to become . . .) employed in the provision of education from its inception to the present day. It is difficult to ascribe only altruistic motives to those who have set goals and objectives. This is especially true if we accept the notion that the pervasive goal of education is to liberate man, individually and collectively, from ignorance. The difficulty arises when one considers that goals are set only when there is motivating purpose. Without there being a purpose, there is hardly a substantial rationale for setting goals at all.

The motives of goal-setters are made didactic when one considers who the goal-setters are. Historically they have been from two cuts of cloth. Acknowledged leaders of men have been goal-setters. These leaders might be expected to be disposed toward preserving, toward sustaining the group they lead as well as their own position of leadership. The other group of goal setters is the antithesis of the acknowledged leaders. Its members have been the vociferous minority. The spokesmen for this group set goals which are in disagreement with those set by the natural or acknowledged leader of the time. Were this not the case, the goals set by the natural leader would go unchallenged and, of course, frequently unquestioned.

A persuasive delusion is frequently at work when goals are ascribed for the public school system. Often these goals seem extremely current, especially when they are congruent with the emotive reactions of people. The most commonly cited example of this in recent years has been the public reaction to Russia's Sputnik I. The magnitude of response to this historic event points up an interesting element in broadly accepted goals for schools— the public school system in the United States was literally caught up in the surge of public sentiment. Almost overnight it was considered bad form not to favor dramatic revision in the curricula associated with offerings of the sciences and mathematics.

Was this evidence of changing goals for public schools? Not really. Remember the differentiation made between goals and objectives in Chapter 1—goals referring to "what we would like to become" and objectives to "*how* we hope to become." The goal then of the American people might be described as a desire not to lag behind Russia in the space race. The impact of this desire upon the public school system was one of redirecting the objectives within the system. Specifically, it called forth a rearrangement in the components of the system and necessitated alterations in how the components would interact. The pervasive goals of the American system of public education were relatively unchanged. Accomplishment of objectives can, however, move goal achievement to greater heights. An oft-mentioned goal of public education is "to let each become all he is capable of being."

The press of public sentiment after Sputnik I did give a new viability to the efforts of those who had been working diligently toward curricular reform in science and mathematics. For that matter, curriculum reformists in general enjoyed support from the public. The people were in a mood to see action—and they were willing to pay for it. Static components in the public school system came under fire, often only because they appeared inert. Public sentiment made it impossible for schools to adopt or maintain a head-in-the-sand posture.

At times it is really fortunate that knowledge exists well ahead of its being utilized broadly in social institutions. Otherwise, there would not be the possibility to inject components of known worth into the system at those instances when the public suddenly decides it is ready for change. It is painful to wait for public receptivity.

The wait, however, is often a wiser course than a pre-emptive insistance, which might sour the public toward the system in general. The argument is really academic since the only elements which have persisted in the system of public education have been those which have won public acceptance. Scholars jumped at the opportunity to get into the public school system curricula and methodologies which they *knew* would benefit youth in school. They knew that some things ripe for use would work and the introduction of these materials and procedures opened the door for further experimentation. Public school systems in significant numbers were budgeting monies for research and curriculum development within the system. It might be said that the very climate of the system was altered.

It should not be presumed, here, that all teachers and administrators have to be shaken into wakefulness by public sentiment. Rather, it must be remembered that the public school system is just that—a *public* system. Changes in objectives within the system require extensive planning. There is always the peril of bandwagonism. Textual materials have to be written, tested, and published. Teachers must frequently be retrained to use new materials; there is, too, the subtle selling task of winning over resistant teachers and administrators who are operating a successful system and are reluctant to try new ideas. As has been found with the inception of the "new mathematics," the parents of school-age youth often need an orientation to the program.

The system of public schools, then, must ever be aware that it is a social institution. A trap lies in either extreme. If the system adopts only the ethic of the local community, it mirrors provincialism and may fail badly in preparing the youth of the community to live as adults in a highly mobile society. If the system moves too far away from the ethic of the community, it may find itself isolated from the patrons whose children it serves.

The increasing interest of the federal government in supporting the public school system may require that broadly accepted goals for the system be viewed more in the context of a national, if not international, community. Whether they are viewed that way or not, broadly accepted goals for the system of public education are, in fact, usually national goals or universal for our system of public education. One reason for this is simply that national organizations are commonly the medium through which these goals are made explicit.

The social strength of dissident goals is noted in historical perspective by one of two phenomena if the goal is strong enough to persist. Either the goal is incorporated into the goals sponsored by the natural leader, or the minority goal is persuasive enough to cause a major upheaval and replace its counterpart, the majority goal. Of course, in the absence of strength or persuasion of some sort, goals set from the minority position merely pass into oblivion. Unfortunately, numerous of these misfires fail even to be recorded as a portion of our historical perspective.

The record of upheavals in education is not large. The acknowledged leaders would seem to have persisted; infact, they have hardly had to envision new goals to any significant extent. One possible explanation for this is the cynical view that from the beginning the goal of education has never been to release man from bondage at all: knowledgable, free-willing man has not always been the intent; rather the goal has often been quite the opposite. It might be argued that the acknowledged leaders and goal setters have in mind an education which will primarily be directed toward what we have described as group preservation, or, in its more insipid form. simple maintenance of the *status quo*. From the point of view of the adult majority that has given leaders their power, either through acknowledgement or acquiescence, a goal such as this might be seen as wholly appropriate. In fact, a more poignant question might be, Is not the leader designated by his followers to perpetuate rather than to be an innovator and a visionary?

Turning now to more recent broadly accepted goals for the system of public education, it can be seen that the leaders are not always complacent. As has been stated in Chapter 1, the visible gains through redefinition and reinterpretation may not be large; however, with each refinement the likelihood of successful evaluation of goal accomplishment is improved.

Education for All American Youth[2] was produced, in part, as a result of inadequate satisfaction with the earlier statement of the Seven Cardinal Principles of Education. As with the Principles, the Ten Imperative Needs of Youth outlined in the book have been generalized from applying only to the secondary schools to include now the system of public education in general. The Ten Imperative Needs are as follows:

1. All youth need to develop saleable skills and those understandings and attitudes that make the worker an intelligent and productive participant in economic life. To this end, most youth need supervised work experience as well as education in the skills and knowledge of their occupation.

2. All youth need to develop and maintain good health and physical fitness.

[2] Educational Policies Commission, *Education for All American Youth* (Washington: NEA, 1944).

3. All youth need to understand the rights and duties of the citizen of a democratic society, and to be diligent and competent in the performance of their obligations as members of the community and citizens of the state and nation.

4. All youth need to understand the significance of the family for the individual and society and the conditions conducive to successful family life.

5. All youth need to know how to purchase and use goods and services intelligently, understanding both the values received by the consumer and the economic consequences of their acts.

6. All youth need to understand the methods of science, the influence of science on human life, and the main scientific facts concerning the nature of the world and of man.

7. All youth need opportunities to develop their capacities to appreciate beauty in literature, art, music, and nature.

8. All youth need to be able to use their leisure time well and to budget it wisely, balancing activities that yield satisfactions to the individual with those that are socially useful.

9. All youth need to develop respect for other persons, to grow in their insight into ethical values and principles, and to be able to live and work cooperatively with others.

10. All youth need to grow in their ability to think rationally, to express their thoughts clearly, and to read and listen with understanding.

William Drake, an educational historian, has outlined in his book, *The American School in Transition,* the American educational ideals as:[3]

1. the educational program shall be formulated and carried out in accordance with the principles of freedom and in keeping with the spirit of scientific truth;

2. equal educational opportunity shall be provided for all individuals;

3. public education shall be free from the control of any class, race, political party, or other group, and shall be operated in the interests of all the people;

4. public education shall be controlled by the people through their legally constituted governmental channels;

5. public education shall be supported by the public treasury at all levels from the preschool child to the adult, and in accordance with the ability of the people to pay;

6. education shall be the guardian and capital of human experience; and

7. education shall be compulsory for the elementary and secondary levels of the public school program.

[3] William E. Drake, *The American School in Transition* (Englewood Cliffs, N.J.: Prentice-Hall, 1955), pp. 23–25.

Drake notes that these ideals have been recognized by other writers in the field, including Ellwood P. Cubberley, Edgar W. Knight, Newton Edwards, and George S. Counts.

The enumeration of these ideals does, in fact, deal with the objectives of American public education more than with the goals for the system in that it describes how we ought to go about the task of providing a system of public education. The ideals do not discuss "what we would like to become" as a result of conducting our system in this manner.

Further statements of objectives proliferate in the literature of public education. One other set of such statements should, however, be mentioned—not because it is unique or especially divergent from other statements, but because of the qualifying comments made with the statements. In 1938 the Educational Policies Commission evolved a series of objectives under the general headings of self-realization, human relationships, economic efficiency, and civic responsibility. The Commission conceded that no single school could hope to accomplish all the goals any more than any single student might be expected to attain full enlightenment. The schools clearly had to engage in some choice-making. The school's task becomes one of understanding the ways in which individuals and societies choose and achieve their goals. The Commission cited the free man as one having "a rational grasp of himself, his surroundings, and the relationship between them." It further states that "the purpose which runs through and strengthens all other educational purposes—the common thread of education—is the development of the ability to think (and, hence, to choose)." In this context, the development of the student's rational powers becomes centrally important.

Sociolegal Goals

It might be expected that the sociolegal goals for the system of public education would evidence a certain rationality. They do. They do especially when one looks *back* at these goals as they mark points of progress in the development of the system of public schools. Looking back, rationality and progress in the system are commingled—the fact that progress was obtained makes easy the ascription of rational action. But is this necessarily so? What do we know of the motives of those responsible for the events which mark sociolegal goals to the present day? Should it not be conceded that the "socio-" elements in these goals emerge from man who is both a rational *and* emotive being? Since law, both statutory and case, is again the product of men, sociolegal goals must be allowed to reflect both man's rational strengths and often his emotive frailties. Specifically, they mirror the conditions of the time as perceived by those who made decisions and set goals.

When the Continental Congress declared in the Northwest Ordinance of 1787 that "schools and the means of education shall forever be encouraged," a tone for the objectives of the time was set. The implicit goal for these objectives is clear. Encouragement of the system of public education was good for society; it would beget the type of citizen who would better serve his personal needs and those of the society. It is important to note that only rarely is mention made of specifically *what* the educated citizen is to become —attention is focused upon *how* he is to get that way. The immense social supposition here is that through the attainment of educational objectives, people will become what they *should* become— and, they will behave in a manner which is complementary to the society. Thomas Jefferson emphasized this faith and trust in human behavior when he said "If a nation expects to be ignorant and free, in a state of civilization, it expects what never was and never will be."

It is really unfair to cite the system of public schools as being unresponsive to societal needs. Granted, the particularization of objectives to meet these needs is time-consuming, leading often to the caustic observation that public schools are not unlike an old and rare formula for the brewing of beer—fifty years behind the times and that's the way they like it. The general criticism is unfair because more often than not progress and change in education are evidenced by social awareness and are frequently accompanied by enabling legislation. Widespread child labor in the mills of New England was followed by legislation for compulsory education. This legislation in New England led to similar legislation in other states, culminating in the early 1900's in nearly all the states having legislated some form of compulsory attendance.

Reference to the emergence of compulsory attendance laws often includes commentary citing society's awareness of the need for education of all the children—in other words, it ascribes motives to the people seeking the legislation. Further, it specifies that these motives were associated with educational goals. Dissenters from this point of view note that the motives may have been quite different. Child labor was causing male heads-of-households to find increasing difficulty in gaining and maintaining employment; often the children in the laborer's family were the primary wage earners. These dissenters point out that the motive behind seeking early compulsory attendance legislation may have been more a desire to get children out of the mills and factories so that adults might find gainful employment than to educate children. Where might these children be placed? If they were all placed in school, their lot as adults might be given more hope for prosperity.

The danger being emphasized here is that a causal relationship between social awareness and legislation for public education does not always exist. Although certain legislation may prove to be educationally desirable, the prompting of the legislation may well have had sources and motives unrelated to educational considerations.

In fairness to the specific example being used, compulsory attendance legislation, it should be mentioned that as these laws became more common among the states, certain of the impetus for the legislation was associated with societal acceptance that education on a public scale possessed an inherent goodness. Immigrants to the United States and organized labor groups early recognized that a system of public education could provide access for their children to a wider choice of opportunities. More thorough treatment will be given to sociolegal goals in Part II. The Systemic Environment, and especially in Chapter 4, The Legal Environment.

Goals of Open and Closed Systems and Their Evaluation

Most societal organizations—systems of people in our society— can be characterized as closed systems. Persistent observers of societal organizations have concluded that organizations are *not* characterized by change. To the contrary, when organizations are viewed over a long period of time, stability rather than change seems to be their outstanding characteristic. This is truly an unfortunate lot when it is considered that the system of public education is one of the more important and one of the oldest of these social organizations.

A closed system is one which, essentially, lacks plasticity; it is not elastic in that its condition is one of containment rather than spread. It is often directed at self-perpetuation with emphasis upon maintenance functions. The closed system may change, but only under those conditions which threaten its very survival. The closed system is not really insensitive; however, the sensitivity it maintains is directed toward preserving that which it has rather than toward an assessment of external environmental needs. This is an important difference between open and closed systems. Although the public schools are usually perceived as a service system in society, their existence as a closed system would cause them to be parasitic in that society.

OPEN SYSTEM

Ideally, the service system in a society should be at least in part an open system—highly sensitive to the changing needs and demands of the membership of that society, even visionary to the point that it *directs* toward a more fruitful existence for the membership. The open system does this by maintaining a flexible posture. The goals of an open system tend to be ideal—so much so that they might be made explicit only in the most general terms. Objectives of an open system are quite the opposite of indoctrination. Components of an open system are arranged to interact in such a manner that individuals being served by the system are individually and collectively prepared to cope with both present and future societal demands.

It is conceded that only calculated guesses can be made in terms of what the future will hold for society. Certainly it would include the provision for critical analyses of the past so that intelligent judgment might profit from both historical error and success. The open system is not irresponsible; quite the opposite. Its sense of responsibility is immense. Where the closed system is able to support the *status quo,* that which is already accepted by the larger societal group, the open system supports more nebulous goals based upon thoughtful conjecture. The society often has not yet grappled with many of the goals for the open system. Societal consideration frequently is limited to those goals which dictate the present ethic controlling its behavior.

CLOSED SYSTEM

Although there is no necessary causal relationship, the system of public education might be described as a closed system on the basis of the historic consistency of its goals. Incidence of modification in the system has more commonly been associated with its objectives than its goals. An example of this might be found in the goal of citizenship education, which has persisted for public schools from the earliest period. Surely the medium of accomplishing objectives has changed through the years. Today we find students engaged in role-playing behavior where they may have at least a vicarious experience in coming to understand how the adult world about them lives as citizens. In an earlier year the objective was the memorization and recitation of "In Adam's Fall, we sinned all." The method has moved away from mouthing moral truths toward the development of understanding and hopefully, an appreciative acceptance of citizenship.

Although there has been significant variation in the mode of instruction, there has not been a commensurate change in the goals of citizenship education. Predominantly, citizenship as taught in the public school system means, in its most broad sense, national citizenship. Often, it does not even mean this. Sectional rivalries, provincialism, and sundry other indulgences tend to overshadow man's citizenship among his fellow man on this earth. Many classes in citizenship today reflect the finest hour of isolationism. The notion that the earth is shrinking, so to speak, would seem limited to communication, trade, travel, and the like. The impact of the idea upon the fellowship among men has yet to be felt. Goals of education have just not moved to the point where citizenship extends beyond archaic and often unrealistic boundaries.

ASSESSING GOALS

As was stated in Chapter 1, it is folly to dispair too much when attempting to assess goal accomplishment. The very utility and worth of our goals for the system require that persistent efforts be made at assessment. An assessment of goal-accomplishment in the closed system is less difficult than in the open system. Unfortunately, this has led to evaluation in education which measures goal accomplishment in terms of the goals for that aspect of the system which is closed. In a sense this is the easy way out.

The system of public schools is *both* an open and a closed system. The degree to which it is more one than the other varies among individual systems and to the degree to which it is responsive to changes in its internal and external environment. Evaluating the goals of the closed system is the easy way out since there is a built-in criterion measure. The question being asked in this evaluation is: Are we continuing to be what we have been—or, how much are we like ourselves? The real misfortune in evaluation of only the closed elements of the system lies in the whole system coming to appear closed. The orientation is backwards. The outcome is often the observation that our system of public schools is backwards.

Assessments of goal accomplishment in the open elements of our school systems are confounded by a lack of clear criteria. However, this is a necessary condition; if there were criteria, a closed system could be formed to meet the goals implicit in the criteria. Broadly taken, the goals of the open system involve facilitating, through behavioral change, the increased possibility that man will continue to have reasonable choices as he lives in our society. The important distinction here involves not our measuring *what* he becomes but rather assessing how pervasive remains the field of his choice. Obviously, there will be some societal judgment regarding what men collectively choose to become, but assessments of the system of public education might better be limited to a determination of how wide a choice exists—and, of course, for how long in the life of man the possibility of choice persists.

The Teacher and Administrator in Goal-
Setting and Evaluation

One of the more observable aspects of how open and closed elements in the system of public education overlap one another involves the teacher and the administrator in the system. Each is intimately involved with goal setting for the system. Some people hold that the ideal condition is one where the goals of the administrator and the teacher are the same—a condition where the energies of the system can be directed toward mutually agreed-upon goals. Others contend that a healthier condition is one where there are competing goals, where there persists an interplay among goals. Which of these notions is better is, in fact, an academic question because the pervasive goal for the system is to enable students to become individuals who can utilize the lessons of their heritage and at the same time enjoy a flexibility of choice in what they will become.

DEVISING GOAL COMPACTS

A principal problem arises when teachers and administrators have not made some compact as to whether they will agree or disagree on the goals for the system. The genesis of the problem lies with how people behave when there are not clear expectancies for them and for those with whom they work. The risk is that parties to goal-setting may behave irrationally in seeking the acceptance of their goals. These ego-bearing components in the system may exert more energy toward getting their way than toward the setting of best possible goals. A further confounding element for relationships between teachers and administrators in the system is that usually, in the structure of the system, administrators are accorded more authority than teachers. The implication here is that the administrator must be tolerant of or solicit the counsel, and possibly divergent thinking, of teachers or leave the teachers with two resources: (1) teachers might choose to acquiesce in the administrators' views, or (2) teachers may decide to challenge administrators and thus risk all the side-effects of confrontation.

Establishing a base of mutual expectancies between teachers and administrators in the system provides at least one other functional advantage. Where these expectations have been made explicit for both components in the system, goal-setting can proceed with the understanding that each of these components has unique tasks and roles. The inference here is that an understanding of expectations will lead to an appreciation of both the similarities and differences in the roles and tasks of teachers and administrators.

Schema 2–1, which describes the school as an open and a closed system illustrates another relationship between the teacher and the administrator in goal-setting. Traditionally, the administrator is charged with what might be called a "local" position; one of his primary tasks is to maintain the integrity of the system. The teacher, on the other hand, may well have a stronger allegiance to the subject field or the grade level in which he teaches than to the particular school system of current employment. Where this is the case, the teacher might be viewed as a "cosmopolitan" in the school system; he is first a teacher of English and only secondly an English teacher in a particular school. The abiding goals for this teacher may be associated more with the goals of English teachers in general than with those goals of the specific school in which he is currently teaching. Increasingly, both teachers and administrators are mobile. Reciprocal certification agreements, expanded position opportunities, and the general increase in the mobility of people may be leading to that point where both administrators and teachers see their goals in a more cosmopolitan context—related more to their professional groups than to the public school system in their community of present employment.

Schematic 2-1. A Narrative Outline of Some of the Open and Closed Dimensions of Public School Systems

Definitions: field—an area within which all forces exist that exert influence on the system.

force—an influencing element within the field.

system—a grouping of forces for particular purposes within the field.

Component—a compositional element within the system which also may be an influencing force.

Statements: 1. A school system may be described as a field comprised of all those forces influencing the system.

2. Each force in the field has a relative strength of influence upon the system.

3. The strength of influence of forces is based upon such factors as proximity to other forces in the field and status in relation to those other forces.

4. Forces may be external to systems in the field or internal components of the systems.

5. Influence exerted by forces in the field may be differentially applied among the components within the system or toward other forces in the field.

6. Influences exerted by the forces will be the result of how each force perceives other forces in the field, the perception of system components in the field, and how the system as a whole is perceived by the forces.

7. Perceptions of forces in the field will be colored by experiences and predispositions of those forces.

8. At any given time forces within the field exert influence toward closure or openness upon the system.

9. The constellation of forces within the field describes the balance between the open and closed dimensions of the school system within the field.

Examples of some possible relationships:

Force¹*—*The administrators* within the system exert influence upon teachers to keep up with current thinking in their teaching specialties.

Force²*—*The teachers* within the school system exert influence upon students to be responsive to an environment larger than the community.

Force³*—*The students* within the school system exert influence upon teachers to moderate their values and those of their parents.

Force⁴ —*The community* exerts influence upon the school system to recognize the local ethic.

Force⁵ —*The state education* agency exerts influence in the field to assure that legal requirements for the school system are met.

Force⁶ —*The federal education* agency exerts influence in the field through making funds available for the establishment of new programs.

Force⁷ —*Systems of education in other countries* exert influence in the field by their success in different approaches to the educational process and the extent to which their ways are popularized and given recognition in the field.

* School system components.

Under these circumstances there is the risk that local values and goals may become submerged; the system may become "too open" and lose its identity with the community. Established communities will not often stand still for this movement toward noncommunity orientation. Even people in newly settled "bedroom" communities who have possibly little agreed-upon heritage tend to desire some constants, to generate some foundational values which will be reflected in the system of public schools. It is the administrator, whether he be local or cosmopolitan in his orientations, who is usually charged by the community with seeing that appropriate constants are identified and observed in the program of the school.

Where there is a sizeable cadre of teachers drawn from the local community (such as New York City) or where the administration is home-grown (again, New York City is a good example), the likelihood exists that local values and goals will be taken into account and will be reflected in the program of the school system. The position being supported here is that extremes of open or closed, local or cosmopolitan, are probably of lesser value than systems which are consciously planned to exist in a state of balance. The viability of the system, then, would depend upon how dynamic was the state of balance, how sensitive it continues to be to the forces which predict needed adjustments in the system.

Emerging Goals and Their Functional Placement in the System

Discussing emerging goals is a bit like playing Nostradamus. Since goals have been defined as that which we would like to become, the concept of emerging goals presupposes some knowledge of future conditions. Apart from outright speculation, one of the wiser approaches might be to suggest that present trends will have a portent for the future. Unfortunately, trend data tend to deal with inanimate aspects of our environment. Occasionally, trends are pushed to the point where it is presumed that people will be swept along by the tides of that inanimate environment. If goals do, in fact, refer to that which we would like to become, a sounder position to maintain might be that men control to a considerable extent what will be their environment. Because man is endowed with free will and is also potentially rational, there is no explicit limit to what might be his goals. The implications of this for the system of public education seem clear—no specific, categorical statement can be made regarding its future goals.

Emerging goals can then be described for the system in terms of what man has done and is now doing—assuming that man will be directed at least in part in his future goal-setting by the past and present. In this context, some generalizations can be advanced. Man would seem to be disposed to a continuing support for his social institutions. Probably at no other time has the system of public education, one of man's social institutions, been more important to the aspirations of man. In an earlier year, the school was seen as a possible aid to achieving higher status and greater prosperity. Today, the system is looked upon as utterly essential for man if he is to be able to cope with new knowledge and new technology and their impact upon mankind.

A commonly projected condition for the future involves the domain of productive employment. It is being said that people will enter the labor market later in life than ever before and will leave it at an earlier age. There would seem to be a likelihood that the need for additional training or retraining will take place more than once even during that short tenure of working years. This condition will extend not only to the laborer but also to the professional worker, who will probably require continuous training throughout his career if he is to keep pace with the expansion of knowledge and changes this expansion has caused.

Enlarged populations and increased automation may very well lead to an extension in the time available for education before employment. With more people and fewer positions for employment, plans must be laid in advance not only to insure the best conditions for the short period of employment but also to enable the persons to use wisely that prolonged time when they will not be employed. Surely, the prolongation will take place if advances in medical science continue to raise the life expectancy of the average person.

What will this mean for the system of public education? Already there can be seen evidence of the system adapting and making functional changes. Operation Head Start was directed toward engaging children in the educational process within the system at an earlier age, with the hope that certain native deprivations of these children might be overcome. The expansion of the junior and community college has greatly enlarged the number of young people enrolled in educational systems beyond the twelfth year. Individual school districts have initiated adult education programs, programs for dropouts, and varied programs of study for regular students K-12.

If the pervasive goal for the system of public schools will be to enhance the possibility for the individual to choose courses of action freely throughout his life and then be able to act in accord with his choices then the system of public education will be altered to the extent that people select, or choose, this system as the social institution which is to have a principal role in the accomplishment of the goal. An important distinction here is whether what the school is now doing is in response to demands made by the people or whether the changes taking place are the result of educators within the system setting goals which they believe will be appropriate for society. Probably it is not one or the other of these but a combination of the two. The real test may well come when society is faced with the decision of choosing the social institution, or system, it will support.

Problems and Issues

1. *How are the goals of the system to be made known so that desired behavioral change in students might effectively be sought?* Although a social system may have goals, their existence is of little worth to systemic components unless the goals have operational meaning. An understanding of goals facilitates the establishment of objectives, which in turn enables the development of specific activities pointed toward inducing desired behavioral change.

Increasing the odds for understanding goals requires that goals must be expressed in different ways, before differing populations, and with a frequency which assures that the system will stray from its intended goals only minimally. How are the goals for the system best explicated?—What are the problems in interpreting goals for different populations?—How do goals assist in devising objectives for the system?—What are the roles of teachers in these tasks?

2. *How can diverse and often conflicting goal-expectations for the school system be resolved?* The most glaring differences of position often exist between the professional components of the school

system and the community in which the system exists. Because the schools are social institutions, the board of education and the professional components of the system should give a fair hearing to all those who have particular expectations for the public schools. Although some persons or groups are better qualified than others to speak about certain goals, this should not lessen the extent to which others are afforded the opportunity to be heard.

The school system has an obligation to provide the organizational structure through which free and articulate communication will be possible. What kinds of organizational arrangements might best facilitate communication between the school and the several segments of the school-community population?—How should the board and professional components be involved in this process?—Are there particular characteristics which might designate a population segment as being uniquely qualified to speak on the subject of goals for the schools?

3. *Does the school system have an obligation to state what goals ought to be invoked now, based upon its predictions of the future needs of youth and society?* American industry has shown the way in establishing research and development units within its organizations. One assumption industry has made is that it must be thinking ahead if it is to continue to be competitive. The larger assumption presupposes that there will be change, that new materials and processes will be found or devised, and that the productive and leisure activities of man will evolve.

The public school system is challenged with a similar problem. The goals for the system stated in here-and-now expectations may be inadequate for our society and its individual members in the next decade. Which systemic components should be engaged in predicting the future needs of youth and society?—How might the system go about this task?—How can "bets on the future" be integrated with existing goals for the system?

Selected References

American Association of School Administrators. *Imperatives in Education*. Washington, D.C., 1966.

Bruner, Jerome. *The Process of Education*. Cambridge, Mass.: Harvard University Press, 1960.

Drake, William E. *The American School in Transition*. Englewood Cliffs, N.J.: Prentice-Hall, Inc., 1955.

Eby, Frederick, and Charles Arrowood. *The History and Philosophy of Education Ancient and Medieval*. Englewood Cliffs, N.J.: Prentice-Hall, Inc. 1940.

Educational Policies Commission. *Education for All American Youth.*
Washington, D.C. The Association, 1944.

Goals for Americans (Report of the President's Commission on National Goals) Englewood Cliffs, N.J.: Prentice-Hall, Inc., 1960.

Keppel, Francis. *The Necessary Revolution in American Education.*
New York: Harper and Row, 1966.

Rockefeller Brothers Fund, Inc. *The Pursuit of Excellence: Education
and the Future of America.* New York: Doubleday and Company, 1958.

Ulich, Robert. *Crisis and Hope in American Education.* Boston: Beacon
Press, 1951.

Whitehead, Alfred North. *The Aims of Education.* New York: Macmillan Company, 1929.

part II

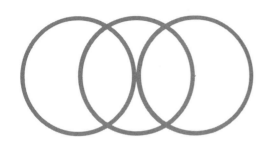

Systemic

Environment

chapter 3

■ *Contemporary American Society*

Of all the environmental forces which seek to mold the character of American school systems, contemporary society would seem to be the most potent. Any educator who has lived through the furor an aroused public has created within a system can attest to the very real power of a society in determining the nature of the education to be provided. Indeed, Brickell's study of how educational change was initiated in the state of New York, makes it very clear that society is a most potent force for changing the nature of public education.[1] He cites as one evidence the massive shift in curricular emphasis which followed the launching of the Russian Sputnik on October 4, 1957. The shift was in no small measure the system's response to an aroused society.

No single chapter can do justice to the complexities of a society. However, an abbreviated review of a few of the many elements which comprise contemporary American society should increase understanding of the motivations which spur political, economic, and legal actions. In addition, it seems appropriate to project some existing societal trends some distance into the future. Such projections seem necessary if strategies are to be developed for mobilizing the power of the populace in support of the educational enterprise.

Urbanization

CENTRAL CITY

The rapid urbanization of the population is one of the most pervasive forces characterizing American society. The farm has long since disappeared as the most common place to live. In its

[1] Henry Brickell, *Organizing New York State for Educational Change* (Albany: State Education Department, 1961).

stead, the metropolis is rapidly becoming the dominant environment, with two out of three Americans now living in the large urban areas.[2] Only 15 per cent of the people lived in the urban areas of 1850, whereas 40 per cent were urban dwellers in 1900. By 1975, 140 million Americans will be residents of metropolitan areas, with about one-half living in central cities and the remainder in the surrounding suburban areas.[3]

Changing concepts of transportation coupled with the rising cost of central city land have been potent forces for changing the nature of the city. The automobile and the truck have extended the radius of the city for both homes and jobs. Primary reliance upon trucks rather than trains to move the products of manufacturing has permitted industry to move to the periphery of the city.

Mobility has also helped free the worker. Home building, as well as plant construction, has grown rapidly in fringe areas. The retail traders, with their shopping plazas and malls, and the household service industries have followed the flow of people away from the center of town.[4]

The core city remains a potent employer. One needs only to view the clogged tenacles of the urban expressway system during the rush hours to understand that people and jobs are no longer located in the same part of town. An interesting phenomenon results in that the daytime population of the central city is often 30–50 per cent higher than the residential population.[5]

The many motivations for human flight from the city's core are only partially understood, but those motivations are important to the educator in suburbia or central city who finds himself having to contend with the residue of some of them. Motivations include dissatisfaction with city conditions (crumbling schools, rising crime rates, and so on), declining property values, and racial prejudice. Increasing affluence and the desire for space also spur the movement.

Into the space vacated by the fleeing middle-income family has come a new, lower-income occupant. In a very large measure, they come from nonwhite minorities. The resulting "gray areas" represent new drains upon city expenditures. The new families have more children and require additional educational, social, health, and welfare services. Each of the requirements is a demand upon the economic resources of the city and tends to accelerate the decline in the attractiveness of the city to the middle-income fam-

[2] Committee for Economic Development, *Guiding Metropolitan Growth*, August 1960, p. 15.

[3] *Ibid.*, pp. 15–16.

[4] *Ibid.*, p. 17.

[5] *Ibid.*, p. 19.

ily. In economic terms, this societal trend seems irreversible with the consequence that more state and federal financial support will be required to aid the metropolitan areas.[6]

The pattern of housing so often follows the white-gray-black pattern. With the emerging concern by both white and nonwhite populations for improving and ultimately equalizing the educational and employment opportunities of the Negro population, racially segregated communities within the city are not to be tolerated.[7] The long-cherished neighborhood school is challenged by a minority group that quite properly recognizes the inherent weaknesses and dangers of an educational system that is socially restrictive. Militancy against a repressive social system is expressed against the local schools. *De facto* vs. *de jure* segregation is no longer the issue, but segregation, regardless of the cause, is. This aroused society is a potent force for changing the configuration of the schools and the attendance policies of metropolitan school systems.

SUBURBIA

Flight to suburban areas is not new, but the magnitude is changing. As early as 1950 movement away from the center of town was being noted. The motivation at that time seemed to be a growing desire to reconstruct the value patterns of the rural community.[8] Early suburban areas were characterized by a rather well-defined ethnic and value pattern. In many ways they were highly segregated on bases of income, belief, race, and, in some cases, religion.

In *Issues of the Sixties,* suburbia is described in terms of values: "The suburban value system is characterized by conformity to middle-class values, 'togetherness,' and familyism in domestic life, and preoccupation with things: the art of keeping the house painted, the heating system going, and the lawn green—the chores of husbandry; autonomy is sacrificed to eternal concern with the man next door, who becomes the mirror in which one's life is appraised."[9]

The same value pattern is carried even farther in the parent-child relationship. With Dr. Spock as a household by-word, the suburban home has become very child-centered and youth-oriented.

The youth himself has a different and difficult task to face in

[6] *Ibid.,* p. 30.

[7] Samuel Moore and Samuel Woodard, "School Desegregation: Localism or Metropolitanism?" *School and Society,* Summer 1966, pp. 269–270.

[8] "The Future Metropolis," *Daedalus,* Winter, 1961, p. 19.

[9] Leonard Freeman and Cornelius Cotter, eds., *Issues of the Sixties* (Wadsworth Publishing Co., 1961), p. 228.

his familial identifications. No longer are father and mother identified by the clothes they wear, the jobs they do, or the household chores they perform—mother wears slacks, works, and pulls crabgrass, whereas father wears shorts, works, and barbecues the dinner. Man may be man and woman may be woman, but the line of demarcation becomes more and more blurred.

Current suburban life is well described by a suburban elementary principal:[10]

The suburb has become less effective as a community than its prototype of 1900. Because of the egalitarian nature of the suburb, there is less capacity for social action. There is more and more emphasis on conformity because the individual is functioning in a peer society. The suburbanite of today did not bring with him a clear image of what he wants his community to be like. All too often his motive was to avoid the undesirable aspects of urban life. Consequently, he has less feeling of identity with his community than his earlier counterpart. Large parts of the population have lost the capacity for acting meaningfully in groups, except when it comes to matters which touch their immediate families. Even the fraternal, benevolent associations have given way to the impersonal agencies of the state or to the United Fund in which lay participation is largely limited to the solicitation of funds. Under the influence of incessant shifting of population, local leadership attracts less support while state and national leaders loom larger on the horizon. The mass of citizens are increasingly defining leadership as distant rather than immediate. This trend will continue.

Mobility

David Boroff has suggested that "the moving van, rather than the vine covered cottage, may well become the symbol of our domestic idyl with certain communities like Levittown, Pennsylvania, and Park Forest, Illinois, simply way stations on the career escalator."[11] His observations very clearly reflect the mobile nature of American society. The Conestoga wagon is gone, but the van lines have provided an adequate substitute.

Seventy-five million Americans now live in homes different from the one they occupied only five years ago. An estimated one-fourth of our population has moved across a state line during the past five years.[12] Los Angeles gains approximately 300,000 new in-

---

[10] Gerald Baughman, "Social Forces," in *Long-Range Forecast of Factors Affecting Public Education in Ladue*. Mimeo. Ladue Public Schools, p. 13.

[11] David Boroff, "Portrait of a Mobile Nation," *New York Times Magazine*, August 26, 1962, p. 69.

[12] "The America the 1960 Census Shows," *U.S. News and World Report*, July 3, 1961, pp. 46–49.

habitants each year. Such figures tend to support contentions that American Society is a very fluid thing, and that any description of it can only suffice for a fleeting moment.

The migrations seem to be of four rather distinct types: (1) migration from rural to metropolitan areas, (2) migration to Florida and the far West, (3) migration of the southern Negro to the northern city, and (4) the migration of the middle-class white from the city to the suburbs. Comparisons of 1950 and 1960 census data highlight the four migrations.

During the 1950–1960 period the following changes were noted:[13]

1. Cities 50,000 and over   — population up 12.9%.
2. Cities 2,500–50,000   — population up 13.9%.
3. City suburbs   — population up 81.6%.
4. Farms and villages   — population down .8%.
5. All "southern" states except Tennessee had declining percentages of non-white population.
6. All "northern" states except Alaska, Hawaii and Arizona had increasing percentages of non-white population.
7. The ten largest cities of the Northeast and all midwestern cities over 500,000 (except Milwaukee) lost population.
8. California gained 5,000,000 new residents.
9. Florida, Arizona and Nevada had increases of more than 70 percent.

These isolated facts highlight the number of families that are uprooted. Not all effects are mathematical, however. In economic terms, 10 per cent of the Gross National Product was spent on various costs associated with migration.[14]

The social and political consequences of mass migration have not yet been completely assessed, perhaps because of the refusal of society to stand still long enough for the measurement. However, some of the consequences seem self-evident. Of immediate danger is the breakdown of local and state government. A short life span within a community or state may be insufficient to develop an interest and pride in local issues.

Citizen activities within government may diminish as home-town ties are broken more and more frequently. As the influx and out-flow of citizens increase, the ability of the local official including the superintendent, to weld a cohesive body of patrons will be sorely taxed. Conversely, the transient population, just passing through, may be impatient with the slow wheels of government; if action is to help them, it must be immediate. The migrant brings with him knowledge of how "it" was done better in another place.

[13] *Ibid.*
[14] David Boroff, *op. cit.*, p. 69.

Increased mobility also changes patterns of family life, which in turn alters the nature of our society. Family dispersion across the continent is very common, and with the dispersion goes one additional unit to which persons have traditionally identified. Increased social accommodation for the problems of old age is another consequence of dispersion, as many families find it difficult to comfort aged parents via long-distance.

Inner family mobility also has increased particularly following increasing affluence. The second (and third) car has permitted the family to go in several directions at once. In no small way, the mobility has reduced the family's ability to regulate morality of its members. Individuals have more contact with values outside the family, and the mobility soon removes the membership from the knowing eyes of neighbors or other family members.

Population Changes

EXPANSION

Of all the changes occurring in the American population, perhaps the most critical is its expansion. From the beginning of man's time on earth, it took until 1830 to achieve the first one billion population; in the next 100 years, the second billion was added; in the next thirty (1930–1960) the third billion was added; and in the next forty, an additional three billion can be expected.[15] Although most of the growth is likely to come in Africa and southwest Asia, one needs only to stand and listen to the steady clicking of the population projector at the Bureau of the Census to be reminded that there will ever be more mouths to feed, bodies to clothe, hands to train, and minds to educate even in the United States.

AGE

Another startling change in the population has been in the age spectrum. During the 1950–1960 period, the number of children under eighteen years of age increased 36.7 per cent and the number of persons over sixty-five increased 34.7 per cent during the same period. Meanwhile, the 18–65 age group increased only 7.4 per cent. The rapidly rising number of nonproductive workers (too young or old) was supported by a relatively constant population of productive age.[16] The next two decades will see another kind of shift as the post-World War II babies enter the productive stage.

[15] "No More Room," *Newsweek*, February 4, 1963, p. 36.
[16] "The America the 1960 Census Shows," *op. cit.*

MARRIAGE

The married status of the population also creates some changes in the nature of society. Between 1950–1960 the number of marriages increased by 14 per cent, and the number of divorces increased by twice that rate. The percentage of widows in the population was up almost 13 per cent, reflecting an increased longevity for women. More importantly, perhaps, was the fact that the age of first marriage was constant throughout the period. Now more than ever young people face the dilemma of an early marriage versus demands for extended schooling to meet the demands of an automated society. Nevertheless, almost two-thirds of all women are married by the time they are 21 years old. In 1960 only 7 per cent of all women never married. Annually, wedding bells ring for about 1.7 million couples.

ROLE OF WOMEN

The emancipation of the female in American society has occurred on many fronts; what the suffragettes did for political freedom, the demands of World War II did for her economic freedom. The Population Reference Bureau provides important data on the role of women in society. To maintain the country's population, each woman needs to bear 2.27 children. The census of 1960 revealed the following: white wives bore 2.6 children; nonwhite wives, 3.1 children; city wives, 2.5 children; farm wives, 3.3 children. Indications are that women now in their twenties will bear an average of 3.1 children.

For the woman, marriage and the bearing of children no longer represent an automatic exclusion from the labor market. On the contrary, over one-half of the working women are married and one-half of those have children under 18 years of age. In 1890 fewer than one in twenty wives was working; by 1950 one wife in five worked; in 1960, one in three.

The pattern of woman's work-life has also changed. "Rosie the Riveter" of the 1940's worked for a few years until she began her family and then quit. By 1960 the pattern had changed. The wife now works, pauses for child-bearing, then hurries back into the labor market. Now a higher proportion (47 per cent) of those women in their late forties work than do those in their late twenties (35 per cent).[17] Increasing college costs may be proving a stimulus for older women to return to work, and the percentage of older women working is almost twice that of 1940.

Dissatisfaction with her dreary dawn-to-dusk existence has proven a powerful motivating force for changing the role of

[17] "Women, Work, Marriage," *Science Digest*, October 1963, pp. 79–82.

women. She seeks and achieves increased respect. She sees less and less need to remain restricted by traditional demands of housekeeping and child rearing. In fact, it appears that the capacity to bear children is the only difference modern woman is willing to accept in her comparison with man, and she seeks to reduce that difference by turning to social agencies for the child's rearing. Kindergartens for three- and four-year-olds, commercial day-nurseries, and preschool activities of all sorts do not lack for enrollees.

Role of the Church

In the earliest days of American education, the church was one of the most potent forces shaping the destiny of those being educated. The curriculum contained unashamed doses of religion and the church fathers were little concerned over the separation of church and state as now conceived. Even the textbooks were designed to convey moral and religious precepts to the reader. In fact a look at a public school curriculum of 1750 would reveal subjects more akin to parochial than to public education.

Although the church was a powerful voice in educational affairs, it was not powerful because of numbers. In 1850 only 16 per cent of the population were church members (Table 3-1).

Table 3-1. Church Membership, 1850–1960[18]

Year	Per Cent Membership
1850	16
1890	22
1900	36
1910	43
1940	49
1950	57
1960	64

Cook hypothesizes that the church is a middle class institution and the rise in membership is well correlated with the expansion of the middle class. The impact of the church upon society is apparently a variable kind of thing. Hoffard reports that "church" holds the greatest attendance appeal for those over 70 years of age.[19] In a study of eleven denominations in Massachusetts, it was determined that attendance fell off between ages 20 and 30 and returned to a more normal figure between ages 35 and 40. Approxi-

[18] Clair Cook, "Technology's Impact on Religion," *Christian Century*, September 2, 1964, pp. 1083–1085.

[19] James Hoffard, "Who Attends Church?" *Christian Century*, May 13, 1964, pp. 654.

mately 25 per cent of church members are in church every Sunday, but only 33 per cent attend on any given Sunday.

But what about the impact of the church and of religion upon society itself? Baughman makes the following suggestion:[20]

It may be an oversimplification to say that the emphasis within the church is swinging from spiritual guidance to social action, from individual salvation to group concern. Certainly the movement is in that direction. One authority says the church is becoming secularized! another says the church is taking on the characteristics of a social age. Both statements indicate a drawing away from problems of the future and a concern for immediate needs. As the church moves toward the role of a social agency it pulls away from dogma and principles of faith. In some instances, fellowship seems to be substituted for faith.

To the social reconstructionists within the church, the new energy spawned within the civil rights movements of the current decade holds hope for creating an institution endowed with the capacity to accomplish social reorganization. The moral activists have seen new life breathed into their religious organizations through participation in social engineering activities. Very likely, the directions of social concern will be ever important on the agenda of churches seeking new roles for religion in this century.

Technology, Automation, and Obsolescence

The changing nature of man's world of work has had great impact on his economic and social life. Technological changes also alter his environment and hence his life's operational pattern. Many of the changes have elicited new pressures for innovations in the educational system.

One obvious outgrowth of automation has been the development of larger industrial and production units. In human terms, automation has drastically altered the traditional concept of the labor markets. The unskilled are unemployed and the demand for scientists and engineers continues to increase. By 1980 it has been estimated that one-ninetieth of the population will need to be scientists or engineers and that 50 per cent of all workers will be on the technical, professional, or managerial levels.[21]

The nonschool education of society has been greatly affected by technological change and the implications for educational systems are staggering. Radical changes in the mass media have altered not only the social pattern of life (as with television) but also the

[20] Gerald Baughman, *op. cit.*, p. 17.
[21] *Issues of the Sixties, op. cit.*, p. 228.

informational sources upon which man bases much of his behavior. On the positive side, Telestar, Syncom, and Comsat have opened new areas of communications which were only dreams in the recent past. Instantaneous reporting from all over the world has helped to shrink the globe. However, other changes are not as positive.

In 1910, thirteen newspaper chains were in existence operating sixty-two newspapers. By 1963, 109 chains were operating 560 newspapers with only 52 cities having separately owned, editorially independent newspapers. Although mergers and the acquisition of radio and television stations by newspapers have come under closer judicial supervision, the trend established is expected to continue with increased responsibility for a free and factual press placed upon shoulders of the news media. Continuation of the trend will also call upon the consuming public to increase its powers of analysis and criticism.[22]

Automation and technological changes also have a role to play in determining society's outlook upon life. As man sees himself as more and more successful in solving his physical problems, his faith in himself may increase. In addition he views industry's increasing capacity to create desirable objects and his own increasing capacity to purchase the objects as opportunities to satisfy his desire to manipulate his physical and social environment. Decreasing hours of work and increasing leisure are powerful allies in creating a climate conducive to making and retaining hedonism and materialism as the prevailing philosophies of the coming decades.

Obsolescence, a term normally applied to out-of-date things, is now being applied to human skills. Rapid technological changes have expanded the number and kinds of tasks to be performed by human minds and hands. However, they also discard the more perfunctory tasks, and other jobs thereby disappear from the labor scene. Persons who find themselves occupationally deprived in an automated society are an emerging social force for restructuring American public education.

Affluence and Poverty

In economic terms, the United States is a middle class country. The vast majority of Americans find themselves with an income which permits them to live in a "middle" ground between the wealthy and the poverty-stricken. Such was not always the case, but taxes have restrained continued growth of income at the top

[22] James Heald, "Scientific and Technological Forces," in *Long Range Forecast of Factors Affecting Public Education in Ladue.* Mimeo. Ladue Public Schools, p. 10.

and the upward pressure of wages has decreased the size of the group at the bottom. John Galbraith reports that in 1938 the 5 per cent of the population with the highest incomes received 33 per cent of the dollars paid as income, but by 1946 they received only 18 per cent.[23] During the same period the lowest 20 per cent increased their income by 42 per cent. The middle-income category has indeed increased its membership. In social terms, Galbraith suggests that persons with rising incomes find little reason to identify themselves with the malcontents, the agitators, the undesirables, or the rabble-rousers.

Since the time of Galbraith's book, affluence has increased markedly. The "good life" now consists of a bedroom for every child and two cars in the garage.

Analyses of the American diet show increasingly proportions of meat and lowering proportions of such low income staples as bread and potatoes. Supermarkets find it profitable to stock gourmet counters and the more expensive, preprocessed food.

One index of rising affluence is the growth of the leisure industries. In 1964, Americans spent $24 billion on leisure-time activities. The expenditure represented about 4 per cent of the gross national product. Boating, fishing, golfing, and camping were only a few of the industries to profit from America's search for pleasure. Two million Americans own second homes and the number increases by 100,000 per year. Another two million leave the United States for travel farther than Canada or Mexico. In the past ten years, the number of stockholders has doubled, and two-thirds of American urban families have $2,800 to spend after paying for food, clothing, shelter, and medical expenses.[24]

In contrast to the affluent, 11 per cent of the urban families have after-tax incomes of less than $2,000. The most common characteristic of the low-income family is the absence of a full-time wage earner, usually because of absence of a father in the home or physical conditions which prevent employment. Another large category of concern is the retired, for 37 per cent of families with "poverty" incomes are retired couples. Nonwhite families represent a disproportionate share of the lowest income group.

The Society and Education

The American educational system holds a distinctive place in contemporary society. Justified or not, the system is looked to as the means by which a greater good will come to prevail. By the

[23] John Galbraith, *The Affluent Society* (Boston: Houghton Mifflin, 1958).
[24] Arnold Chase, "Income and Expenditures of Low Income Families," *Monthly Labor Review*, August 1964, pp. 889–890.

conservative, it is charged with retaining the current culture; by the liberal, it is charged with forging a new and better society; and by all, it is charged with giving to children the opportunity to survive in any potential society. Faith in the public schools may well be one of the dominant cultural characteristics of the twentieth century. American society is so convinced that education is the key to future improvements in the lot of man that the society has seen fit to require children to attend for a period far longer than required of most children in the world. As a matter of course, the society has made refusal to attend a legal offense. Today, American children are in school—like it or not.

The society of the United States has not always valued education to the same degree. In 1870, there were only 16,000 high school graduates, representing about 3% of the seventeen-year-old population. In 1963, over 70 per cent of the population was graduating from high school and 91.4 per cent of the fourteen- to seventeen-year-olds were in school on a full-time basis.[25] The American student attends school about 180 days per year for slightly less than 6 hours per day.[26]

The economic value of education is continually reported to society. The working press cites study after study of correlations between education and income. School bulletin boards continually display articles showing improved income resulting from increased education. The economic aspect is a common lever employed by the counselor attempting to dissuade the potential dropout. In short, society is well convinced of education's economic value and the strength of its faith in the system is in large measure due to its opinions about economic worth.

When society is aroused to a common concern, the school is often looked to as the common solution. If all children need immunization against a new epidemic—use the schools; if Civil Defense housing is inadequate—use the schools; if American diets are inadequate—use the schools; if housing patterns create segregation—use the schools; if patriotism wanes—abuse the schools. Schools get the call to serve the common need and the criticism when all the needs are not met. Nevertheless, despite its failures, the educational system retains the faith of the society.

Perhaps history would show that the various subcultures comprising American society have looked to education for different purposes over the years. To the Negro population, the educational system holds a particular promise. Foremost in the minds of the

[25] N.E.A. *Research Bulletins,* XLI (February 1963) and XLII (February 1964).

[26] Raymond Whitfield and Eugene Egger, "School Attendance of Swiss and American Children," *School and Society,* April 17, 1965, pp. 254–256.

leadership has been the faith that equal and integrated education is the greatest hope that the minority has for removing the social, cultural, and intellectual barriers of two hundred years of subjugation. In the South and North, each with different problems, new solutions are sought which will justify the faith of the Negro population. Out of education's most crucial problem may come the greatest opportunity to realize the dreams of those who would contend that the schools must develop a new social order.

All social classes and subcultures do not have the same respect for education. Despite the general faith alluded to above, some very real differences exist in the way in which segments of society use the schools. To the American Indian with his struggle to maintain his own culture, school may be simply an interruption of the other processes by which he can retain his Indian identity. Other feelings, just as real, occur in other segments and are manifested in many ways.

In a study of attendance, it was found that in the sixteen–seventeen age bracket, the percentage of children from high-income families was about 22 per cent higher than children from low-income families. By age twenty to twenty-four the percentage from high-income homes was three times larger than from low-income homes.[27]

Studies of activities undertaken by youth from the various social classes show that when confronted with choice, curricular decisions differ.[28] In general, the higher economic classes elected to participate in the college preparatory curricula. The general and commercial curricula were more often chosen by those from the lower economic classes. It should not be assumed that all the choices were unguided and free. It may well be that a secondary relationship, existing between social classes and intelligence quotients (reported by Hollingshead), serves to promote placement into the various curricula.

Brookover, in *A Sociology of Education*,[29] suggests several expectations which American society holds for its educational system. Many of his contentions are based upon findings from Elmo Roper's famous *Fortune* survey.[30] The first set of expectations centers

[27] Bernard Karpinos, "School Attendance as Affected by Prevailing Socio-Economic Factors," *School Review*, LVII (1943).

[28] See Lloyd Warner and Paul Lunt, *Yankee City Series* (New Haven: Yale University Press, 1942); and A. B. Hollingshead, *Elmtown's Youth* (New York: John Wiley and Sons, 1949).

[29] Wilbur Brookover, *A Sociology of Education* (New York: American Book Co.), 1964.

[30] Elmo Roper, "Higher Education: the *Fortune* Survey," *Supplement to Fortune*, September 1949.

around "training for a vocation." Society has come to expect that
formal education will contribute to the skills required to get a
better job or to make more money.

Secondly, it is suggested that society expects children to acquire
some basic skills through the process of education. Although not
specifically listed, these expectations probably include skills involved with reading, with oral and written communication, with
mathematical calculation and so on.

Transmission of accepted cultural values is the third societal
expectation. Radicalism with regard to cultural patterns is not
condoned, and the school is expected to actively encourage virtue,
good character, and high morals.

Social adjustment is yet another hope held for education. Society
is disturbed by members whose behavior deviates significantly from
societal norms. Educational systems are expected to be normative
institutions with the capacity to encourage and reward normative
behavior on the part of future members of the society. "Successful"
schools operate well within the tolerance limits of their society.

Opportunity for social mobility is another type of need which
society exhibits. The higher the level of education the more mobility power education has. The lower the social class, the greater the
appeal of the social mobility concept. Of all the expectations of
society, this is one of the most universally accepted as a reality.

Protecting Society

It would not be fitting to close this short discussion of contemporary American society and its relationship to public schools
without mentioning the manner in which it protects itself from a
system too socially upsetting to be tolerated. The common actions
available to society are legal, economic, and political. These actions
and their manifestations are more thoroughly discussed in the
following three chapters.

For many years, the "society solution" to the disruptive influence
was to dismiss the objectionable element. Thus, leadership, which
by its nature demands some distance from the norm, was punished
by the process of firing the offender. When it became apparent that
Mr. X was teaching things "dangerous" (e.g., the United Nations,
evolution, integration) to the retention of the *status quo*, Mr. X
was released from his position to seek employment in an area
where his pronouncements would be less disruptive. In this way,
society could at least slow down the rate at which the behavior of
its children was being changed.

The teaching profession rebels at such unilateral and uncompli-
mentary behavior on the part of employers. Tenure legislation has

been achieved in many states as a counteraction to unwarranted teacher dismissals. At the national level, sanctions against school districts judged as undesirable places of employment have been added as leverage against a resistive society. Even strikes have been used on occasion. The reaction of society to these leverages and their impact on the faith which society has invested in public education will be developments worthy of study for years to come.

Problems and Issues

1. *What kind of positive and negative potentials do various societal forces have for extending their influence into the classrooms of specific subject matter?* Although it is quite easy to conceive of a local community as having a modal behavior which can be described in sociological terms, it is more true that a local society consists rather of diverse segments, with each segment having its own motivations and goal-directed behaviors. Upperclass bankers and lower-class factory workers do not exhibit similar characteristics and the kind of pressures they generate can be expected to be dissimilar.

Specific forces generated by society are often focused in topical areas. Some will be organized and potent, others random and impotent. The capacity of various social segments to exert pressures on their educational system also varies over a broad continuum. An educational system will be the recipient of many social pressures—from what direction?—from whom?—directed at what?—satisfied how?

2. *What characteristics of American society shall its educational system elect to support and promote?* The American public school system, in accepting a responsibility to change the behavior of young people, takes upon itself the responsibility for transmitting a system of culture to the student components. The diversity of the American society guarantees that many patterns of value will prevail among the human groups comprising the society. The preservation of society and its smaller groups requires that its value patterns be instilled in its youngest members. If this were not the case, young members in the maturation process would bring disruptive and destructive forces to bear on the alien culture in which they find themselves.

The segmentation of American society illustrated by the large number of groups which comprise it, guarantees that not a single value pattern is appropriate to all groups and to all individuals. Patterns of religion, politics, and economic beliefs which characterize the various social segments represent divergent forces with which the schools must contend.

Choices must be made by educators. Consideration will be given either consciously or tacitly to a pattern of total values. Students, during the educational process, will sample the values, will compare them with those outside the school, and will ultimately accept or reject those being promulgated by the educational institution. In determining its social posture, the school must consider—what values?—at what support cost?—by what process?—with what effect?

3. *Through what kinds of administrative arrangements can a public school system remain flexible enough to meet the great diversity of societal needs with which it is confronted?* When a school accepts the development of each student component to its maximum potential, it accepts an impossible task. Each child in and of himself brings an almost infinite number of potentials to which the school must address itself; for example, the child has potential to jump long and high; a potential to play a clarinet or a bass drum or a piano; a potential to write, to spell, and to speak; a potential to draw or to paint; and so on. Most commonly, schools have elected to attack the problem of student development by organizing those students which are somewhat alike into groups of moderate size and then attempting to provide the groups with educational experiences designed to foster development of potentials.

In addition to student needs, society itself makes continual expressions of its requirements. The term "teacher shortage" is a reflection of the fact that society has been unable to obtain the quantity of teachers it seeks at the quality level it desires. Such an expression is one of need. Governmental prognostications that this country will be short by X number of scientists and engineers by 1970 is an expression of need. When a society demands civil rights actions to bring full citizenship to all of its population segments, it is an expression of need. Multiple societal expressions result in multiple pressures upon educational systems. The system must respond to what kinds of needs?—from what sources?—through what organizational arrangements?—and finally, when demands exceed capacity, by what criteria shall selective decisions be made?

Selected References

Brookover, Wilbur. *Sociology of Education.* New York: American Book Company, 1964.

Freeman, Leonard and Cornelius Cotter, eds. *Issues of the Sixties.* San Francisco: Wadsworth Publishing Co., 1961.

Galbraith, John. *The Affluent Society.* Boston: Houghton Mifflin, 1958.

Goslin, David. *The School in Contemporary Society.* Chicago: Scott Foresman, 1965.

Harrington, Michael. *The Other America.* New York: Macmillan, 1962.

Hollingshead, A. B. *Elmtown's Youth.* New York: John Wiley and Sons, 1949.

Hunter, Floyd. *Community Power Structure.* Chapel Hill, N.C.: University of North Carolina Press, 1953.

Presthus, Robert. *Men at the Top.* New York: Oxford University Press, 1964.

Sociological Abstracts

U.S. Census

Warner, Lloyd. *Yankee City Series.* New Haven: Yale University Press, 1952.

chapter 4

■ *The Legal Environment*

The Federal Constitution and
Supreme Court Decisions

The federal government has no inherent powers. Powers
which do exist are delegated to the federal government by the Constitution directly or through interpretations of the Constitution by
the Supreme Court of the United States. Historically, education has
been a function of the several states. The near-unilateral control of
education at the state level has been attributed to the Tenth
Amendment to the federal Constitution, which states that, "The
powers not delegated to the United States by the constitution, nor
prohibited by it to the states, are reserved to the states respectively,
or to the people."

Apart from implied powers which the federal government may
have over education, the principal direct power might be found in
the General-Welfare Clause in the Preamble to the Constitution.
This clause gives Congress power to, among other things, provide
for the general welfare of the United States. It was not until 1936
that arguments over how this clause should be interpreted were
resolved. The Supreme Court in deciding *United States v. Butler*
chose to accept the reasoning of Alexander Hamilton, who had held
that the general-welfare clause gave Congress broad and extensive
powers and that these powers were not limited only to the purposes
enumerated. As yet there is no clear and unmistakable authority
for the federal government to manage public education under the
provisions of the general-welfare clause. Specific instances of
federal involvement and intervention, such as in Little Rock, Ark.,
1957, have been viewed by some as explicable under these provisions.

More recently the Elementary and Secondary Education Act of

1965 (PL 89-10) had as its stated purpose the meeting of a national problem. An explication of this purpose indicates that the Act is directed toward meeting a problem of our people in general. There are no words in the Act which specifically usurp state powers. Statements supporting the urgency of the Act cited concern with elementary and secondary education foundations which are of varying quality and adequacy, national draft rejection rates, and problems of employment and manpower retraining. Since these concerns are national in scope it might be contended that national problems require action from the national level.

CONSTITUTIONAL PROVISIONS AND INTERPRETATIONS

Under the provisions of the Constitution certain limitations are placed upon the states (for example, the states may not pass legislation which will impair the obligations of contracts) ; however, state legislation is usually seen as a mere expression of present policy—statutes are not often found to be in the nature of contracts. The states have distinct domain in exercising their legitimate police power—the power to act as the public good may dictate—to the extent that the Supreme Court will review only whether the power exercised is, in fact, legitimate. The provisions of the First Amendment assuring religious freedom have been interpreted under the Fourteenth Amendment to extend to both the federal government and to the several states. There has been a heritage of separation of church and state which recently was evidenced by the Supreme Court in its now famous prayer decision in *School District of Abington Township, Pa., v. Schempp* (1963) ; however, at this same time there is increasing evidence of plans for shared time and dual enrollments of pupils between public and nonpublic school systems.

The position of the Supreme Court in relation to the Constitution is fundamentally important when one considers that excepting amendment to the Constitution or a Constitutional Convention, the highest court is the final interpretor of that document which sets the tone for our legal existence. The Supreme Court has actively engaged in the review of state exercise of police power for only the last one hundred years; however, since the turn of the century there have been increasing instances where the court has taken note of not only our heritage and legal precedent but also of current societal conditions and occasionally portents of the future. The Supreme Court has also been willing to review its own position. In *Brown v. The Board of Education of Topeka, Kansas* (1954) the court reversed a position it had held regarding "separate but equal" education since *Plessy v. Ferguson* (1896). The 1954 decision called attention to intangible factors which had not heretofore been considered, and that the historical setting in 1896 was described as making the two cases not really comparable situations. The *West Virginia State Board of Education v. Barnette* (1943) case saw the court reverse the position it had taken in *Minersville School District v. Gobitis* (1940) regarding the requirement that pupils salute the flag. These alterations in the posture of the highest court reflect not only its attention to the rights extended through the Constitution but also the many and diverse elements on which its decisions might have impact. At this time a pupil may not be required to salute the flag, separate schools are not considered equal, and public school systems may not include prayer in the curriculum.

LAW AND SOCIETY

The very fact that the Supreme Court is rendering decisions based on much more than legal precedent, places the system of public education in the role of a medium through which our people are able to test certain existing laws. Since we are a people who have chosen to govern ourselves by laws of our own making, it seems wholly appropriate that we use our social institutions as media through which laws might be challenged, altered, affirmed, or overcome. Our society allows the system of public education to serve a multiple role; it fosters our heritage while at the same time it points to the future. It is a medium which must exist in constant flux if it is to be attentive to the full measure of its responsibility as a social institution. Components within the system of public education miss a distinct opportunity if they do not both observe and participate in society's use of its own institution. The system is in a position to assure that laws are observed and their value taught, at the same time assuring that equivalent attention is given to existing means for challenging laws.

Although the federal government has traditionally maintained only an advisory and, purportedly, noncoercive role in its relationship with public education, participation in government-sponsored programs has typically meant complying with certain stipulations (for example, at one time, disclaimer affidavits). The practical impact of this has been that federal monies, raised at large, have been readily available only to compliant school systems. The systems have had the choice of accepting federal assistance with compliance, rejecting these monies (as has sometimes been the case with both financially poor and rich institutions), or challenging through the courts those stipulations for compliance.

One further variation in the law as interpreted through Supreme Court decisions should be mentioned, namely, that the Supreme

Court may or may not choose to review a case submitted in appeal from a lower court. In the now-famous Louisiana Textbook Case, *Cochran v. Louisiana State Board of Education* (1930), the highest court affirmed the right of the State of Louisiana to provide free textbooks to the school children of the state. This decision had specific application in only Louisiana. Until the recent Elementary and Secondary Education Act was passed, only the State of Mississippi affirmed also the right to provide free textbooks. In New York, South Dakota, and New Mexico that right has been tested in the courts and forbidden. Similarly, Iowa, Washington, New Mexico, Missouri, Alaska, and Wisconsin have ruled, as states, against the Supreme Court decision in *Everson v. Board of Education* (1947) wherein it was permitted that local boards of education in New Jersey might provide transportation services or reimbursement for transportation costs for both public and non-public school students.

Because of provisions in the state constitution, the State of New York has taken the position that certain activities sponsored under the Elementary and Secondary Education Act must be fully paid for with federal funds. Support of an educational enterprise which is wholly or in part under the control or direction of any religious denomination violates the state constitution, hence no state and federal monies may be commingled in New York. Each state, then, must determine whether and to what extent it may legally participate in federal programs which support education. The federal government has not yet mandated that any state comply with a particular educational program—indeed, it remains to be seen whether a rationale for such a mandate might be found in the federal Constitution.

State-Local District Relationships

DISTRICTS OF STATE

Systems of public education exist in each of the several states as a result of provisions in state constitutions, charters, and legislation. The notion of a "local" school district is, in fact, a fiction bred from the historical development of school districts in the United States. Essentially, school districts exist at the pleasure of the state. The state may extend certain privileges to its school districts; however, the duties of the district are obligations imposed—no contract exists between the local school district and the state. Theoretically, any state could modify or dissolve its organization of school districts. Since the state legally created its school districts, all school property is state property held in trust by the local district for the state. The local district has no vested rights in this school property. Further, the local district is accountable in the last analysis to the state, not to only the people of the local district.

That the local district is a quasi-corporate arm of the state is further evidenced by local boards of education or trustees being state officers; in fact, they are the only legally constituted education officers for the district. Although these state officers may be appointed or elected by the constituency of the district, their duties and obligations are set by the state, and it is only the state to whom they are answerable. It must be conceded that local school district trustees gain and lose their office at the will of local voters or appointing officers and that local constituents commonly expect "their" representatives to act in keeping with local needs and desires. It may be this very schism between the local ethic and state control which forebodes the lessening power and ultimate extinction of local boards of education as they now exist.

ESTABLISHING DOMAINS

The relationship between the state and local school system is very much a function of the character of legislation for education in the state and the influence of the state agency established for the supervision of education. Where the state education law is broadly prescriptive, the local district may sense that there is little domain within which it might exercise discretionary judgment. Conversely, where the state education agency is under-financed and undermanned its impact upon local school districts is only marginal. Probably the extent to which prescription for education at the local level and support for the state education agency exist is indicative of the general disposition of the state toward where and how educational decisions ought to be made. It might be inferred from this that states sponsoring strong state education agencies and/or extensive prescriptive legislation for education have come to posit decision-making at the state level, thus leaving the local school district and boards of education in a rather impotent position.

In most states, however, there is either stated or implied some provision whereby the local board of education, within its powers and duties stipulated by the state, is charged with the responsibility for initiating those activities which will best serve the needs of those being educated in the district, so long as those activities do not violate state law or the state and federal constitutions. This provision is not unlike the General-Welfare Clause in the Preamble to the Constitution; it is a conditioning statement under which trustees may exert broad leadership in their decision-making. Surely, certain of what school trustees do under this provision will be challenged, possibly even in the courts. To the extent that these state officers in local districts do not choose to invoke this mandate to act, they default in their legal responsibility as state officers and thereby support the case for prescriptive legislation and a commensurate reduction in the powers of local trustees and board members.

STATE CODES

In many states the principal body of education law pertains to the fiscal relationship between the state and its local school districts. The state education agency has as one of its primary functions the supervision of expenditure of state monies distributed to local school districts for educational purposes. Guidelines exist for major expenditures to assure that at least minimal standards are maintained. Typically, these guidelines cover such matters as schoolhouse construction, borrowing money through the sale of bonds, minimum teachers' salaries, curricular syllabuses, and so on. A further major concern of the state is to set standards for the certification of professional personnel employed in local school districts. The state sets minimum standards for personnel in various positions; however, the local district may well set higher requirements for professional positions than those set by the state. When a state issues a license or certificate to an individual, it indicates only that the individual is eligible for employment—no promise is made that the person will be employed. By this issuance the state recognizes that the certificate holder is competent and qualified to teach. This recognition is absolute in that only the state or issuing agent may revoke the certificate. The local district may challenge the competence of one of its employees and may as a consequence of this remove that person from employment in the district but this in no way affects that person's certification unless the state should take action.

States also provide through statutes tenure or continuing contracts for certain employees in local school districts. Although the decision to place an employee on tenure is made in the local district, it is only through enabling legislation that the provisions for continued employment can be maintained. Generally, tenure has been held not to be a contract between the state and an employee of the local district; rather it is only an expression of current legislative policy. Where tenure statutes do exist there are usually specific provisions under which a person may be removed from tenure. These provisions commonly include such matters as insubordination, immoral character, conduct unbecoming to a teacher, inefficiency, incompetency, physical or mental disability, or neglect of duty. Where the provisions for removal from tenure are specifically enumerated the teacher may not typically be removed for any cause other than one or several of those causes enumerated in the provisions.

The relationship between the state and its local districts is then a proprietary one; the state has created the local school districts and assumes in varying degrees a supervisory responsibility over them.

The Local School District and Teacher Personnel

EMPLOYMENT

Teachers may be employed by the local school district only through the action of the school officers convened in a legally constituted meeting and acting as a group. This means that only the trustees or board of education may legally employ a teacher for the local district. Recruitment and preliminary procurement may be undertaken by persons serving as agents for the board of education; however, the contract for employment must be made with the only legal officers of the district. Certain states require that the contract for employment be executed in writing. In agreeing to a contract with a school district, the teacher also agrees to abide by all the policies, rules, and regulations of the board of education, whether or not they exist in writing, and those which the board might promulgate during the tenure of the contract. There is no requirement that the employed teacher be notified or advised of existing policies, rules, or regulations. Failure to observe policy may cause the teacher to be guilty of insubordination, which is usually one of the legitimate grounds for dismissal from contract.

A teacher who makes a contract with a school district is assumed to be certified; in the absence of proper certification the contract is null and void. The general rule is that where a district accepts the services of a certified teacher even though a contract has not yet been legally effected, the action of making the contract can be ratified so long as the contract could have been effected in the earlier instance. Even such events as appointment to tenure or a continuing contract are overcome if it is determined that the teacher does not have a valid certificate or license to teach. Technically, a teacher has not been employed until final action has been taken on the contract by both the teacher and the board of education. Since action on contracts typically requires that a record be made in the minutes of the board meeting, the contract is not fully made until the *following* board meeting, at which time minutes of the previous meeting are read for approval and acceptance. In practice teachers will be interviewed and procured by a variety of district personnel and the contract, signed by the teacher, will be delivered to the board of education for action. It might be said that the whole matter of personnel procurement operates on the extended premise of good faith.

PROBATION AND TENURE

Commonly, it is expected that a new teacher serve a period of probation in the school district before a decision is reached regarding a tenure appointment or continuing contract. It is frequently required that the chief school officer (really a professional *employee,* not a legal school officer) in the district, typically the superintendent, recommend to the board of education the names of teachers who he feels should be candidates for continuing employment. The board of education may or may not accept his recommendations, and if they choose nonappointment there is no requirement that reasons be made known to the teachers involved. Removal from appointment during probation often leaves the teacher with no legal recourse against the district or the board of education, even if the action was capricious and arbitrary.

Once a teacher has been appointed to tenure or a continuing contract, he can usually be removed only for cause. Although most statutes specify the precise reasons for which a teacher may be removed, others add the provision that the teacher may also be removed for "good cause." Once a teacher has attained tenure, it becomes the burden of the district to demonstrate why he should be removed from the employ of the district.

Lest these conditions appear too bleak, it should be noted that responsible school districts make distinct efforts to keep faith with their employees. In these districts brochures outlining district philosophy, policy, rules, and regulations are made available to all teachers and to candidates for teaching positions in the district. Extensive supervisory programs exist to assist the probationary teacher toward development as a valuable asset on the teaching staff. Long before recommendation for tenure is carried to the board of education, both the teacher and administrative personnel have given considerable time to discussing the strengths and weaknesses of the probationary teacher's performance.

As with other large groups of employees, teachers tend to form and take membership in organizations. Boards of education are free to employ any teacher certified in the state. The law may specify conditions of organizational membership. After a teacher has been employed by a board of education, that board may find it difficult to control his choice of organizations to which to belong.

It has been uniformly held that teachers as public employees may not legally strike. Where teachers have struck, the invocation of penalty measures provided for under the law against the striking teachers has had differential effects. Statutes stipulating harsh penalties rarely have been invoked. Refusal to enforce the full penalties of New York State's Conlon-Wadlin Act is a case in point. The spread of professional-negotiations acts among the states will make it incumbent upon teacher groups to begin to police themselves or to risk the enactment of legislation which may impose further external restraints upon their behavior.

Teacher-Administrator Relationships

Since the only legal officers for the local school district are the members of the board of education or board of trustees, both teachers and administrators are employees, not officers, of the district. Normally, the relationship between the teacher and the administrator is one of subordinate to superordinate. The administrator is charged with the responsibility and, hopefully, is given the authority to carry out the policies, rules, and regulations adopted by the board of education for the district.

SUPERIOR-SUBORDINATE RELATIONSHIPS

The criterion usually applied to test rules and regulations established for teacher conduct is that of *reasonableness*. Rather uniformly the courts have refused to examine whether decisions of boards of education are wise decisions—it has been presumed that these public officers always attempt to make wise decisions—only the matters of reasonableness and prudence are examined. The relationships among three principal components in the system— the teacher, the administrator, and the board of education—are sometimes confounding: The board is the employing agent and makes the decision regarding re-employment, whereas it is the administrator who commonly recommends the course of action to the board; the administrator is responsible for the supervision of the curricular and instructional programs, whereas it is the board which adopts and approves for use in the district curricular format and instructional methodologies; the professional teacher has as his responsibility the task of best employing his skills and knowledge to the conduct of a fruitful teaching-learning environment for children within the system. Obviously, there are times when these three components will disagree as to how and when certain elements within the system will be invoked. These differences do not necessarily mean that selfish ends are sought by one or several of the components, only that there are differences of opinion regarding appropriate timing and media for accomplishment. The legal environment of the local district is such that the board of education has clear domain to prevail in its desires to the extent that those desires do not violate a higher authority (state or federal).

An optimum condition for the system might be one where there exists a mutual respect among the components—a condition in which consensus of judgment is sought and compromise can be successfully reached. Since these components include both professional personnel (teachers and administrators) and nonprofessional personnel (members of the board of education), it is imperative that each recognize the legal and professional positions of the others. To a lesser extent possibly, the administrator often must defer to the teacher as the board of education might to its professional employees. The question here becomes one of determining which components within the system are best qualified to pass judgment or make decisions on particular problems. The administrator does not have to seek or accept advisement from subordinate components in the system—his legal responsibility is still to the board of education; however, his responsibility as a professional educator may color his ethical conduct with both subordinate and superordinate components of the system.

Teachers who feel aggrieved in their relationships within the system may always carry this concern to the next higher levels within the system. Increasingly, school systems are adopting grievance procedures whereby employees have the opportunity to be judged by both their peers and superordinates. Frequently there is an appellate stage in this procedure which provides for extensive review before the matter is brought to the board of education. It should be noted that such grievance procedures are usable only to the extent that discretionary judgment may be invoked to give relief—conditions fixed by law or regulation are not legitimate grievances since even the board of education may exercise no judgment or discretion in these matters.

NEGOTIATIONS

There is a rather broad absence of enabling legislation that permits boards of education to negotiate with employees in such a manner that the negotiation will be binding upon the board. The trend, however, would seem to be toward such legislation. Boards of education may choose to negotiate in the absence of this enabling legislation; however, that which is agreed upon continues at the pleasure of the board and is, in fact, not really negotiated. This places the administrator in a strategic position between the teacher and the board of education. It is he through whom the teachers will most often work in seeking board action. The position of the administrator requires that this component represent to the board for himself and the rest of the professional staff the best thinking for the conduct of education, at the same time invoking the policies of the board of education with himself and the remaining professional staff. It is clear where and to whom he is legally responsible. How he behaves as a human component in the system predicts his moral and ethical disposition to those with whom he works.

One other condition is unique for the system. Relationships between and among teachers and administrators are wholly professional; each component is an employee in the system and relationships of components vary as the teacher works with pupils and the administrator works with teachers and the board of education. The character of the fully professional relationship is one where knowledge and skill are presumed, whereas in the situation of a professional working with nonprofessionals there may be marked variations in both knowledge and skill as it would apply to systemic operation.

Teacher-Pupil Relationships

Precedent in law has established that the teacher has an *in loco parentis* relationship with pupils—a relationship of "standing in place of the parent." Equally, precedent has established that boards of education may make and enforce any reasonable regulations to govern pupil conduct. Where reasonableness is tested the courts will deal only with the particular case in application—not with the general reasonableness of the rule or regulation. The teacher, then, has a remarkable freedom in dealing with pupils. His domain of control extends outside the classroom and even off school grounds and outside the regular school hours. He may legally attempt to control student behavior which tends to bring the school or its employees into disrespect.

Attendance and Decorum

Although most states have some form of compulsory education law, attendance in the public school is generally described as a privilege not a right. The child may enjoy the privilege of regular attendance so long as his conduct does not place in jeopardy the legitimate rights of others to the educational opportunities of the school system. The teacher in his classroom relationships with pupils has the task of developing particular talents and abilities, while assuring that individual differences among pupils do not extend to that point where they impinge upon the equal rights of other students.

The responsibility of the teacher for decorum in the classroom is usually tested by a judgment of foreseeability—a determination of whether a hypothetical reasonable person in the same situation would have been able to foresee the event and the extent to which it might have been averted. The teacher cannot be expected to foresee all of the possible consequences of an activity; however, he is expected to take normal precautionary action in advising pupils of potential danger and to adjust activities to the sex, size, maturity, and general preparedness of the pupils for the activities.

These same adjustments apply to the use of corporal punishment with pupils. In the absence of a regulation forbidding its use, the teacher may at his discretion use corporal punishment with pupils. It is expected that the punishment will be adapted to the nature of the offense, will be meted out without malice, and will cause no permanent injury to the pupil. Certain of these conditions might seem to place the teacher in a rather precarious position. He might feel that the punishment is necessary soon after the act if the pupil is to associate the punishment with the act performed; at the same time, he may have concern that immediate punishment might seem malicious and emotive, lacking in rational reflection. Commonly, the courts have given the teacher the benefit of the doubt and have protected the teacher from liability where it could not be shown clearly that the punishment administered was excessive and unreasonable.

NEGLIGENCE AND LIABILITY

Historically, the school district has been held by the courts to lack the capacity for liability in negligence since the schools are quasi-corporate arms of the state. The state was seen as sovereign and enjoyed the extension of the notion that the "King can do no wrong." This historic immunity has had no application where the school maintains a nuisance or where criminal liability accrues to a teacher. In recent years the Doctrine of Immunity enjoyed by the schools has been appreciably eroded. Court decisions are coming to recognize that the system of public schools is "big business" and that the system engages frequently in large-scale money raising ventures (such as athletic contests for which admission is charged). School districts and teachers in recent years have undertaken to carry liability insurance and the courts have sometimes taken the position that to carry the insurance presumes the possibility of liability. In a few states there are provisions in the law which require that local school districts also be sued when the teacher is sued, and it follows that the district assumes a liability for those acts which it has directed the teacher to initiate and perform as a part of his regular duties as an employee of the district.

The whole matter of teacher liability regarding pupil behavior makes it imperative that the teacher clearly understand what are the activities endorsed by the board of education in which he has responsibility for initiation and supervision. To the extent that he elects to go beyond that which falls under board sponsorship he is, in a sense, on his own and is certainly much more open to personal liability. If this discussion of teacher-pupil relationships has a rather punitive slant, it is because most of the legal literature regarding this relationship is directed toward cases in which teacher negligence has been charged. Possibly because there is an absence of cases, little legal literature treats the intimate relationship between the teacher and the pupil in the teaching-learning situation—the relationship which would include the responsibility for maximum learning under everyday circumstances.

BOARD REGULATIONS

Although the board of education has extensive power to regulate pupil conduct, the relationships between pupils and teachers will usually be the by-product of how these regulations are perceived and effected in the classroom. It is possible that the board will set generally prescriptive regulations, whereas the teacher might be willing to forego certain compliance with these regulations. The thought that learning, even teaching, could better prosper in a permissive atmosphere may tempt the teacher to take less seriously regulations set by the board. This course of action is perilous and, in fact, insubordinate, no matter what desirable learning outcomes result for pupils. Where teachers feel that particular regulations have no real bearing on the teaching-learning situation in the classroom or on the desired socialization of pupils in the school, it behooves them to take their case through the administration to the board of education, trusting that the board, since it makes the final judgment, will have the best educational interests of pupils at heart. Teachers who ignore the regulations set for teacher-pupil conduct repudiate the foundations of a society of men who govern themselves by their own laws—the very society for which pupils are candidates.

Legal Aspects of Curriculum Development

The state is the highest level at which prescription regarding curricular observances may be set. Although the Supreme Court has acted in protecting individual rights, such as permitting non-observance of the flag salute and denying the right to use prayer in the school, it rarely has reviewed *what* may be taught (see *Meyer v. Nebraska* 1923) and has chosen to review how teaching is done only to the extent of protecting the rights of teachers to pursue the teaching of that for which they have prepared.

STATE ROLE

The several states have by law and regulation established minimum standards for their public schools. Frequently it is the responsibility of local boards to assure that nonpublic schools in the district also meet the standards set by the state. These minimum standards typically refer to particular courses which must be offered at certain grade levels, the amount of time which must be devoted to instruction in particular subjects, and the observation of particular commemorative days during the year. Here again, the state is prescriptive—it is mandated that the board of education as officers of the state for the local school district see that these standards are included in the regular program for the school. There is no discretion for the board of education in those standards mandated by the state. The board of education in each school district is free, however, to choose to exceed the minimum standards set by the state. More importantly, it is left to the local districts to determine *how* those elements mandated for the curriculum shall be taught.

In states where the agency for education is strongly supported there are often suggested syllabuses prepared by state agency employees in conjunction with groups of teachers and resource persons from the schools. In subject areas where there may be a state-wide examination to determine pupil achievement it is not uncommon for the suggested syllabuses to be coercive in terms of what is actually taught. It is not unlikely that national examinations may intrude certain of this same coercion into the classroom. It is also common practice for states to recognize lists of textbooks from which individual school districts may choose those they wish to adopt for use in their classrooms. The breadth of choice among books varies from state to state.

DISTRICT ACTION

The board of education is in a pivotal position in the adoption of curriculums for the schools. All decisions beyond those conditions mandated by the state must be reached by the local board of education. Usually these decisions are reached upon the advisement of the chief school administrator of the district who, in turn, has sought advisement from appropriate subordinate staff members. In districts where the decisions regarding curriculum are made wholly by the board with little or no advisement from the professional staff, there is a blatant denial of the competency of the professional employees to act in one of the capacities for which they were hired.

Likewise, the professional staff of the school has a responsibility to the board of education to put into practice those curriculums which have been adopted by the board. The haziest area in the legal aspects of curriculum development is in teaching methodologies employed by the professional staff. Although curriculum development and methodology may be seen as separate concerns, it seems unlikely that curriculums can be rationally evolved without consideration being given to the teaching media. The general contention has been that this is wholly a professional matter—that the act of teaching can only be resolved by professionals, and then often only on an individual basis. It might be contended, however, that the method employed becomes, in fact, part of the curriculum for the student and if this is true then the board of education has a legal concern in this area.

While the state will suggest syllabuses which intend assurance that all the public school pupils in the state are given exposure to a necessary, if minimum, content in subjects, the local board of education is relatively free to expand or contract the courses of study so that the joint desires of the board and local professional employees might be met. Local desires might take the character of heightening the emphasis upon a particular subject field, of developing and offering study in subjects not commonly taught, or of integrating content which will draw attention to local heritage believed worthy for consideration by pupils.

As the board of education adopts curriculums for the schools, it undertakes a further responsibility to seek out professional teachers who will have and employ the necessary talents and skills to properly present the curriculum in their areas of competency. It means too that as changes in the curriculum are undertaken, experienced teachers in the school system may need orientation to revisions and changes. Where boards of education make the decision to keep abreast of the times and point to the future in curriculums adopted for the schools, they must also face the decision of supporting programs for the professional staff which will assure a continuing ability to understand and teach what is adopted. The language of the law is very general in this matter but it usually says, in effect, that boards of education have the *duty* to do what is necessary to secure the best educational results.

MATERIALS AND COPYRIGHT

One further area of legal concern in curriculum development involves the use of materials which the school does not own. Specifically, legal considerations obtain when materials under copyright are reproduced for use, either by mechanical or electronic means, without the prior consent of the owner. Commonly this problem arises when a teacher wants to reproduce materials from published writings or wishes to tape a musical selection from a record. Although it is difficult for the owner of material which is widely disseminated to monitor the use of that material, it is clearly the responsibility of the user to obtain permission or, at the least, to give credit of authorship. In the case of certain materials (i.e., dramatic productions) payment to the owner of the material may be required for its use. Materials which may be used freely usually contain a statement to this effect. Since the review by Congress of present copyright legislation, attention has been drawn to the possibility that the use of copying devices for the reproduction of educational materials may be further restricted under the law.

When it is not clear who owns published materials, communication with the publisher will usually establish whether the publisher or the author(s) or both retain ownership. Materials which are not commercially published or do not have copyright may be used at the discretion of the teacher or school system, however, when it is clear that the materials are the product of an individual or an agency which can be identified, the courtesy is often extended to request permission for use. The simple courtesy note may evoke information which will enhance the use of the material or lead to other and newer materials appropriate for use.

LOYALTY OATH

Recently the Supreme Court established that the disclaimer oath as administered in one state (New York) was unconstitutional. The court was widely split on the issue, which might indicate that oaths are yet another "gray area," subject to further interpretation. The question seems to remain, "Who is protecting whom from what?"

Problems and Issues

1. *How might professional components within the public school system suggest the direction which law should take?* The public school teacher is in a paradoxical position. He is charged with teaching children an appreciation of our heritage as a people who govern themselves. At the same time, he may feel a professional obligation to suggest the direction which law should take for the betterment of society—a direction which may predict the need for change in the law. As a professional public employee there may be some constraints upon his civil liberties as an individual. Yet,

the teacher must make some sense of his paradoxical position if
he is to function effectively as a human being and as a teacher.
Are there constraints placed upon a teacher as he performs his
professional tasks?—If so, what are the implications of these
restraining forces? Do teachers have a right (an obligation) to
suggest the direction which law should take?—If so, toward what
population and by what means should their efforts be focused?

2. *How can the federal government comply with its obligation
to provide for the general welfare while acknowledging the rights
of the several states in the matter of public education.* There are
not equivalent educational opportunities for all students in all
states. The federal government has an abiding obligation to each
citizen while at the same time it has a similar constitutional mandate to observe and respect certain freedoms extended to the states.
Congressional enactments in recent years have been pointed toward
improving educational opportunity for all youth. In some cases,
individual states have charged that participation in federal programs has amounted to coercion and placed in jeopardy state decisions having to do with how education will be conducted in that
state. The questions which may be asked is whether the individual
is more important than the state. The individual is both a citizen
of the state and the nation. Which governmental body shall have
the controlling influence over how his education shall be conducted?
—If there is to be a compromise of control, in which dimensions
will the state have particular rights?—In which will the federal
government have domain?—How might teachers engage themselves
in this process to assure that the legal outcomes reflect a thoughtful consideration for the education of youth and the future of
society?

3. *Do public school systems have a proper role in challenging
existing law through test cases?* Where the public school system
desires to do something which it considers to be good for youth
and for society but acknowledges that existing law forbids the
action, the system must make a decision. The system can comply
with existing law, it can seek through other agencies or persons
to influence legislation which will amend existing law, or it might
ignore existing law and risk a legal challenge of its activities.

Since the policy and operation of public school systems is jointly
arrived at by lay and professional judgment, there may exist some
genuine conflict when it is asked what is of the greatest worth:
observance of the law or sponsoring activities which are believed to
be good? Since our people are typified as a society which governs
itself by law, the latter choice of action might extend civil disobedience beyond reasonable limits. How might national referendums be used to determine the broad texture of public opinion

regarding what is good?—By what means might the process of altering existing law be hastened where time may be an essential factor—How might political expediency be avoided in legislation which has particular impact upon public education?—What might be the proper roles of professional educational components in this task?

Selected References

American Association of School Administrators. *Code of Ethics.* Washington, D.C.: The Association, 1966.

Edwards, Newton. *The Courts and the Public Schools,* rev. ed. Chicago: University of Chicago Press, 1955.

Flowers, Ann, and Edward C. Bolmeier. *Law and Pupil Control.* Cincinnati: W. H. Anderson Company, 1964.

Fulbright, Evelyn R. and Edward C. Bolmeier. *Courts and the Curriculum.* Cincinnati: W. H. Anderson Company, 1964.

Garber, Lee O., and Newton Edwards. *School Law Casebook Series,* I–IV. Danville, Ill.: Interstate Printers and Publishers, 1962–1964.

Gauerke, Warren E. *Legal and Ethical Responsibilities of School Personnel.* Englewood Cliffs, N.J.: Prentice-Hall, Inc. 1959.

Nolte, M. Chester, and John Phillip Linn. *School Law for Teachers.* Danville, Ill.: Interstate Printers and Publishers, 1963.

Zelermyer, William. *The Process of Legal Reasoning.* Englewood Cliffs, N.J.: Prentice-Hall, 1960.

chapter 5

■ *The Economic Environment*

Support for the System

Public school systems as institutions of society are both producers and consumers. The method of economics provides one way of inspecting how the system operates in society. Only one form of "capital" placed in the system appreciates in value—the student; the appreciation which takes place benefits both the individual and the society. Other investments in the system are essentially consumable. A bench measure of the efficiency of the system might be the extent to which these other investments in the system do in fact support the appreciation in value of the student component. Conversely, investment in the system which does not support appreciation of student components becomes an expenditure which might be described as overhead—an expenditure necessary to the operation of the system but less closely related to the students. The system often could not exist without expenditure for these overhead items.

Support for the system from without—from society—takes two forms. It involves the extent to which youth are placed in the system for the purpose of education and the extent to which the system is provided with what it needs to accomplish this task.

There is also an internal support mission for the system which might be described as the plan for management within the system of those investments made from without. Internal support, then, involves planning and providing system-sponsored activities for students and procuring the necessary personnel and facilities for these activities.

There has been great popularity for describing the support of education in terms of the tax effort made by the local community to support the local school system. While it is true that local students attend local schools and that monies are raised, in the main, from what might be called local sources, there would appear to be a trend for the increased state and federal support of education. In a financial sense, this is local money being returned to local communities; both the community from which it was raised and other communities in which the need for the money might be greater.

Support for the system must, then, be seen in a context much larger than only the local community. This becomes especially obvious when it is considered that monies raised by state and federal governmental units are not directly approved by the people. The people, where they vote on the local budget for the public school system, actually determine the extent to which they will be able to participate in available state and federal monies. By example, state aid to local school districts is often determined, in part, by the local efforts made to support the public schools. Certain federal and state funds are available only to those school systems which elect to carry a shared cost for those programs being sponsored by higher governmental units.

Where a state or the federal government offers to underwrite a significant percentage of the cost of an educational program, the local school system may take the position that it cannot afford not to participate in the program. This is a little like the person who buys something on sale only because the article is such a tremendous buy; there is no reflection on his need for the article. School systems participating in such "bargain" programs are no less guilty than the shopper unless they have clearly established a rationale based on appreciating the student for bringing outside-sponsored programs into the activities of the system.

While economic analyses tend to deal in the main with the external support of the school—both in terms of dollars allotted for public education from several sources and in terms of the incidence of human capital entrusted to the system for formal education—there is also the matter of the internal economics of public school systems. Since "local" school systems are quasi-corporate arms of the state, the tool of economics must be used in any given school system with the clear understanding that the system is not an entity unto itself but has dependent relationships with intermediate units (county and area districts set by the state) and with the state itself.

Consideration of the internal support for the system probably replicates to some extent the external support mission. The principal difference lies with how the system chooses to distribute its wealth among its several components. Certain of this distribution is set by law. Other choices of distribution are made by the local board of education and represent the value structure of the local school unit. Presumably, the law of the state *requires* local school systems to dedicate particular portions of their resources to programs or tasks which the state has elected to value highly. As the valuing of the state becomes prescriptive for the local district (a condition in which the local district seems to have less and less discretion in deciding how it will distribute its resources), the public school system might be seen as a "state system." In states where there is a high degree of variation in the distribution of resources among the several school districts it might be said that there is an acknowledgement of or support for "local control" or this might be the result of a long heritage of local control with a commensurate lack of power or leadership from the state level. As local control is greater, there is a concurrent need for a greater rapport between the school and the community—especially if the community has a voice in what resources will be made available to the local school system. It might even be suggested that where local control is strong there is a concurrent strength of reflection of the community (its values) in the local school system.

Enumerating the Economic Aspects of the System

Economics as an analytic tool is useful in describing the relationships between the goals for the system (in this case, the desired behavioral changes in students) and the resources at the disposal of the system (both real and dispositional and including the student). It is an especially applicable tool where there are alternatives or options to be chosen among in the distribution of these resources. The output of the public school system (the student for himself and the student as a member of the society) can be "measured" only in very gross terms. Finite determinations of the outcomes of public schools are at best speculative. With these conditions given, the task of the public school system is one of attempting to best deploy its resources to achieve the desired behavioral change in students.

Apart from the student, the principal resources of the system are money (or some other exchange medium) and the dispositional postures of those who have a voice in systemic decisions. In using its resources the system must decide upon how it will invest in *time, personnel,* and *facilities*—the three principal commodities at its disposal to effect the operation of the system. None of these three commodities can be viewed alone since each bears a dependent relationship to the other two. Often the law of the state will prescribe some limits upon time. Frequently, there will be statutes which obligate the school system to offer certain of its program for a specific number of minutes each day and possibly each day of the school week. This decision of time commitment has been made for the local school system. Its freedom is limited to what *other time* it chooses to commit for these required programs and also the time it chooses to allot to other aspects of the curriculum which the statutes do not control. If it is accepted that there are a reasonable number of hours in the school day and that teaching effectiveness remains constant, granting that the limits of both are somewhat flexible, then time allotted for one element in the curriculum of the system necessarily is at the expense of other elements which might have been offered or which must be presented in a restricted time period.

Where time is allotted for particular activities there must be space (facilities) in which the activities might be conducted. There will usually be professional staff members (personnel) associated with the supervision of these activities.

Investment in personnel for most public school systems involves strategies of procurement, deployment, and retraining. The last strategy is especially important in those states that have tenure statutes or continuing contracts. The public school system will probably devote each year about 70 per cent of its current expenditure budget to instructional services. A commitment of this magnitude might suggest that the system has chosen to value most highly (in terms of aspiring toward systemic goal accomplishment) the services of its instructional personnel. An alternate view is that instructional personnel (fully certified professional components) are often required by statute and that the school system must increasingly devote a larger segment of its resources to their procurement and retention if it is to comply with the law.

In either event it might be expected that the public school system would be especially thoughtful in procuring and deploying this "high cost" item. It might also be expected that the system would expend other resources to assure that professional personnel are "freed" so that the best use might be made of their time. Such is not always the case. Often disproportionate amounts of their time are being devoted to tasks other than the preparation and presentation of the curriculum. Where professional components are assigned to tasks peripheral to instruction, not only is instructional and planning time lost but the efficiency of performance at professional tasks may be diminished.

Relationships Between Expenditures and Quality

The impact of education on the national economy is often described by citing the increase in aggregate income and employment as scarce resources are committed to education. In general, this is a social impact of expenditures for education. On a more individual basis it has been anticipated that our citizenry will have a heightened earning power as more people persist in school and matriculate to higher levels of education. None of these relationships, however, deals with how expenditures for the system of public education affect the quality of the system itself.

ASSESSMENT

An assessment of the quality of the system and its relationship to expenditures for the system requires that some criteria be established to permit inspection of the system at a given time *while students are in it*. Although outcomes for students in later life are of critical import, the probability of desired outcomes can only be enhanced by direct attention toward what is now being done within the school system.

Within the systems the principal relationship between expenditure and quality depends upon the extent to which the educational program for the system predicts the expenditure pattern. In a sense it is here that criteria are set, that priorities for expenditures are set in terms of the perceived educational needs of the system. Where the reverse takes place (and this is too often the case) the educational program becomes no more than a chance reflection of the monies available at a given time. The first move toward achieving quality for the system is to assure that monies are being allotted to sectors of the system on a priority basis where the priority order is clearly in terms of the goals for the system. Implicit in this is, of course, a systemic recognition of the needs of youth and society as both recipients and sponsors of the system.

If it is accepted that the future is difficult to predict and that it is the task of the school to prepare youth to be able to successfully cope as adults, then one expenditure area for the public school system must receive more attention than it has heretofore. School systems must become actively engaged in research and development. Among other things this means that school systems must be willing to expend some risk capital—and they must be willing to accept that there will be a relatively high loss ratio. The pay-off, of course, lies with what can be discovered and done within the system as a result of this expenditure. Research and development will also tend to offset the liklihood of the school system becoming too fixed in its ways. It will create a healthy ferment within the system while at the same time giving evidence to the public that eternal answers to curriculum and methodology have not yet been found.

What is being suggested is that for any given school system its quality is a transient thing, dependent upon its sensitivity to personal and societal needs, the capabilities of the system, and its preparation for the educational needs of the future.

Assumption of Risk

It might even be said that the public school system has a responsibility to assume some risks concerning the future—risks reflected in the support mission for the present school program. Two kinds of risks seem especially dangerous. One is the "averaging" of an expenditure program in that it expresses an inability or unwillingness of the board of education and practitioner administrators to take risks. It is predicated upon the assumption that each element of the school program will have its ups and downs, that all elements of the program have equivalent import, and, worst of all, that significant movement toward improving quality cannot be achieved by differential expenditure among the several elements of the program.

The second bad risk would appear to be more pervasive in public education, probably because it is often seen as a characteristic of humans in organizations. This risk is that what is being done in a "well-known," "good" school system is equally applicable to other school systems. Heightened accent on innovation in education often has led to this attitude. The danger lies with the fact that the "well-known" school system may be in only the exploratory stages of the innovation and may be still collecting data to test whether it should be made part of the regular program. The other school systems which, in reality, *adopt* the innovation through risking emulation are counting on the transfer of quality. If these bandwagon school systems are correct in their approach to seeking quality, then serious consideration ought to be given to a greater standardization of educational practice. Citing this approach to quality education as a bad risk presumes that we know as yet too little about human behavior and that what little we think we know would seem to indicate that there are more differences than similarities in expenditure practices which provide quality education.

The stigma of the second risk is further confounded by the pressure brought upon the public schools from the public sector. It is not unreasonable or unnatural for citizens to want "their" public school system to be "like" systems which are meeting with particular favor on the national scene. It falls to all the professional components and especially to administrative components in the system to be alert for innovations which *may* be adapted for use in their particular system. Equally, it is incumbent on the professional components in the system to resist pressures from whatever sources suggest that the public school system should borrow the trappings of instant success.

The school system which seeks quality education from its expenditures may well not be typified by widespread innovation; evidence of "change" may be difficult to discern in a dynamic state. However, in seeking quality through careful expenditure the school system has the opportunity to build a sound rationale for phasing in and out particular elements in its program. The absence of abrupt changes in the program of the school not only predicts thoughtful planning and testing of its worthiness for inclusion but also improves the chances of the change being acceptable to those who must implement it.

Overcoming Economic Disadvantages

ATTACKING DISADVANTAGEMENT

The principal approach to overcoming an economic disadvantage has been to merge the school district with one or several larger districts. Expanding the geography of the district has sometimes expanded the economic base of the school system. It has also meant, in some cases, that instead of having a small disadvantaged district, merger has resulted in an enlarged disadvantaged district. One of the elements of economic disadvantage has been the persistent reliance upon taxation for raising monies to support the district.

Taxpayer resistance coupled with an inflationary spiral has resulted in many school districts not being able to keep pace with the economy. Deficit spending becomes necessary. Delays in taxpayer approval of capital improvement (for example, the erection of new buildings) often have made the improvement much more costly than originally anticipated. Increases in state taxes for noneducational purposes have held relatively stable the proportion of state aid to local school districts. The impact of these conditions has been that school systems have had to spend more each year to "keep even" and that the increased spending has relied upon monies raised locally.

Although the state has not kept pace with increased spending needs in local districts, the federal government has provided through the several titles of the Elementary and Secondary Education Act monies for particular purposes. In the main, these federal monies are used to reduce problems of disadvantage. The federal monies are, however, initiatory or "seed" monies in the sense that it is expected that local districts increasingly will take over these programs. Too, there is no assurance that there will be a constant flow of federal monies or for what specific purposes federal money will be available. Hypothetically, the economically disadvantaged local school system is not in bad shape if its disadvantage is one defined as such by the federal government at a particular time. Where the problem arises is in those districts where there are *other* forms of disadvantage for which external monies are not available.

SYSTEMIC REACTIONS TO DISADVANTAGEMENT

One of the simplest economic disadvantages found in most school districts today is meeting the demands for teacher salaries (instructional services). Since these services often represent some 70 per cent of the current operating budget, districts which cannot compete in the market of teacher procurement are also faced with losing presently employed teachers to other districts. The result often is accepting procurement of teachers of lesser quality or training than is desired and acquiescence to the loss of present personnel at an abnormally high rate. There are also teachers in each district who might be classified as "captive" teachers—professional components who probably will not leave the district because there are other reasons why they have elected to remain in the community.

Granting that disadvantaged districts will continue to try to procure high caliber personnel, their present position might suggest that available resources be deployed to both retrain the existing professional components and extend supervisory services. It may also necessitate a retrenchment in the educational program for the system. Although this last alternative is less than an optimum condition, it acknowledges that there are priorities in the educational program of the system.

It behooves the disadvantaged public school system to assess carefully whether the conditions of disadvantage lie within the system or whether they reside in its environment. In the case of the student himself being disadvantaged, the problem is complex since the student has an existence both within and external to the system. Where the external environment, frequently the local community, is the source of economic disadvantage, the school may solicit community acceptance of a narrow program as an alternative to adequate economic support. Unfortunately, public schools have frequently "withdrawn" elements of the program which have high community support (for example, interscholastic athletics, hot lunch programs, and bus transportation) in an attempt to "blackmail" the community into accepting the total support package which the school seeks. These efforts often refute the priorities for the educational program of the school while coercing the public into believing that if the school cannot have what it wants then the community cannot have those elements of the program in which it has the most interest. There is little wonder that voter resistance heightens as the school portrays the role of Peck's bad boy or that communities question whether in fact there really are priorities in the educational program of the public school.

Capitalizing on Economic Advantages

FINANCIAL ADVANTAGE

Concern with the scarcity of time is pervasive for all public school systems when it is considered that students are "passing through" the system at a relatively constant rate. While plans for time usage may be improved over the years, individual students must rely on what is happening now.

The economically advantaged public school system also has the opportunity to engage in broad-based planning. If it is committed to *public* education and the assumption that the professional components are agents for society at large, then there is the likelihood that the advisement of many people will be invited as the educational program is framed. Analogous to the saying that the rich get richer, the system which involves many people representing the spectrum of society in the framing of the school program will probably be the system which continues to elicit strong support. It is the system where the economic support for education continues to rise as articulate communication between the school community and society is sought and maintained.

Economically advantaged schools may drift toward oligarchy. The select few who really decide what will be done may be resident in the community or the school. Or they may represent both camps but be like-minded, since they are bred and nurtured in closed environments the persistence of their goodness is based upon a great deal of guessing and a strong reliance upon chance. The history of social institutions would seem to indicate that sooner or later the people in their larger numbers will be heard. When their voice has to be eruptive the impact on the educational program may be disruptive if not disastrous.

LUXURY AND RISK

The economically advantaged school system which is also supporting education can afford the luxury of error. It is in the position of being able to take more risks in its program for education. An element of the educational program in such a district may have only fifth level priority and yet be stronger than the same element in the program of a less advantaged district. Since the advantaged district is in a position to employ more professional components, it can, in a sense, create time. When "time is gained," there can be more choices for students toward which they might be directed for any given segment of the school day.

If the general educational program is uncommonly strong, there is the added risk that weak elements in the program may persist as the system assumes a self-satisfied posture. While the advantaged district may drop and add elements in its educational program as it is deemed necessary or wise, there are still the problems of dealing with the professional components who must effect the transition. It might be suggested that where the program is strong there has obtained a certain amount of bureaucratization hence there are built-in resistors to change.

The advantaged district must live with the paradox of being proud of how sound its program is, yet not becoming so committed to the program that it loses the ability to alter or discard it should other, more appropriate approaches be discovered. Such a program requires professional personnel and a community disposed to placing a strong value on constantly striving for the best possible educational program. The advantaged district which becomes complacent not only does a disservice to its students but also to society since it portrays a static model of what is purportedly good—a model which refutes the possibility of improvement and begs adoption rather than adaptation.

Generating More Appropriate Economic Bases for the System

SOURCES

There would appear to be two distinct sources of wealth which are sought by the public school system; dollars and favorable attitudinal dispositions. These principal bases for the support of the system are not necessarily concurrent nor does the express giving or offering of one or both necessarily predict support for the public school system per se. Dollar support for public education may mean only that the community fathers have discovered that one means of attracting industrial wealth to a community is to provide strong public schools, even if it means a higher tax rate. Attitudinal support for public education, including aspiring to membership on the board of education, is frequently considered politically wise by those who seek other public office. The basic question is whether dollar and attitudinal support for public education reflects a concern with public education or is it a means to several other ends having to do with the education of youth and betterment of society. What will be the answer to this question? Probably, it will never be known. There will always be professed rationales for support of

public education. Whether they are the true reasons is conjectural.
Those concerned with motives have long been vexed with this
problem. A more pragmatic approach directs attention to garnering
the support and being less concerned with the motives which elicit
it. In any event *someone* must be reasonably convinced that support
of public education is important, or else there would not be support
for it by those who seek public favor or the improvement of their
own image.

Traditionally, education has been a state function. There is an
equal tradition for the several states to extend considerable discretion to their local school districts. Historically, strong reliance has
been placed upon the property tax as a means of raising dollars for
public education.

LOCAL RESISTANCE AND REACTIONS

Recently attention has been drawn to a number of events which
deviate from the tradition and at the same time establish prece-
dents. Boards of education in local school districts are meeting
increasing resistance to raising monies for public education through
local property tax. State legislatures would seem to be extending
less discretion to local boards of education. At the same time, while
state tax revenues are increasing, there has not been a significant
increase in the share of these revenues being devoted to public
education. The federal government, especially through the Elementary and Secondary Education Act, has clearly become concerned
with and directly involved in providing fiscal support for educational programs in local school districts in the several states. Pressures at the federal level have created some anxiety over whether
federal support will be continuing or serve only an initiatory function. At all levels of government—local, state, and federal—there
is a keen competition for the tax dollar. While the federal government may awaken states and communities to the importance of
education in our society, the support mission (raising tax dollars)
is still principally a local task. Although states are increasing their
aid to local districts in dollars, the share of state revenue committed
to education remains approximately the same and leaves the local
school district in the throes of a long-standing problem but with
increased citizen interest in improving public education.

FEDERAL ROLE

Generating *appropriate* economic bases for the support of public
education requires a value judgment which can be made only by the
people, by society. The value judgment is manifest in the social,
economic, and political sectors of our society. Bolstering the economy in some ways (for example, a "war economy") may defeat the

hope for increased support for education while giving an overall impression of economic strength. But as national resources are marshalled to support the demands of the Department of Defense there is a concurrent shrinking or increased scarcity of resources for other socially sponsored institutions such as the public schools. Economists often suggest that a careful balance must be maintained between progressive and regressive taxation on the assumption that there must be an equity in taxes levied among peoples of varying resources and with different consumption patterns. The decision then is one of national scope. To what extent do we as a people choose to value (and hence support) public education?

If education is deemed to have a national importance then it would appear reasonable to solicit for the raising of monies where they exist and the expenditure of these monies where they are most needed. Obviously, this suggests differential expenditures. While different dollar amounts would be raised through local, state, and federal taxation from available sources, equity could be sought in the *effort* made by persons or institutions to support public education.

Accepting the federal concern for the General Welfare of the people, it is possible that the principal collector of taxes might be the federal government. Relief in local communities might be sought permitting them more flexibility in raising *additional* monies if they so choose to sponsor locally desired programs or to enrich elements in the basic educational program which might be deemed desirable for all public school systems.

A means of distributing this money which has been suggested is the "rebate" to the several states of a fixed percentage of what has been collected from the state in federal income tax. While this alone would not compensate for the distribution of monies to where they are most needed, it would accomplish at least the gathering of money in such a manner that equivalent effort to pay would be observed.

If education is not seen as a national problem with commensurate federal legislation clearly directed toward its support, then it must be concluded that sufficient conditions are being met by leaving the decision of the extent to which education will be economically supported to individual states and to local school districts. Where the decision is reached to support the latter—an optional local support for education—it must be understood that there will continue to be immense variation in the support missions performed and that the quality of public education will remain a chance condition of political and economic geography.

In essence then all the people must be confronted with the decision of whether they wish to support education—whether they give it a high enough priority in the national economy that it can withstand the many other passing demands for scarce resources. Once this decision has been affirmed, one way or the other, the existing legislative and executive structure of our government are fully capable of effecting the support mission.

Problems and Issues

1. *How do economic environments vary from system to system?* In the process of preparing financial support plans, the state gets recommendations from potential recipients about the most equitable means for distributing tax dollars to equalize the educational opportunities of children served by the educational programs of the state. A common concern in metropolitan areas is expressed over the differences in noneducational requirements facing urban centers. "Municipal overburden" is claimed to make support needs of central city different from those of out-state communities.

Under the concept of overburden, the city maintains that its citizens have only a limited amount of funds to expend for tax purposes. That finite quantity must cover streets, lights, police and fire protection, local welfare, and other city-provided services not generally reimbursed by the state. Because the cost of services provided by cities is *proportionately* higher than the services provided elsewhere, and because the city tends to provide services at a higher level than elsewhere, "municipal overburden" reduces the amount of money available for local educational programs. Because education is a legal function of the state, the cities have turned more and more to the state legislatures for larger and larger shares of financial support for public education. In some cases, educational need, increased by influx of poorly educated persons, is also cited as justification for differentiating support payments. Given the overburden argument, what should be the out-state response?— What real differences in need are apparent among districts?—How shall differences be accommodated in a democratic society—What stands should professionals take?—What is the federal role?

2. *How shall education be "equalized?"* In an era of rapid transportation and great population mobility, school systems across the country become the almost constant recipients of new students educated in adjacent districts, elsewhere in the state, or in some other region of the country. Such mobility has placed new demands for educational equalization on broader and broader scales.

Compounding the problems created by humans in transit is the inequality in the location of wealth from system to system or from state to state. Equalization has been attempted in many ways within states. The broader questions now seem to be, should educational opportunity be equalized on a federal basis?—How might it be accomplished?—With what attendant dangers?—At what cost to state programs?—At any level, how is equalization best achieved?

3. *What are the dimensions of "advantagement" and "disadvantagement?"* From a standpoint of wealth, advantagement can be viewed in many ways—the location of factories, utilities, and railroads; the location and value of residential property; the location of sources of income; the location of the income producer's home; the location of intangible properties; the source of sales tax collections; and so forth. Secondarily, advantagement may refer to an educational condition arising from high-quality students, attractiveness of the system to outstanding teachers, a history of creative leadership, and so on. Given the distance between advantagement and disadvantagement, how can the distance be reduced?—When reducing disadvantagement is accomplished at the cost of reducing the educational quality in the advantaged system, how can it be justified?—Under what conditions?—For what ends?—At what political risk?—At what educational cost?

Selected References

Benson, Charles. *The Economics of Public Education.* Boston: Houghton Mifflin, 1961.

Benson, Charles. *Perspectives on the Economics of Education.* Boston: Houghton Mifflin, 1963.

Burkhead, Jesse. *State and Local Taxes for Public Education.* Syracuse, N.Y.: Syracuse University Press, 1963.

Carlton, Frank Tracey. *Economic Influences Upon Educational Progress in the United States, 1820–1950.* New York: Teachers College, Columbia University, 1966.

The Cost of Education Index. (Prepared annually by the editors of *School Management.*)

Galbraith, John. *The Affluent Society.* Boston: Houghton Mifflin, 1958.

Harris, Seymour E. ed. *Challenge and Change in American Education and Public Policy.* Berkeley Cal.: McCutchan Publishing, 1965.

Harris, Seymour. *More Resources for Education.* New York: Harper & Row, 1960.

Miner, Jerry. *Social and Economic Factors in Spending for Public Education.* Syracuse, N.Y.: Syracuse University Press, 1963.

National Committee for the Support of Public Schools. *Changing Demands on Education and Their Fiscal Implications.* Washington D.C.: The Committee, 1963.

Tiedt, Sidney W. *The Role of the Federal Government in Education.* New York: Oxford University Press, 1966.

chapter 6

■ *The Political*
Environment

In addition to the legal and economic institutions and forces created by a society to serve as expressions of its will, a third group of institutions and forces has arisen to satisfy society's political requirements. These constitute the political environment in which public schools must operate. Just as an educational system must be responsive and sensitive to legal and economic forces so must it exist simultaneously in several political environments each of which carries unique potentials, stimuli, restraints, and pitfalls. The administration of a public school system in a contemporary American community is, in no small measure, a political adventure requiring the administrative head to be politic in the discharge of his duties.

Unfortunately, the term "political" does not always convey a wholesome picture. Somehow the term has often become associated with partisanship; thus, an act done for "political purposes" carries a connotation of selfish or one-sided advantage. Fortunately, other adjectival usage carries less of a colored connotation. For example, a "political subdivision" should simply imply a geographic region in which the qualified populace can carry forth particular governmental functions. Even so, some would conjure an image of gerry-mandered real estate.

Politic is meant to imply wisdom in the conduct of the various affairs of state. Differentiation in perceptions about what is wise serves as the genesis for partisan bodies devoted to the pursuit of their individual beliefs. Conjecture about the wisdom of particular governmental activity "before the fact" forces a magnification of the differences between bodies, and the use of the term *political* to convey the differences is calculated to put the term in the poorest of lights.

For purposes of clarification, the term *political* shall be used in association with (1) the various ways in which society as a whole attempts to develop its institutions to reflect its own desires and (2) the various ways in which the institutions themselves attempt to be responsive to society in its segmented parts. The first portion of the definition requires a review of the formal and informal structures through which society expresses its desires upon the institutions. The second half requires an investigation of institutional behaviors arising from forces in the political environment.

Formal Organizations and Activities

Over the past centuries, American society has established a multitude of formal political organizations to serve as the primary agents of the society's political purpose. The organizations are in themselves expressions of the desires of society and are generally responsive to an electorate comprised of a large segment of that society. In addition, society establishes formal regulatory agencies charged with overseeing the activities of both political and non-political organizations. The latter agencies remain responsive to society through less formal, but nonetheless real, means than the primary organizations. Among the primary political institutions would be such organizations as the United States Congress, a state legislature, a city council, and a board of education. Among the regulatory agencies are the Interstate Commerce Commission, the Federal Reserve Board, port authorities, and regional sewer authorities.

The formal political organizations, whether of a primary or regulatory type, have some common characteristics: (1) the organizations operate under specifically approved instructions from society in the form of constitutions, by-laws, rules, court orders, and so on; (2) the organizations all have formal means for change and modification controlled in some fashion by the sponsoring society; and (3) they operate in ways which permit public review of the decisions enacted by the organization.

FEDERAL OPERATIONS

Over the past two hundred years an increasing amount of federal activity has been directed at educational institutions and programs. In large measure, activities have been focused on items of national interest, although some were aimed at remedying the short-sightedness of more provincial state agencies. In the most recent years, some obvious attempts have been made to supply federal funds and federal forces to overcome the inequities existing in inter- and intrastate geographic regions.

Interpreters of the United States Constitution unanimously point to Amendment Ten as the basis for placing the fundamental responsibility for public education in the hands of the various states. Amendment Ten states "the powers not delegated to the United States by the Constitution, nor prohibited by it to the States, are reserved to the States respectively, or the people." How then are large federal programs related to education authorized and financed at the federal level if education, neither delegated nor prohibited, is truly a function of the various states? The answer to this apparent dilemma is found in Article I, Section 8 of the United States Constitution which authorizes the Congress "to lay and collect Taxes, Duties, Imports, and Excises, and to pay the Debts and provide for the common Defense and the general Welfare of the United States." The "general welfare" provision has been interpreted to authorize the Congress to tax for broad social purposes including education.

In the most direct way, the federal government is involved in educational programs through the establishment and operation of schools. The several service academies are federal schools at the college level; the reservation schools operated by the Bureau of Indian Affairs and the dependent schools operated by the Department of Defense for the children of servicemen stationed overseas are examples of federally operated schools at the elementary and secondary level.

Other operations are not nearly as direct as the actual establishment and operation of schools. It is generally conceded that federal activity in the area of education began in 1785, four years prior to the adoption of the federal Constitution, with the Northwest Ordinance which reserved the 16th section in each township and the income derived therefrom for educational use. By 1850, the concept established by the ordinance had been enlarged to include two sections per township. Fourteen states were admitted to the Union following the change and thus their educational institutions received a double endowment.

A similar kind of endowment was made to higher education with the passage of the Morrill Act in 1862. The act granted 30,000 acres, for each senator and representative, for support of a college in various states. Although not very important to the study of public school systems, the passage of the Act does reflect the importance of national interest on federal legislation, for the colleges established by the land endowments were to include study of agriculture, mechanical arts, and *military tactics*. President Buchanan vetoed the bill as introduced in 1857. However, by 1862 the need by the Union Army for military leadership was more apparent, and President Lincoln signed the act into law. National interest, or general welfare, prevailed.

In 1867, a Department of Education was established by an Act of Congress. The Department, later to be named the United States Office of Education, was charged with the responsibility of (1) collecting data reflecting the condition of education in the States, (2) diffusing information respecting the organization and management of schools and school systems, and (3) promoting the cause of education throughout the country. The limited purposes conceived at the time the Office was created have been expanded to include the responsibility of administering the various enactments of Congress as they relate to education.

FEDERAL PROGRAMS

Among the various enactments of the Congress which relate to public educational systems, seven seem to be of paramount importance because of their impact upon society and its schools. Each of the enactments, in its own way, has been a political force which has helped shape the public educational institutions and systems.

The G. I. Bills

Public Law 16 established a program to guarantee the financing of vocational rehabilitation of servicemen following World War II. The second act, Public Law 346, provided general assistance to veterans desiring to continue their education in schools or colleges. Modifications and amendments to the original bills have extended the benefit concept to the veterans of both the Korean and the Vietnam conflicts. Approximately 750,000 veterans have taken advantage of rehabilitation provisions, and over ten million have participated in the school and college program. Without doubt, the bills, have dramatically changed the characteristics of the college population. In addition, the educational level and its attendant economic consequences have been powerful determinants of the characteristics of contemporary society.

The National Science Foundation

In 1950, President Truman signed the bill establishing the National Science Foundation. The Foundation was "to promote the progress of science; to advance the national health and prosperity, and welfare; to secure the national defense; and for other purposes." From the Foundation has come support for basic research in science, mathematics, medicine, engineering, and so on. Financial support, through the Foundation, has been made to fellowship and scholarship programs as well as to colleges and universities for the development and operation of specific academic programs in the sciences and mathematics.

The Cooperative Research Act

For those concerned with the paucity of research-based data pertaining to education, the Cooperative Research Act of 1954 was particularly welcome. The Act provides financial support for basic and applied research. The support has provided great stimulus to educational and other research from behavioral sciences that pertain to the educative process. The Act may prove to be the historical marker from which is measured progress toward supplying a more scientific base to education.

The National Defense Education Act

In 1958 the NDEA legislation was passed "to insure trained manpower of sufficient quantity to meet the national defense needs of the United States." There is reason to believe that NDEA received massive grass-root support which had begun to swell with the successful Russian Sputnik I. Although the Act as now amended goes far beyond the areas of science and mathematics, one of the earliest provisions was for financial aid to encourage the purchase of scientific equipment for the laboratories of the nation's secondary schools. Subsequently the Act has been amended and embraces such diverse activities as loan and fellowship programs, research in foreign languages, experimentation in educational media, preparation programs for counselors, improvement of academic curriculums, and academic institutes for many kinds of teachers including some of the social sciences and the humanities. The NDEA has been a powerful force for improving the teachers and the teaching facilities of public schools.

The Vocational Education Act

Deep concern for the technologically displaced and the vocationally unprepared led to the enactment of the Vocational Education Act of 1963. The authorization of federal expenditures caused states to re-examine concepts of vocational training and to develop long-range plans for upgrading the skills of the unemployed. New vocational uses were found for existing school facilities, and part-time jobs were developed for young people to permit them to remain in vocational training programs.

The Civil Rights Act

The Civil Rights Act of 1964 called for drastic action to improve the general lot of minority peoples who had been disenfranchised from their constitutional rights through the prejudicial actions of others. Among the specific provisions were guidelines and instructions for overturning attendance policies resulting in segregated classrooms. Concern for integrating school classrooms is also an expression of the Act, although both the desegregation and integration aspects are still in the process of testing in the courts by those districts questioning the constitutionality of the provisions. Nevertheless, the Civil Rights Act of 1964 will be a landmark in the attempts to equalize educational opportunities for all citizens.

The Elementary and Secondary Education Act

The ESEA of 1965 will continue to have impact on the public schools and on the philosophical arguments put forth, both pro and con, on the wisdom of federal aid to education. Among its five major titles are provisions to finance local educational programs designed expressly for disadvantaged youth, to improve the quality of public school libraries, to promote projects which accelerate creativity in education, and to promote projects designed to strengthen state departments of education. The fifth provision, actually Title IV, extends and amends the Cooperative Research Act. The ESEA seems particularly important in that it more closely approximates outright federal grants to public education than ever conceived before. Its provision to extend some aid to nonpublic school students also makes it a landmark act. Its impact on those it was to serve can only be measured in years to come.

STATE CONTROLS

The overwhelming power, whether exercised or not, influencing public education rests at the state level. Each of the states has evolved a unique set of institutions and operating arrangements to serve its specific educational requirements. In all of the states, with the possible exception of those operating as a single district, most of the decision-making actually takes place at the local level within a framework of guidelines supplied at the state level. However, it should be emphasized that the state legislature can assume the decision-making role at any point which it might deem appropriate.

Within the political structures of the states several areas seem to receive almost universal attention. The more important of these are educational program and financial assistance and control because of their day-to-day implications. The certification of personnel, approval of buildings, the development of transportation systems, and the control of such tangential programs as school lunches and health care programs are other common areas of concentrated state attention, but program and finance seem far more crucial.

EDUCATIONAL PLANNING

State educational agencies engage in many activities designed to control some aspects of curricular programming. Such actual items as specifying the minimum length of a school day or a school year are program determinants. Normally state agencies express their will through the establishment of minimum and maximum limits or through specific pronouncements related to one isolated curricular activity.

Examples of minimum and maximum limits are laws, still on the books of some states to govern such things as the minimum number of minutes to be devoted to a recess period. Such limits, if enforced, would also be determinants of program. Some limitations are designed to be more constructive, however. Minimum days for a school year and minimum school district size are limitations normally enacted to *raise* the standards of educational programming.

Specific curricular announcements are normally well intentioned but often turn out to be quite bizarre. For example, state pronouncements about the exact number of minutes to be devoted to bird study, the evils of tobacco and alcohol, or the deification of a local hero are often in the categories of the unimaginative. Other specific rulings need not be so restrictive. For example, the state-wide adoption of basic textual materials in reading would leave some local initiative while providing a basic uniformity among districts.

FINANCE

The normal pattern among states is to provide some financial assistance for local school districts. Universally, the local districts view the amount of state support as inadequate to the task with which the state has charged them. In defense of the states, they have raised taxes at a far faster rate than the federal government, but they have been unable to cope with the burgeoning demands. They find themselves with more roads to construct, more programs of mental health to finance, more crime to fight, and more welfare programs to administer. These programs along with the unbelievable increase in children to educate following World War II have found few states able to meet the local educator's demand for increased aid.

State financial support is a potent force not only in the amount of general aid but also in the manner in which it is collected and distributed. Taxing programs can be as rewarding or as punishing to rich or poor districts as the state deems just. Taxes collected are very often distributed in a manner which partially equalizes the wealth available to educate children in districts of varying economic potential.

The appropriation of the collected funds is often used to stimulate desired action on the part of local districts. For example, district reorganization and consolidation can be encouraged by changing distribution formulas to reward such behavior. Transportation and special education projects are commonly launched by offering financial advantages to districts which initiate the desired programs of state legislatures. The reward approach to the distribution of funds seems to be a more palatable way to obtain desired ends than prescriptive legislation which forces program adoption.

STATE POLITICAL ORGANIZATION

Although each state has unique institutions, there are some rather universal similarities. All of the states have legislative bodies elected by the people on the basis that the person voted for best reflects the desires of the voter. They are, of course, political manifestations of society. State legislatures have recognized the need to establish a separate agency to discharge the state's responsibility to public education. Similarly, the states have the services of a chief state school officer and a department of education to superintend the affairs of the state educational agency.

THE LEGISLATURE

In spite of the seemingly endless power of the legislatures in determining the course of public education in their respective states, some restrictions do exist. They may not go against the state constitution in passing legislation or the legislation may be overturned by a state supreme court. Similarly, when challenged, a piece of legislation may be overturned by the United States Supreme Court if it is found to violate provisions of the federal Constitution.

The number of bills pertaining to education is very high in each state legislature because of the number of educational decisions which only the legislature is empowered to make. To reduce the load, a committee system is normally employed with the usual values and limitations in attendance. The committees are subjected to the pressure tactics of large taxpayers, local district superintendents, mayors, educational organizations, and all other individuals or agencies which stand to gain or lose from the enactment of a particular piece of legislation under consideration.

THE STATE EDUCATIONAL AGENCY

Although every state has a state agency to supervise and coordinate its educational affairs, there is no unanimity in the manner in which the membership achieves the office. Figure 6-1 illustrates the proportion of methods by which state boards of education (many have other titles) are created.

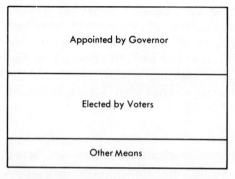

Figure 6-1. Creation of state boards of education.

The main functions served by the state board are (1) the appointment of a state superintendent (in some states); (2) the development of legislative proposals for consideration by the legislature; (3) the presentation of a budget to the governor describing the educational needs of the state; (4) the formulation of educational policy in accordance with existing statutes; (5) the exercise of general control over educational programs in operation within the elementary and secondary schools of the state; (6) the encouragement of sound programs by subordinate educational agencies; and (7) the coordination of all educational activities within the state. The last function would include higher education activities in a few states. A most important function not served by state boards is that of taxation. Absence of taxing authority weakens their power considerably.

THE CHIEF STATE SCHOOL OFFICER

The chief state school officer goes by many titles including state superintendent. Titles notwithstanding, he is many things to many people, depending upon his relationship to the state board of education. He achieves his high office in many ways (Figure 6-2).

Variations in patterns of office achievement by state boards of education and state superintendents create three major combinations: an elected board-appointive superintendent; an elected

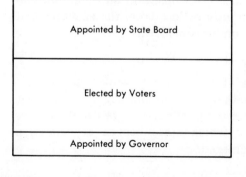

Figure 6-2. Manner in which the office of chief state school officer is achieved.

board-elected superintendent; appointed board-elected superintendent. In those cases where the board is elected and the superintendent is appointed, he is normally conceived as the executive officer of the board. This pattern seems to be gaining favor.

The state superintendent carries many responsibilities. Among them are: (1) execution of the policies of the state board of education and provisions of the law enacted by the state legislature; (2) administration of a professional staff comprising his department; (3) recommendation of staff appointments to his department; (4) development of a budget for consideration by the state board of education; (5) recommendation of desirable legislation for consideration by the board and subsequently the legislature; and (6) administration of any state schools (orphanages, blind, deaf, and so on).

Much of the state superintendent's leadership capacity resides in his lines of communication with other politically potent bodies, particularly the State Board and the State Legislature. His capacity to stimulate effective legislation and his ability to mobilize the resources required to carry forth imaginative programs are the ultimate measures of his leadership. Staff competency is important to the superintendent. Their credibility with public school officials can often predict the leadership potential of the state agency.

LOCAL SCHOOL BOARDS

With state legislative and regulatory agencies far away and otherwise concerned, the local board of education takes on a powerful political role. Through their local boards of education, the district citizenry has a most responsive agent. The local issues are better known and more clearly delineated; the local man on the board is more subject to political pressures; local interest is high and educational endeavors are exposed to public view. All of these factors make the local board a most critical feature of the local system. No board does as much as it could do, and no board fulfills only the minimum requirements. What it does elect to do is normally a fair reflection of the placement of education by the community on several continuums between many extremes.

At the local level, citizens become primarily involved in the affairs of education through two activities: elections and referendums. As in other matters of their governance, society is unwilling to delegate all decision-making power in a board of education. Because society never perfectly trusts its elected representatives, it retains constraints upon their power to enact provisions more extreme than the society can tolerate. For this reason, most school systems are fiscally dependent upon a direct supporting vote of the populace to obtain funds necessary for operation. Likewise, society retains for itself the capacity to decide if it should pledge its resources through bonding for capital improvement.

Educational projects not directly dependent upon community financial support are nevertheless subject to community approval and political support. Controversial curricular changes have a way of uniting adversaries against candidates seeking re-election to boards of education. On the other hand, controversy sometimes supplies the rallying point for the election of new membership to the board. In either event, the board of education finds itself responsive to a society that has a rather specific image of what its educational system should be like.

Informal Organizations and Forces

Formal organizations are designated by society and licensed by that society to represent it. The operations of the formal organizations are normally open to public attendance without regard to special interest. On the other hand, informal organizations are designated by less than the total society and, therefore, cannot be licensed to speak for the society. In almost every case, the informal organizations which impinge upon public education are special interest groups comprised of citizens holding a strong interest in some aspect of the educational system. No interest group, in and of itself, has the *official* power to change the system. However, all of them do have power, in a political sense, to force an expression of their will upon persons who reside in power positions of the formal organization. Examples of organizations that sometimes bring forces of relevance to bear on the educational system are the Parent-Teacher Associations, Music Parent Organizations, Booster Clubs, and Library Mothers.

The *modus operandi* of informal organizations takes various forms. Will expression is normally entrusted to a representative of the informal group. On occasion the superintendent of schools is first contacted and apprised of wishes and desires of the membership. On other occasions, individual board members are contacted with the hope that these individuals can seek appropriate action through the formal system. One of the most effective manners used in accomplishing the ends of the informal organizations is that of the hearing. At an open hearing, large numbers of the rank-and-file membership can be present to lend credence to the expressions of the representative. Persons elected to political office, such as boards of education, cannot help but be impressed more by an expression from a group than by the expression of an individual speaking for himself alone.

There have been hints in the preceding paragraphs that the

expressions made by informal organizations are forces which are generally illegitimate in nature. Such, of course, is not the entire case. It is through the expressions of individuals, formal organizations, and informal groups that representative bodies come best to know the feelings and reactions of the various segments of their constituency. Without such expressions, the elected representative would be required to rely solely upon his own judgment. Such sole reliance would not seem to be in the best interest of democratic government.

Yet, another kind of informal force also exists. This is the force created by the various minorities generally overlooked in processes of mass representation. In its most illegitimate sense, the force consists of minorities who cannot stand the vote. Such minorities, when dealing with educational institutions, utilize the same techniques which larger legislative bodies have long been subjected to. Delaying decisions, dividing the opposition, seeking leadership positions in high office, referrals to committees, rumor campaigns, and subtle innuendoes are all ploys recognized by these kinds of minorities as effective ways of creating forces consistent with their own desires.

Playing the role of the "squeaky wheel" has often proven to be an effective way of stimulating change in an existing system. The squeaking minority is indeed more likely to get the "oil" than the nonsqueaking majority, and the knowledge that organizations abhor squeaking is a powerful tool in the kit of the extremist minority.

Responding to Political Forces

To the laissez-faire administrator, charged with conducting the affairs of a dynamic system, diverse political forces pose no real problem. Within his operational philosophy, he can accommodate the diversity of the forces by simply responding to each force in turn. Such an administrator's response is traditionally just sufficient enough to dull the barb of the force. But to the conscientious administrator concerned with carrying the entire system forward in pursuit of its goals, each of the forces requires a calculated response which is representative of a long-range strategy.

The strategy itself must consist of many alternatives open to the administrator facing various contingencies. These strategic points might be illustrated as follows: (1) when the goals of professional organizations are at variance; (2) when teachers and school boards are at disagreement over salary terms; (3) when pro and con tax groups are in operation; (4) when controversy arises over methods or materials; or (5) when staff is concerned over the dismissal of a co-worker. In each of these examples, the vested interests are likely to be applying political pressure to the system administrator and to the board as they approach the decision setting.

In general, the system administrator's chief concern is with the political forces which may be restrictive of his capacity to move his organization forward toward its goals. Without the capacity to so move his organization, he loses his ability to lead. Without leadership, he is powerless to proceed with the tasks with which he has been charged. On occasion, he must mobilize new forces to achieve the potentials of the organization: he must mobilize his forces to induce political or other restrictions upon his organization: and at times he must mobilize force sufficient to overthrow a restrictive element either within or without the organization.

Vector theory would suggest that the largest movement follows the largest force. As was mentioned earlier, the launching of the Russian Sputnik was indeed a potent force for stimulating interest and organizational change within the educational enterprise. But the system administrator has no Sputnik to launch into orbit. He must seek his power from other sources, and like it or not, he finds himself required to marshal sufficient power to accomplish the goals of his organization. When those goals have antagonistic opponents, even more power is required.

From what sources can a systems administrator draw power?

1. *Power of personal-professional persuasion.* Recent studies from the field of communication arts have demonstrated that the credibility of the person giving an oral or written communication is an important factor in the acceptance of that communication by the listener or the reader. The administrator who has commanded respect throughout his community is a credible source capable of commanding the respect of his audience. His very charismatic nature is a political force. It should also be noted, however, that the administrator's credibility is also related to the closeness of his message to that which the receiver would like to hear. Therefore, it seems reasonable to assume that the administrator tends to lose credibility as his pronouncements deviate farther and farther from the mean position of his community. At times, the administrator must use other more credible sources to carry the message to the society.

2. *The power of group-professional persuasion.* The educational system's chief administrator is normally the highest ranking professional in a group of professionals. As a leader of a large professional staff, it is possible for that administrator to mobilize others within his staff to his own position. Such mobilization then provides him with all of the political power inherent in groups. In

most communities, the public school is the largest single employer. As such, a mobilized work force committed to a particular position is indeed a potent force for making change or for retaining a position consistent with the goals of that work force.

3. *Power of public opinion.* The public relations documents prepared by many educational systems are designed to convince a public that its schools are in fact providing an education consistent with the desires of that public. With that as its major objective, the document can go on in small steps to lead the public to new positions. The public position at a given point in time is a potent force when mobilized for action. The administrator can call upon this force when its position is consistent with that being sought. However, it is apparent that that same administrator must be wary of allowing public opinion to mobilize people in a direction not consistent with the system's goals.

4. *Power of law.* The systems administrator often finds it easier to convince a limited number of individuals of the appropriateness of a particular action than to convince an entire public. When such a movement best serves his needs he is well advised to seek the consensus of the smaller group which is his board of education. He can oftentimes legitimize an organizational direction by having that direction become a part of legally adopted school-board policy. Outside of his own district, he is also free to solicit help in making desired changes at the state level. His professional organizations and the boards of educations are potent forces for convincing legislatures of the desirability of particular legislative action.

5. *Power of the Majority.* When an organization is being deterred from accomplishing its goals because of harassment by small minority pressure groups and when the harassment is clearly an attempt to prohibit organizational change, the system's administrator can often call forth the power inherent in a majority population. As indicated earlier, minorities cannot stand votes and as a result they must operate outside of the formal organization. The converse of this is a powerful tool in the hands of the administrator. A common maneuver is to force consideration of the issue at hand in a formal meeting of the formal organization. Its placement on the agenda and the subsequent requirement for action is a legitimate way of resolving the issue, even though it may leave the minority unsatisfied.

6. *Power of the Minority.* As a corollary to the power of the majority, the system's administrator may also use the techniques of the minority to accomplish the goals of the organization. His political behavior often requires that he keep issues from reaching the agenda and the floor of the formal group where action would be required. His control over the agenda is one matter in which he can

accomplish this end. His power to delay through referral to committees and other kinds of slow-moving groups, often results in delaying an undesirable issue to death.

Problems and Issues

1. *How can the nature of political forces in a school community be ascertained?* Just as a social environment is comprised of many segments, so is a political environment. Each of the various political forces which impinge upon the operation of a public school system represents a desire on the part of individuals or groups to accomplish a change deemed to be in the best interest of the sponsoring agent or agency. The forces thus generated may be pointed or subtle, but all are designed to be will-expressive.

A measure of the political will of the entire constituent body of a local school system is occasionally gained through the use of elections and referendums. However, the vast majority of decisions having political overtones must be made by the representative body—the board of education. Because the board is a representative body, its members will in some measure be cognizant of the political will of friends, neighbors, business associates, and other societal segments. A small board in a fairly large community cannot, unfortunately, be knowledgeable about all of the desires of all the people. In varying degrees, therefore, the public school system will remain ignorant of the political will of the total society. To this end, it seems important to ask, *who* are the power figures that consistently represent various political segments?—How strong is the leadership?—How potent the force?—By what means can the forces be identified?

2. *Upon what bases shall a public school system elect to respond to politically inspired forces?* It has been suggested that the political forces with which a public school system must deal come from many directions. Federal, state, and local laws are enacted and enforced. Duly adopted constitutions affect the affairs of school systems governance. Local political conditions, in the form of ordinances and unwritten understandings, attempt to instruct those concerned with managing the affairs of the educational enterprise.

Other kinds of forces are also in evidence. Some types of legislation *demand* that particular and specific action be undertaken; some legislation and some resolutions attempt to convey the spirit of the legislative body through the form of requests that units of government, including public school systems, undertake specific action, and finally some legislation has been passed which *enables* school districts to modify their educational affairs when, and if, they desire to do so. Other kinds of forces have their origin in partisanship or in special interest sources, and both may be reflected in informal ways dissociated from legal or legislative action. Faced with a host of possibilities for responding to political sources, how shall a system plan its reactions?—By what criteria?—When does the system generate counterforces?—When is resistance legitimate?

3. *Under what conditions should teachers and administrators within public school systems attempt to involve themselves in local political affairs?* Both teachers and administrators are developers and consumers of political forces. As citizens within a democratic community, they have certain unalienable political rights which they are free to exercise. From their position within the local system, they can view the impact of external political forces upon the functioning of the system, and as a result, they are in a good position to make discretionary decisions about their own political behavior. Nevertheless, they must decide, when to become involved?—On what issues?—With what degree of vigor?—At what professional risk?

Selected References

Antonio, William, and Howard Ebrlich, eds. *Power and Democracy in America.* Notre Dame: University of Notre Dame Press, 1961.

Bailey, Stephen, *et al. Schoolmen and Politics.* Syracuse: Syracuse University Press, 1962.

Bloomberg, Warner, and Morris Sunshine. *Suburban Power Structure and Public Education.* Syracuse: Syracuse University Press, 1963.

Dahl, Robert. *Who Governs?* New Haven: Yale University Press, 1961.

Kammerer, Gladys, *et al. The Urban Political Community.* Boston: Houghton Mifflin, 1963.

Kimbrough, Ralph. *Political Power and Educational Decision Making.* Chicago: Rand McNally, 1964.

Zeiglar, Harmon. *The Political World of the High School Teacher.* Eugene, Ore.: CASEA, 1966.

part *III*

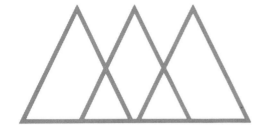

The Major
Components

chapter 7

■ *The Board of Education*

Unwillingness on the part of local communities to grant absolute and free rein to the local school master probably gave rise to governing bodies which were ultimately to emerge as boards of education. The nature of the body which governs individual school systems varies in many ways from one system to another. Nevertheless, the responsibility to the system and their responsiveness to their constituency is fairly constant across the country.

In 1647, only a few years after its first settlers came, Massachusetts enacted a law which required each town to maintain a school. The school's formation and its means of financial support were left to the selectmen of the respective towns. Thus it was that the early public schools remained under the control of local city governments. School policies and administrative matters regarding the public schools were discussed and determined at town meetings. The 1647 law even had a penalty of five pounds to be levied against communities failing to maintain public schools.

It was not until 1826 that Massachusetts saw fit to change the method of governing the local public schools. In that year a law was passed requiring that school committees be separated from the municipal authorities and simultaneously that the school governing body be given the right to take "general charge . . . of all public schools." Many authorities point to the 1826 law as the beginning of local boards of education.

Although Massachusetts saw fit in 1826 to separate local boards of education from municipal governing bodies, not all school systems in contemporary America have been made independent from such governing bodies. In many of the larger cities and in some of the Eastern states strong ties continue to exist between educational and municipal governing bodies. The legal provisions of most states entering the union after 1850 make explicit the dichotomy between the two governing forms.

What is a Board of Education?

In its strictest sense, a board of education is the agency designated by a state as the governing unit responsible for the educational affairs within a local school district. The board is a trustee for the state. As an elected body, it represents a particular geographic region and its society. That society normally charges its board with the responsibility of developing educational policies capable of generating programs holding promise for meeting the educational needs and desires of the community. Because most of the states place the responsibility for the operation of public schools within local districts, boards of education become primary agents of the state as well as the representatives of the people residing within the local district (see Figure 7-1).

Local school districts are generally recognized as quasi-corporations licensed to conduct the educational affairs of a local district within a larger framework of state law. State law provides each of the local boards of education with general guidelines for operating their affairs. Outside of those limitations specifically listed in the law, the boards of education have generally been free to operate their educational systems in a manner most consistent with the wishes and desires of the local society. Rather than specifying the kinds of activities in which boards of education may not engage, state laws and regulations are normally more positively stated. They usually advise local boards on appropriate means for compliance with the regulations of the larger state society.

The action of local boards of education within a given geographic region are very much alike in spite of the freedom found in the clause, "to do anything not inconsistent with this act," a common phrase appearing in state laws granting general powers to boards of education. As boards engage in activities "not inconsistent" with state mandates, the activities tend to become routine practice and, if good, are subsequently copied by adjacent school districts. Thus, boards tend to operate more uniformly than the law would require.

Restrictions on the activities of local boards are not limited to those imposed by state laws or state constitutions. Court cases and opinions of the state attorney general may also guide the behavior of the local board in the absence of legislative action. In addition, state boards are empowered by the state to make rules and regulations consistent with state law. The rules and regulations of the state boards are generally binding upon the local school district and serve as restrictions upon their local autonomy. In some states

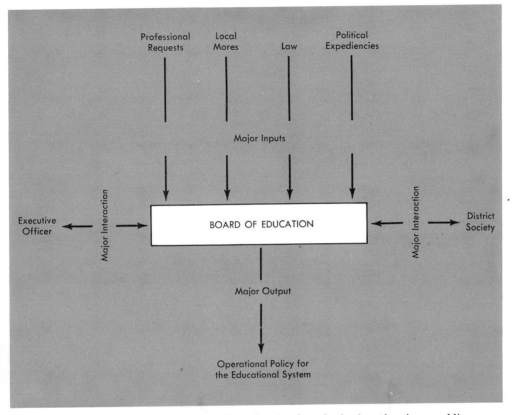

Figure 7-1. Conceptualization of the role of a board of education in a public school system.

it is possible for city charters to restrict some aspects of board operations. Those cities that have charter provisions tend to be the same ones that show a political relationship between municipal and educational government.

The community in which the board of education is functioning will also have some unwritten guidelines, in the form of local mores, as to appropriate board behavior. These guidelines are tacitly accepted over long periods of time as binding upon the boards of education. Operationally, unwritten community expectations can be as powerful as law in determining the courses of action chosen by local school boards.

Because boards of education are primarily concerned with the efficient operation of a professional staff, the ethics of the profession involved may also limit the board's activities. Should the board ask the professional staff to engage in behaviors contrary to the established ethic, this would create systemic dissonance disruptive to the system's operation.

In an era of negotiations with professional groups, boards of education are increasingly finding themselves with new sets of operating restrictions. More specifically, in some states by legal enactment and in others by coercion, boards are being required to sign restrictive contracts with employees. The provisions of the master contracts are so stated as to guarantee that the behaviors of both groups entering into the contract will be consistent with the agreements reached in the negotiating processes. The contract provisions are binding upon the boards and thereby serve as additional guidelines to their decisions and as additional restrictions on their autonomy.

Relationship to a School System

As a major component of an educational system, boards of education have roles to play which are both unique and integrated. The unique aspects of their spheres of responsibility are those items which are made explicit in law. There are roles which *only* they can perform. These unique roles may not be delegated nor can the boards of education be relieved from the responsibility of their accomplishment.

Operationally, boards of education have few unique roles. Many of the items for which they are responsible are accomplished through the behaviors of various school board employees. Responsibility in these kinds of matters is largely supervisory in nature and requires that the boards see that the tasks are, in fact, performed.

Thus, within the framework of a dynamic system comprised primarily of human components, boards of education find themselves with two general responsibilities to the system. They must provide components of a quantity and of a particular professional capacity to see that the organization continuously moves forward toward its goals. Secondly, the wise board recognizes that organizational movement towards a goal in a school system requires human interaction. Therefore, conditions conducive to goal-seeking interaction are to be highly desired by school boards.

General Characteristics of Boards of Education

Although boards of education are alike in many ways, their similarities are hard to characterize, but some generalities can be drawn. School board size is one such example. In general, the size of the board is related to the size of the system being governed, with the larger boards being found in the larger school districts. Over one-half of the school systems of 100,000 or more student enrollments have boards of education comprised of nine or more members.[1] The median number of school board members found in districts from 12,000 to 100,000 students is seven members. In school districts under 12,000 enrollments, almost half are governed by five-member boards of education.

The method of selecting local school board members also varies according to the size of the school district. About two-thirds of the districts enrolling more than 12,000 students have boards of education elected on a nonpartisan basis; another 10–15 per cent are elected on partisan ballots; and the remainder are selected through an appointment process involving the city mayor, the city council, or some other group empowered to make the appointments. In districts smaller than 12,000 students, the percentage of school board members elected on a nonpartisan ballot increases considerably, and in rural areas almost no board members would reach their position by means of an appointment by an outside agency.

The nomination of candidates for positions on local boards of education can occur in any of a number of ways. In some states, the prospective school boards member files with a county clerk a petition signed by a small percentage of the voting public. In other states, an announcement may be made by the candidate to a county clerk which is sufficient to put him on the ballot. In still others, nominations may be made by independent or political caucuses. In a few instances, primary elections precede the final balloting.

The question is sometimes raised about the desirability of electing boards of education versus the appointment of membership. The arguments, pro and con, tend to be about the same whether the governing body under question is a board of education or another type of agency. Those who favor the appointment of school board members by another agency tend to feel (1) that all of a city's governmental operations should be placed under the responsible control of an all-inclusive governing body; (2) that many highly qualified persons who do not wish to engage in the political activities surrounding an election will consent to an immediate appointment to a board of education; and (3) that appointments can be made on the basis of individual merit as opposed to enthusiasm generated around a particular educational issue. Those who favor the election of school board members generally feel that (1) elections are in the best interest of a democratic society; (2) board members can be made more responsive to the populace because of the voter's capacity to remove an individual from office; and (3) boards of education can be kept separate from other political agencies, normally those governing an individual city.

[1] *N.E.A. Research Bulletins* periodically report on the make-up of American school boards.

Responsibilities of Boards of Education

The kinds of activities in which school boards engage would provide substance for a very long list indeed. The scope of their activities as defined by state statutes is very broad. The additional dimension of items not listed in state statutes is, of course, very nearly infinite. However, the major activities engaged in by most boards of education can be enumerated under the following seven categories:

1. *Establishing Local Operational Policy.* Policies are general guides to action by board members or by its executive officers and employees. The determination of policies is a normal result of debates concerning the most appropriate courses of action for the membership of the school system. The clarity with which board policies are written is in no small measure related to the manner in which the policies are executed. The modification of policy is also a legitimate province of the school board, closely related to the changes in the society which created the system.

Even professionals within the system often misunderstand the role of policy. Policy does not tell *how* a particular goal is to be established, pursued, or accomplished. Rather, policy points out the direction to be pursued by the system, leaving the "how" to the discretion of the executive staff.

2. *Determining the Nature of Local Educational Programs.* With the exception of the requirements inherent in state codes, the local board of education is free to determine and establish its educational program. It is possible, in the absence of state adopted materials, for a board of education to elect to utilize a particular curricular program over a different or competing program. In addition, the length of time which students spend on a given curricular area, if not in conflict with state requirements, is also well within the province of the local board.

Not all restrictions on educational programs are legal, however. As an example, many secondary schools have found it advantageous to seek membership in the various accrediting associations. To retain this membership, the school district must maintain an educational program equal to the standards set by the association. These standards are responsible in very large measure for the configuration of secondary education in this country.

3. *Selecting Its Executive Officer.* Many members of boards of education serve their entire tenure without having to participate in the process of selecting a superintendent of schools. Without doubt the selection process is the most important single act in which a school board can engage. Because of the limited number of board sessions during a year, most of its work must be carried on, in its

absence, by its executive officer. The degree to which the board and the superintendent are compatible, and the degree to which they can tolerate each other's differences, is an important ingredient in moving forward the business of the educational enterprise.

4. *Providing Educational Facilities.* The local board of education must provide facilities for the educational program of the district in a number of a quality sufficient to guarantee that the program can be carried forward.

When necessary the board of education can exercise its power of "eminent domain" to acquire sites for school facilities. Few boards are anxious to exercise this particular right because of the animosities such action usually engenders. When possible, school sites are purchased from willing sellers at reasonable prices without the necessity of resorting to condemnation procedures. Nevertheless, as an agent of the state, boards of education have been granted the power to carry forth state programs even when the actions are contrary to the wishes of individual property holders. However, the board in a condemnation proceding must still be governed by the legal processes which protect the property rights of the landowner.

In addition to providing school facilities in the form of sites and buildings, boards of education also must provide the day-to-day operational materials required for an educational program. Provision of various kinds of equipment, furniture, and educational aids, as well as many consumable supplies required to operate an educational program, are the responsibility of the local board of education.

The related action of establishing local attendance area boundary lines is also within the province of the local board. Boards of education cannot justify the construction of school sites solely on the basis of convenience to a neighborhood. Weighed against that convenience is the cost of such additional facilities, which must be borne by the entire school district. The compromise of providing convenience while retaining the fiscal responsibility is often accomplished through the shifting of attendance boundary lines. Boundary line shifts are seldom popular with persons who find their children having to change schools between two particular grades. Nevertheless, when the inconvenience of a few is balanced against the cost to the many, the board's obligations often become clear.

Boundary line shifts may also be precipitated for educational as well as economic reasons. General population shifts may alter the student populations in given neighborhoods, thereby disturbing class sizes and pupil-teacher ratios. Relocation of attendance boundary lines may be calculated to redistribute the students into group sizes that can be more easily accommodated.

5. *Employing Professional and Other Staff Members.* In addition

to selecting its own executive officers and administrative staff, boards of education are responsible for filling other personnel vacancies within the educational system. In the smallest school districts, many boards do, in fact, hire every teacher and nonprofessional employee. In larger districts, however, responsibility for recruiting, selecting, and recommending employment to the board of education is usually left to the chief executive officer.

Although professional administrators recognize the legal responsibilities of their boards of education, most will express the feeling that the accomplishment of educational goals is most likely to occur in an organization where professional harmony prevails. Knowledge about the professional tasks to be performed is far more likely to reside in a professionally trained executive head than in the lay membership of a board of education. For this reason, many boards of education perform the employment function in only a most perfunctory way at the request and on the recommendation of the chief executive officer. As a general rule, boards will have established some policies to direct the administrator's behavior in securing the various staff members.

The board of education must also concern itself with problems concerning the retention or dismissal of staff members. Again, board-developed policies are likely to guide the executive officer in affairs related to retention and dismissal. There has been a general tendency over the recent past to establish more careful procedures for the dismissal of professional employees. School boards across the country are losing or have already lost the power to dismiss a teacher without just cause. Today's enlightened boards of education make provisions within their operating framework for teachers under threat of dismissal to have a private hearing of charges and evidences. The professional associations to which teachers belong have, in large measure, been responsible for strengthening dismissal procedures.

6. *Authorizing Elections and Referendums.* Boards of education often find it necessary to assess the will of the public through election or referendum procedures. Some procedures are required by law whereas others are proposed to the people so that the board may be advised of the feeling of their community. A third type of referendum, for the establishment of long-term bonds for the construction of school facilities, is also a normal legal requirement, although it is usually done on an ad hoc basis. Examples of those normally required by law would include the establishment of an annual operating tax rate or the annual election of school board members. The decision to establish a local school bus system or to annex an adjacent school district may well follow advisory referendums held by the board to receive community help in reaching

a final decision. In some states, referendums to establish junior college districts are only advisory to boards of education.

7. *Maintaining and Publishing Required Records.* In every state, legal records must be kept concerning actions taken by local boards of education. In addition to the minutes of regular meetings, which become legal and public documents, state regulations will normally require that many other kinds of records be maintained. Included in the normal records requirements would be such things as attendance records, the degree to which teachers meet certification requirements, financial records, and the like. As a general rule, the executive officer of the board is responsible for compiling the records and documents, which the board subsequently approves and publishes.

8. *Evaluating Goal Directions.* Because the local school boards have responsibility for establishing the organizational and educational goals of school systems, some provisions must inevitably be made for evaluating movement of the organization toward established goals. The evaluation process may take many forms, but it must inevitably be concerned with the adequacy of the system's components to interact in a fashion deemed appropriate for goal accomplishment.

The evaluation process serves two ends. Data collected in the evaluation process are used to measure both the speed and the direction of the organization toward the goals of the system. In addition, however, the evaluative process also provides information that may accentuate the necessity for revising goals or for the development of new and better goals.

The manner in which a board of education serves the evaluation function is exceedingly important to a system whose human components are essentially professional. Inquisitions which cast aspersions on the professional competence of an individual component are not likely to be well received by the professional community. On the other hand, boards which capitalize on the natural desires of a professional group to improve its own operations are likely to be much better received by the organizational membership.

The Modus Operandi

Although much of the way a board of education may govern its affairs may be controlled by legislative requirements, a great deal of freedom remains for individual operating procedures. The business of a board of education must be conducted in a legally established meeting with a quorum of the membership present. The size of the quorum will normally be established by state law. Agenda for board meetings are normally established by the chief executive officer and include items of business which he judges as necessary for board understanding as well as items requested for inclusion by the membership of the board. Regular meetings of boards of education are normally held once a month.

Special meetings are also often called. The term *special* refers to any meeting held at a time other than that established by state law or by local by-laws. They are called because of the press of emergency business, the inability of the board to accomplish all of its business at the regular meeting, or to carry on a function which may be lengthy or which will require the undivided attention of the board membership. Examples of two kinds of special meetings would be: (1) An organizational meeting following the annual school election when the law requires that the board be organized in a time period shorter than that intervening between the election and the next regular meeting; and (2) a special meeting might be held to examine a display of school furniture being offered via bids from various equipment manufacturers. The examination of the merits of school furniture would take more time than would be warranted by such an agenda item in a regular meeting.

Within both regular and special meetings of boards of education, "executive sessions" are sometimes held. The law in most states recognizes that some board business is of such a nature that public disclosure could result in irreparable damage to an individual. Frank discussions of conditions surrounding a recommendation to dismiss a professional employee would be such an example. Another type of condition which justifies the use of an executive session is one that might involve expenditure of public funds. For example, premature knowledge of a proposed location for a new school building might result in the land under consideration being subdivided with both the price of the land and the difficulty in securing it increasing tremendously. Such action would not be in the best financial interest of the total district and early discussions might best be held in executive sessions.

Executive sessions should be concerned with discussion only, and their number should be very limited. The final disposition of a case would require formal board action and such should be taken in a regular meeting and duly recorded in the minutes thereof. Excessive use of the right to closed "executive sessions" is an abuse which can lead to well-justified public distrust of the work of the board.

One of the more debatable aspects of a board's operating procedure concerns the use of a committee structure. Some school boards, particularly the larger ones found in metropolitan areas, prefer to conduct their business through standing committees. Study is done by the smaller subgroups, with recommendations for action being brought before the total board. In smaller communities where the membership is limited and standing committees would consist of one or two or three persons, boards of education tend to conduct their business as a "committee of the whole." The trend even in the larger cities has been away from the standing committee type of organization.

One of the great weaknesses of the committee system is the inordinate amount of time spent by committees and the board as a whole on activities only tangential to instruction. Monthly reports from committees such as finance, personnel, athletics, transportation, buildings and grounds, and instruction seem to imply that each of the committees has equal weight and worth. The investment of the committee member's time in the work of his committee also tends to build a commitment to the topic of his working group which may be out of proportion to the worth of his topical area to the total educational system. When the board meets, its crucial task is to draw out and refine ideas—not to set them in opposition to one another, with the outcome of endless haggling.[2]

The Policy Development Role

Although local operational policies established by boards of education may just be "understood," most often they are written records of discussions concerning a particular topical area. The record serves as a subsequent standard against which related problems, suggestions, and recommendations will be impersonally compared and judged. The policy documents outlining the general tenor of a board of education are invaluable aids to the executive officer who is required to make decisions in the absence of that board.

In addition to developing policy, boards of education also legally enact bylaws, rules, and procedures. Bylaws describe the legal manner in which the board will be organized and conduct its business. Rules are exact statements to govern behavior in specific contingencies. Procedures are statements of how a particular type of act is to be performed. Bylaws, rules, and procedures, when not in conflict with higher statutes, have the power of law within the local district and are binding upon the board, district employees, students, and their parents.

With regard to policy, three individuals or groups of individuals have a close relationship to policy development. The superintendent of schools, alert to the problems he faces, may often request an expression of the board's feeling to guide his actions. In this way,

---

[2] Samuel Moore, "Policy Formulation: A Group and Individual Effort," *Journal of the New York State School Boards Association*, June 1966, 23–24.

he stimulates development of board policy. In his other role, he is a consumer of policy and must govern his actions by it.

Teachers are taking a new role in board policy and as professional negotiations take their particular emerging course, teachers are more often being consulted about various personnel policies. Although most boards have historically considered teacher welfare in their policy deliberations, teachers are now demanding to be partners in the development of policies affecting their welfare.

The public is also concerned with policy because it is through the policy statement that community will is given due concern. Policy antagonistic to the general will results in operations which receive little support from the public, at best, or arouse antagonism, at worst. Policy arising from the will of a narrow majority is likely to result in administrative acts which prove to be highly controversial if they disturb the *status quo* which the majority views as protective of its interests.

In playing an appropriate role within the system for which they are responsible, many courses of action are open to local school boards. The very best boards fulfill their responsibilities by encouraging, stimulating, questioning, facilitating, supporting, and conserving, when conserving is done for the sake of efficient resource allocation. The poorest boards on the other hand serve their roles by criticizing, executing, administering, investigating, and conserving purely for the sake of conservation.

Problems and Issues

1. *How can interactions between boards of education and teachers be improved?* The very nature of the administration of American public school systems requires that much interaction take place between the administrative staff and the local board of education. The superintendent of schools, as the executive officer of the board of education, has many opportunities to participate with the board. Teachers, however, do not enjoy the same position. They are somewhat isolated from the board of education and their major interactions tend to be with other teachers and with building administrators. Without interaction between boards of education and the teaching faculty, understandings are difficult to achieve. Even more serious is the difficulty in creating a mutual respect of one group for the other.

The ultimate accomplishment of school board policy often resides with the classroom teacher. If the policy received by teachers is always and only received following an interpretation by an intermediate administrator (or administrators), then the intermediary represents a potential communication block to the total understanding of the policy. To the degree that teachers can be involved with primary communication directly from boards of education, potentials for misunderstandings are reduced. To improve teacher-board relationships, how can the number of interactions be increased?—What should be the bases for interaction? —With what teachers should the board react?—What dangers might be involved?—What should be the role of the interactors?

2. *What should be the requirement for school board membership?* The responsibilities of boards of education are many and varied. It has already been suggested that they must help to establish local educational policy, to determine the nature of local educational programs, in selecting executive officers, to provide facilities, to employ teachers, to authorize elections and referendums, and so forth. In a more general sense, the board of education must accept responsibility for providing to its society an educational system capable of meeting the needs of individual students, the local society, and society at large.

Individuals coming to boards of education from varying backgrounds and with varying kinds of interest may represent varying societal segments, various political and economic points of view. All of these background elements will contribute to the ultimate decisions being made by that board member in the official sessions of the governing body.

As a representative of society, regardless of whether he has been elected or appointed, the board member carries additional responsibility to his office. His actions must be reflective not only of his own desires and motivations, but also of the wills, the desires, and motivations of the groups being represented. To the degree that the individual member is successful in welding his individual desires into the larger pattern of community will, representative government is well served. In view of the responsibilities of the office, are there personal characteristics holding high potential for good school board membership?—What are they?—How can people exhibiting these characteristics be encouraged to seek elective office?—To what extent should teachers and administrators participate in encouraging qualified persons to run for school board office?—What risks and dangers are involved with in-system participation?

3. *What larger political roles should local boards of education serve?* Responsibilities of local boards of education to supervise the administration of a local school system are well known and well founded in law and precedent. Their responsibilities to local school districts have been enumerated and are well known by both professionals and local communities. On occasion, however, boards of education find themselves facing problems and responsibilities larger than the local resources are capable of meeting. The educa-

tional aspirations sought by the system governed by the board of education may exceed the economic capacity of a community to attain them. The board of education may find itself with aspirations higher than the aspirations of the community it represents. Under any condition, what kind of a role can be played outside of the local district?—Through what means can boards of education mobilize external resources?—Should local boards engage in "power politics" at the state level?—How can the interests of local school boards be impressed upon superordinate bodies?

Selected References

American Association of School Administrators. *Roles, Responsibilities, Relationships of the School Board, Superintendent and Staff*. Washington, D.C.: AASA, 1963.

American Association of School Administrators. *School Board–Superintendent Relationships*, 34th Yearbook. Washington, D.C.: AASA, 1956

Gross, Neal. *Who Runs Our Schools?* New York: John Wiley and Sons, 1958.

Pierce, Truman, *et al. Community Leadership for Public Education*. Englewood Cliffs, N.J.: Prentice-Hall, 1955.

Wayson, William. *Improvement of School Board Relationships*. Chicago: University of Chicago, Midwest Administrative Center, 1962.

White, Alpheus. *Local School Board: Organiations and Practices*. Washington, D.C.: United States Office of Education, 1962.

chapter 8

■ *The Administrator*

James Lipham in the LXIII NSSE yearbook of 1964 suggests that "the administrator . . . may be identified as the individual who utilizes existing structures and procedures to achieve an organizational goal or objective." In his analysis he differentiates administrative behavior from leadership behavior by defining leadership "as the initiation of a new structure or procedure for accomplishing an organization's goals and objectives or for changing an organization's goals and objectives."[1] Although the dichotomy suggested by Lipham is useful, this chapter will consider the administrator as the individual whose position requires that he be responsible for moving the organization toward its goals, whether the process requires utilizing new or existing procedures. Hence, he is conceived as leader and administrator.

Although the number of administrators in a complex school system is quite large, this chapter will consider the four most common kinds of positions: the superintendent, the building principal, the business manager, and the curriculum coordinator.

In studying the roles and responsibilities of the various administrative positions, several concepts need elaboration; the first of these is the line-staff concept. Although the military organization has proved to be efficient in many ways, the nature of the goals being pursued by the military is so different from those pursued by other organizations, analogies drawn from the military tend to be less than perfect. Nevertheless, the line and staff relationships developed by the military do have some similarities to those in educational systems. The line position is one in which power is directly delegated from the superordinate governing body. With the

[1] *Behavioral Science and Educational Administration*, National Society for the Study of Education, LXIII Yearbook, Part II (Chicago, Ill.: University of Chicago Press, 1964), p. 122.

power should come the responsibility for accomplishing tasks decreed from above and the necessity for reporting to the superior body. Staff positions involve different kinds of responsibilities and normally carry a different reporting function. The staff officer tends to be an aide to some line position and often serves an intermediary role between a line position and the subordinates serving below. Because the staff officer lacks power to "force" compliance of subordinates to his decisions, his techniques tend to be limited to those involving persuasive powers. The staff officer is directly responsible to a line officer rather than to the superordinate body, and his reports are generally made to the line officer.

A second concept needing elaboration is that involving authority, power, and responsibility. Authority, in its simplest sense, is the right to proceed. An administrator attains this right through a process of authorization, which comes in the form of instructions from a superior body or at the consensual request of subordinates. In either case, the administrator is "permitted" to launch a particular activity. The administrator may also receive authorization to participate in a particular kind of an activity through the provisions of law, operating procedures, and does, in fact, receive tacit authorization from such nebulous sources as local custom.

The concept of power implies the capacity to accomplish a particular task, and in a physical sense would also be concerned with the rate at which the task was accomplished. In most cases, administrators are not forced to consider the problems involved with rate unless a stringent deadline has been applied. The power to accomplish various administrative acts may come from many sources. When human and physical resources are involved superordinates can sometimes provide these resources to the administrator facing a particular task. A more potent power, however, comes from the willingness of subordinates to be governed in the style represented by the administrator's behavior. The converse is, of course, also true. For when subordinates are at odds with the manner of their governance, the responsible administrator finds it exceedingly difficult to move his organization forward—or in any direction, for that matter.

Responsibility involves accountability. Within an organizational system, the receipt of authority and/or power carries with it responsibility to accomplish the administrative task at hand. It is mainly responsibility which separates the various levels in an administrative hierarchy. As one advances from the lowest administrative position to the highest, his direct accountability to the governing body increases.

There is a relationship between the line-staff concept and the authority, power, and responsibility definitions. Both line and staff officials can be granted at various times both authority and power. The superintendent of schools can authorize his building principal, a lower line officer, to proceed to carry out a particular board directive. This authorization coming from a superior line officer serves as an instruction to the principal to accomplish the delegated task. In addition, the superior officer can supply power, when the appropriate power can come from external sources, or the subordinate can marshal power of his own from the various resources at his command and at his level of the hierarchical structure.

In a similar fashion, a superintendent of schools could authorize a staff officer to proceed with a given task. Lacking the power inherent in a line position, the staff officer is then likely to develop his power resources from those available within his area of operation. However, although the line officer can authorize and can make a staff officer accountable to him, he must bear the responsibility and the accountability for the accomplishment of the task to his governing body. In short, he cannot delegate responsibility given to him by his superior governing body. He can make the staff officer responsible to him but not to the governing agency.

The power available to line officers is often great and holds the potential for being insidious. The following are most potent weapons in the line officer's power arsenal: (1) recommendations for promotion, (2) recommendations for salary increases, (3) recommendations for dismissal, and (4) recommendations for tenure. Even in an enlightened age when administrators recognize the organizational disasters which can follow the indiscriminate use of their power, the recognition that such power does exist is nevertheless potent in the determination of subordinate behavior.

In summary, administrative officers within a public educational system are the responsible agents to the local board of education for moving the organization and its human membership toward the desired goals. Because of their relationship to the local board of education, administrative officers find themselves in an accountable role to the society represented by the system. While the teachers within the system may be responsible for ultimately accomplishing the instructional goals of the system, the administrative officers in the discharge of their duties find that they are accountable for seeing that appropriate instruction does take place and for making change within the system when the instructional program is failing to accomplish the goals set for it.

The Superintendent of Schools

The American Association of School Administrators in attempting to define the unique role of the superintendent of schools, has made the following suggestion:[2]

The superintendent of schools is employed by the board of education as its executive agent. He is the professional advisor to the board, chief administrator of the schools, the leader of the staff, and the focal point of responsibility within the district. He is in a strategic, if trying, position to help both boards of education and teachers, singly or in groups, as they work through their common problems. He is the professional advisor to whom the board looks for recommendations on policy, the chief administrator of the schools, the leader of the professional staff, and the protector and defender of the rights of children to the best and most appropriate educational opportunity. He is a professional educator and a professional school administrator.

Some disillusionment has arisen in recent years over the position of the superintendents of schools. Superintendents, by and large, have chosen to attempt to develop their position so as to allow them to serve as the educational leaders of the professional staff. Changes in the direction taken by teachers' groups are forcing a reconsideration of the unique role served by the superintendent. In a legal sense, there is little doubt that the superintendent of schools must be the educational officer within a public school system who is responsible for carrying forth the policies adopted by the local board of education. When board policy, which he must execute, comes in conflict with the desires of other professionals within the system, the superintendent of schools is legally committed to serve as the executor of the policy. He is legally bound to align himself with the policy of the board.

Superintendents have not all been prone to accept the either/or relationship of being a "board man" or a "teachers' man." Instead, they have attempted to carve out a different basis for their administrative operation. The new ground involves a resolution of conflict between governing boards and the practicing professionals. Most often the strategy is to strengthen the goals of the educational system, which tend to be accepted by both the board of education and the practicing professionals, so that the goals may be held in higher order than policy. Thus it is that the human components in conflict within the system may rally their energies around a point of agreement—the goals—and thereafter seek resolution of their differences in ways that do not disrupt goals.

[2] American Association of Secondary School Administrators, *Roles, Responsibilities, Relationships of the School Board, Superintendent and Staff* (Washington, D.C.: AASA, 1963), pp. 4, 15.

EXECUTIVE POWER

The superintendent of schools is generally recognized as the most influential member of the educational system. Because of his unique position within the system and because of the powers which are normally delegated to him, he finds himself with the capacity to facilitate or to deter organizational movement towards systemic goals.

As indicated in Figure 8-1, the major output from the superintendent is the executive decision. It is precisely that decision-making power which makes the superintendency the most potent component in the educational system. Henry Brickell, following his study of how change took place in New York State, reached the following conclusion: "An administrator is powerful because he can marshal the necessary authority—if not the necessary leadership—to precipitate a decision. . . . Authority is a critical element in the shaping of institutional decisons. Schools depend heavily upon administrative authority in decision making. Consequently, the control center of the institution, as schools are managed today, is the administrator. He may not be—and frequently is not—*the original source of interest in a new type of program,* but unless he gives it his attention and actively promotes its use, it will not come into being."[3] Thus, we find the superintendent of schools with not only the power to make decisions, but with a second type of power —the ability to keep a decision from being made.

ROLE OF THE SUPERINTENDENT

Within a public educational system, the superintendent of schools has three major responsibilities which outline his role. His first responsibility is the execution of school board policy. Depending upon the nature of the policy under consideration and the explicit instructions he may receive from his board of education, the superintendent is free to embark upon a course of action to accomplish the letter and the spirit of the enacted policy. When the policy is explicit and his instructions direct, he has little alternative but to follow the instructions and to initiate the required activity. With less explicit, more broadly developed policy, he has a great deal of freedom to develop strategic and tactical plans for reaching the desired end. How he elects to execute the policies of his board will be subject to their review and may be modified upon their instruction. Excessive modification by a governing board judging "after the fact" can become a very real source of friction between the superintendent and his board of education.

[3] Henry Brickell, "Organizing New York State for Educational Change," *The Role of the Public, the Board, the Administrator and the Teacher* (1961), pp. 23, 24.

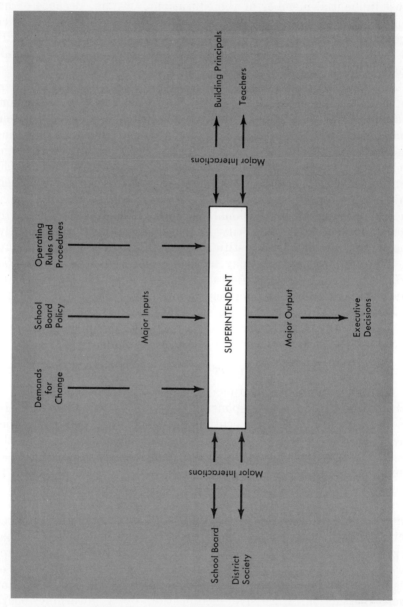

Figure 8-1. Conceptualization of the role of the superintendent in public school systems.

The superintendent's second responsibility is the administration of the affairs for the entire system. If Lipham's definition for administration is accepted, then the superintendent, as an administrator, is responsible for the ongoing, day-to-day operational problems which occur in complex systems. We would expect to find him, therefore, maintaining the established order, procedures, and goals which serve as the basis for the system's continuance. As an administrator, he finds himself with routine tasks which by their very systematic nature tend to be recurring. As an administrator his creative capacity is not taxed but he does, in this role, seek to maintain the solid foundation from which reasonable systemic deviations could be launched.

His final responsibility is that of leadership. Experts in group dynamics notwithstanding, the superintendent in a public school system is, by his office, in a leadership position for two reasons. First, the highest official job classification within a hierarchy is a leadership position in spite of the characteristics of the person occupying this position. Secondly, the superintendent of schools will be charged by his board of education to make changes within the system, and as Lipham has suggested, leadership is "the initiation of a new structure or procedure for accomplishing an organization's goals and objectives or for changing the organization's goals and objectives."[4] If the superintendent is fortunate enough to behave in a way considered appropriate by other components within the system, he may add the third dimension of leadership, which has its genesis within the mind of the perceiver.

Leadership arising from the superintendent's office is not all directed at the subordinate components of the system. In a dynamic society changes are also required within governing bodies. As a result the superintendent has a moral responsibility to upgrade the operational capacity of his board of education. In a similar fashion, the superintendent concerned with the societal environment may wish to be an agent of change within that society. In serving this latter role, he becomes a leader, not only of the system, but also of the environment of the system. Leadership with his board of education is largely an educational affair. With his decision-making power, he can elect to provide the kinds of information to his board that will move them to change.

The superintendent is often called upon to be the visionary of the system. He is required to project needs and to plan for the mobilization of significant and sufficient resources. Risk-taking may often follow his prognostications. In fact, his success may be measured by his ability to guess right.

[4] NSSE, LXIII Yearbook, *op. cit.*

ENVIRONMENTAL ENGINEERING

Organizational movement and continual change is probably inevitable—organizational direction is not. In an effort to serve a determining role in the system, the superintendent has the role of environmental engineer. He recognizes that an organization changes its behavior in much the same way that the human organism does. He soon realizes that forces do have an impact upon organizational direction and that many of these forces are at his command.

To some individuals, environmental engineering poses a real moral dilemma. They are unsure of the desirability, or, in fact, of their right, of marshalling external or internal forces and applying them to make organizational change. Acceptance of the fact that the organization will change in spite of the leadership is requisite to the leadership accepting the task of environmental engineering. Engineering carries with it the expectation that planned organizational change is likely to be better than random change. Random change leads in desirable directions only by chance while planned change improves the odds that the organization will move in desirable directions.

Once the desirable change has been defined, the environmental engineer marshalls his resources to affect the nature, strength, and direction of existing forces. When altering existing forces proves to be insufficient to the task, the engineer has the task of effecting new forces calculated to stimulate desired movement. New forces may spring from untapped areas within the system, or forces inherent within the social, economic, and political environment of the system may be called into play.

In summary, the superintendent of a public school system is responsible for making executive decisions. As the chief executive officer of the board designated to govern the system, the superintendent must make decisions in light of existing school board policy and with the recognition of the operating rules and procedures of the system. His decisions are normally precipitated by demands for change either on the part of the professional subordinate or from the governing board. Given a propensity for change, the superintendent interacts with his governing board, his society, his subordinate administrators, and his teachers to develop decisions capable of directing the organization toward its goals.

The Building Principal

The historical position of the principal places him in a dilemma not much different from that faced by the superintendent of schools. Historically, the principalship predates the superintendency and evolved from the concept of "principal teacher." As educational systems became more and more complex, governing boards found that the local school building needed an individual who could coordinate the affairs of that building with the desires of the governing board. As a result, one of the teachers, usually an older person on whom the board felt they could rely, was chosen to serve this part-time role. Thus it was that the "principal teacher" was responsible for gathering together information for state forms, county surveys, and so on. At this point, there was little doubt that the "principal teacher" was primarily a teacher.

With the advent of the full-time building principal, perceptions about the principalship began to change. Building principals became more and more professional and many, in fact, earned advanced degrees in the field of administration. Principals began to come from the ranks of administrators instead of being designated from the staff of a particular building. Nevertheless, the administrators normally carry a teaching background and have a close identification with the professional teachers. Thus it is that the principal finds himself with the dilemma of serving the administrative role, namely, carrying out board policy in a building setting, or attempting to serve as the "principal teacher" when these two roles come in conflict. Fortunately, the principal is seldom faced with the either/or dichotomy. He, like the superintendent, can use his energies to prevent much of the conflict which would force him to take sides.

Unlike the superintendent, legal descriptions of his position and responsibilities tend to be far less explicit. Nevertheless, it seems clear that the building principal is an administrator, not a teacher. As an administrator within the system, he is ultimately responsible for moving the organization forward toward all goals, both instructional and noninstructional. It is largely the latter area, the noninstructional goals, which will differentiate his behaviors from those engaged in by teachers.

Role

The conceptualization shown in Figure 8-2 suggests that the major outcomes of a building principal's work are organizational decisions and the execution of line decisions made by the superintendent of schools. In either case, the principal finds himself most often interacting with teachers on his staff and with the superintendent. His occasional interactions will include those with the board of education, the curriculum coordinator, parents, and students.

The building principal has problems most normally related to demands for a change in the status position. In arriving at his

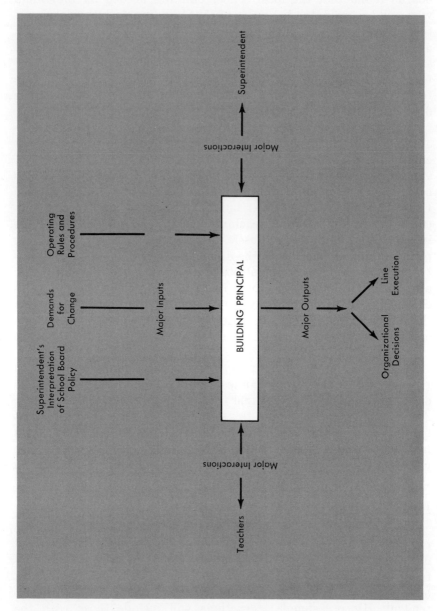

Figure 8-2. Conceptualization of the role of the principal in public school systems.

decisions, he takes into account existing operating rules and procedures and the interpretations of board policy available to him.

Organizational decisions are those involving changes in how the
components in his building are organized to accomplish the missions
set for the building. The principal is responsible for placing components, whether teachers, students, cook, custodians, or bus
drivers, in an appropriate constellation for the desired outcomes to
emerge. For example, when the outcome is learning the principal
is responsible for placing students and teachers in an environment
conducive to learning. He sees that the home economics student is
in the kitchen at a time when the cooking teacher is available to
direct the learning endeavor. He places the woodworking student in
the shop with the woodshop teacher and the chemistry student in
the chemistry lab with the chemistry teacher. The amount of time
and the time of day in which interaction between components will
take place is largely the principal's responsibility. He is also responsible for developing a system to secure the materials required
for the teaching act.

The formation of committees, the developing of organizations
both student and teacher, the utilization of space, and the development of personnel are all decisions of an organizational nature
with which the building principal must wrestle. It should not be
implied that these decisions are his to make unilaterally, although
in many systems he has that power to make such decisions. Rather,
the decisions are normally arrived at through a process of the
interactions outlined above. He seeks consensus on the decisions,
but the lack of consensus does not absolve him from the responsibility for making the decision.

The principal's second function, the execution of decisions made
by the superintendent, generally removes some of the creativity
associated with the principalship. In organizational decisions, the
principal ordinarily has the freedom to determine both "what"
and "how." In executing a decision made by a superordinate, the
subordinate line administrator—in this case the building principal
—no longer is free to establish the "what." Interactions between
the principal and the superintendent do make it possible to establish the creative limits within which the latter's decision is to be
implemented. As an example, the superintendent may inform the
high school principal that the book rental fee for the following year
will be $5.00. The principal then finds himself in a position of being
told what the subsequent policy will be, but he may remain free to
establish the procedures for implementing the change.

The Business Manager

Throughout a long period in the history of American public education, the superintendent of schools served as manager of the business affairs of the system. It was largely through his office that materials were purchased, teachers were hired, budgets were drawn, accounts were kept, children were accounted for, inventories were maintained, and the facilities were planned and maintained. In many communities, then as now, the superintendent was charged by his governing board with providing an educational program, of dubious quality, at the lowest possible cost to the district taxpayers. The superintendent's success was largely measured in terms of total cost rather than on a quality criterion basis.

Increasing complexities in the curricular experiences being offered to children and an increasing concern on the part of the lay public with the quality of educational programs have combined to stimulate a re-examination of the role of the superintendent of schools. As he accepted this new responsibility as instructional leader, new demands were placed upon him which have required the institution of a new office within the enterprise—the business manager.

Although the business manager is conceived in many different ways in the various districts which employ such a person, some generalizations can be drawn about his role. For example, in most systems, the business manager is expected to be able to translate educational plans into fiscal requirements. He normally transmits the translation, in the form of a budget, to the superintendent of schools and subsequently to the board of education. Upon approval of the budget document and upon receipt of the funds to carry forth the educational program, the business manager is given the responsibility of administering the funds in a fashion calculated to facilitate the development of the educational program which elicited fund procurement.

In addition to developing and administering educational budgets, the business manager supervises the day-to-day operations of the system. In most systems he is largely responsible for the conduct of all noninstructional programs and for supervising the personnel that carry them forth.

As indicated in Figure 8-3, the business manager is conceived as receiving his major instructions from the board of education and from the superintendent of schools. His behavior in carrying forth the requirements of his job would be governed by the operating rules and procedures in effect at a given period and time. Secondary inputs are day-to-day requests for action which are forwarded by professional and nonprofessional personnel concerned about the

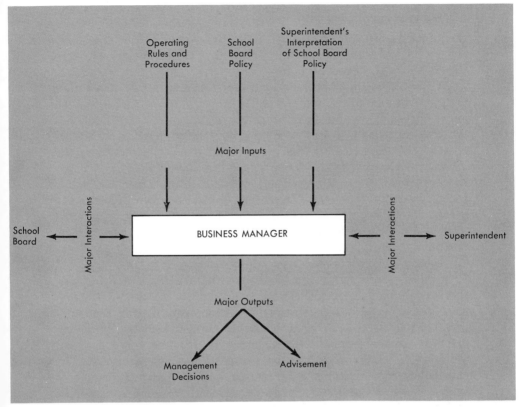

Figure 8-3. Conceptualization of the role of the business manager in public school systems.

capacity of existing resources to serve their function within the system. In carrying out his responsibilities, the business manager's major interactions tend to be with the board of education and with the superintendent of schools. His administrative governance is largely with nonprofessional personnel, which might include such persons as accountants, bookkeepers, custodians, cooks, bus drivers, and so on. The output of his administrative behavior will be management decisions—decisions about the most appropriate courses of action to guarantee that the business affairs of the system will be making a positive contribution toward the accomplishment of the system's long-range goals.

The Curriculum Coordinator

In an age of specialization the superintendent of schools is no longer able to be an expert in all subjects at all grade levels—if, in fact, he ever was. The responsibility for developing appropriate educational experiences for young people throughout an educational system has become a delegated function. At the elementary level the function is often vested with the principal; at the secondary level heads of various academic departments are often involved in the departmental process.

With children moving year by year from one grade to another and from one building to another, the process of developing unified experiences has become exceedingly complex. In addition, the mobility of young people from system to system has placed an additional strain upon the capacity of a given set of experiences to meet the diverse needs of a total student population. For these and other reasons, new positions have been created within American public school systems to carry the responsibility of coordinating the diverse and segmented experiences prepared by professional teachers into a gestalt reflective of the system's goals. These new positions generally carry the label "curriculum coordinator" or "director of instruction" (see Figure 8-4).

In an effort to retain his identity with instructional programs, the superintendent of schools has tended to place the curriculum coordinator in a staff position with a responsibility for reporting directly to him. As a result of his training, the curriculum coordinator tends to stress the desirability of utilizing persuasive and noncoercive means of satisfying the position responsibilities. The curriculum coordinator has not usually been assigned the power to hire and fire, to promote and to recommend for tenure by virtue of his job description. In the conduct of his duties, the curriculum coordinator normally relies upon the superintendent's interpretation of school board policy and decisions about the appropriateness of a particular action. He, like others within the system, must operate within the framework of rules and regulations.

The curriculum coordinator must be particularly sensitive to developments arising from curricular research. He recognizes that neither the superintendent nor the board of education can be experts on all aspects of the "alphabet soup" represented in present day curricular programs. SMSG, BSCS, PSSC, and ITA are only a few examples of curricular programs touted by outside agencies as worthy of consideration by a local school district. The curriculum coordinator is largely responsible for digesting the potentials of the various programs for application within the school system. Therefore, he must serve an information and recommendation function about the appropriateness of various curricular experiences.

In addition to interactions with professionals external to his system, the director of instruction also finds himself constantly at work with teachers, principals, and the superintendent of schools.

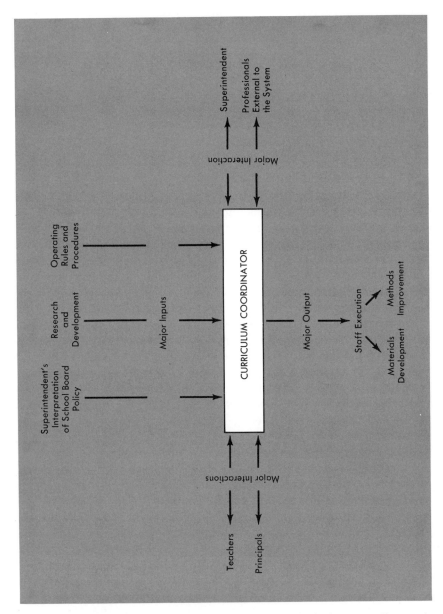

Figure 8-4. Conceptualization of the role of the curriculum coordinator in public school systems.

His coordinative function can only be served through an ongoing series of interactions between the individuals responsible for articulating the experiences of various grade levels and in various school buildings.

Because instruction is his responsibility, he develops systems for improving methods of instruction and for developing curricular materials. His work with instructional supervisors, either line or staff, is pointed toward improvement in instructional methods. His office, in concert with the business manager, must provide the means whereby instructional aids are procured or manufactured for use within the learning environment.

Line and Staff Relationships

Although the terms *line* and *staff* have been used throughout this chapter, no suggestion is being made as to the desirability of school systems emulating military organizations. However, they are convenient terms to partially convey the relationship of various human components within a functioning system. Organizations do have hierarchies and governing bodies, and some way must be used to describe the manner in which authority and responsibility get transmitted from one part of the system to another.

Those who have chosen to emulate the more clearly defined military model are those to whom legalism appeals. More enlightened districts attempt to dull the edges of lines of authority, and "teaming" is becoming far more common as an operating method. With teaming comes the opportunity for persons from low hierarchical positions to exercise a particular expertise, with appropriate respect, at a higher level of responsibility. Superintendents in such districts are mobilizing competent resources according to need, with little regard for position title.

Nevertheless, governing bodies and the society they represent will continue to demand that accountability be located in a visible position and not hidden behind the skirts of "The Committee" or the "Group Decision." Responsibility will continue to follow hierarchical lines in order that accountability may remain visible, but the human interactions within the hierarchy need not resemble the military. Rather, patterns of leadership and its exercise will change while the patterns of community and professional expectations will continue to seek more visible routes to fulfillment.

Problems and Issues

1. *What are the impacts of line and staff relationships upon teachers seeking professional status?* To the physician, engaged in personal practice, the question of line and staff relationships is of

little import. As a professional in private practice, he is little concerned with subordinate or superordinate bodies, and in fact he functions in organizational isolation. Traditional educational organizations place teachers in low positions in the hierarchical order. Because he is neither self-employed nor free to set his own fees, the teacher also finds himself in an employer-employee relationship and under the supervision of an intermediary officer designated by the employer. The teacher does not have organizational isolation.

In the process of becoming educated, teachers have come to expect increased degrees of freedom. To the extent that organizational arrangements prevent the exercise of freedom, the teacher feels threatened and unfulfilled. On the other hand, he enters a school system with the knowledge that that system has expectations for his professional behavior. He also comes to realize that the organization has goals which it shall seek with or without his assistance and that the organization is bigger than any individual member. He finds his greatest satisfactions in professional situations where his goals are congruent with those of the organization. In view of the above, how will administrative behavior affect teacher behavior?—How do line and staff behaviors differ?—Are they perceived differently?—In what areas of a teacher's professional life would one relationship (line or staff) be better than the other?

2. *By what means can administrators utilize the differentiated talents of their teaching staff in furthering the accomplishment of systemic goals?* Each teacher employed in a public school system brings to the system unique talents. Such, of course, is also the case with the administrators. Neither teachers nor administrators have a corner on all talents. Consequently, administrators desiring to further systemic goals find, if they are honest with themselves, that they are inadequate to accomplish all tasks in and of themselves. Assistance is required from other administrators and from teachers. Hierarchical arrangements which place administrators in superordinate positions to teachers have often prevented the creative utilization of teacher competencies.

It seems logical to assume that within the teaching faculty there resides unusual expertise concerning students and the students' interaction with the educational curriculum. The teacher is a daily observer of children and of the capacity of various curricular experiences to accomplish the objectives set for them. On the other hand, the administrator is in day-to-day contact with the systems operation. As he becomes more experienced, he gains knowledge about the manner in which systemic components can be arranged into effectively functioning configurations. Given these differentiated capacities, how can teachers and administrators collaborate to accomplish systemic goals?—In what areas?—Through what processes?—Under what conditions of respect?

3. *Under what conditions can the chief executive officer of a school system be both administrator and leader?* Accepting Lipham's definition of administration and leadership, the chief executive officer finds himself in a functional dilemma. In administering the affairs of the system, he must retain current and ongoing processes and he must direct the energies of the systems' components toward predetermined goals. Leadership, on the other hand, carries with it perceptual connotations. The follower, if he is to follow, must perceive the leader as an individual capable of contributing toward the accomplishment of his own personal and professional goals. In the case of the chief executive officer, the board of education selects a superintendent of schools on the basis of its judgment about his capacity to further its goals. Teachers are not given the opportunity, normally, to participate in the selection of their chief executive officer, and as a result, they may not ascribe "leadership" to the superintendent as an automatic consequence of his appointment by the board of education. Given these conditions, can there be "administrative leadership?—Under what conditions?—By what kind of a person?—By what behaviors?—How does an administrator become a leader?

Selected References

American Association of School Administrators. *The Unique Role of the Superintendent of Schools.* Washington: N.E.A. Educational Policies Commission, 1965.

Culbertson, Jack, Paul Jacobson, and Theodore Reller. *Administrative Relationships. A Casebook.* Englewood Cliffs, N.J.: Prentice-Hall, 1960.

Hicks, William V., and Marshall Jamieson. *The Elementary School Principal at Work.* Englewood Cliffs, N.J.: Prentice-Hall, 1957.

Jennings, Eugene. *Anatomy of Leadership,* New York: Harper & Row, 1960.

McCleary, Lloyd, and Stephen Hencley. *Secondary School Administration.* New York: Dodd-Mead, 1965.

Miller, Van. *The Public Administration of American School Systems.* New York: Macmillan, 1965.

NSSE. *Behavior Science and Educational Administration.* LXIII Yearbook, Part II. Chicago: University of Chicago Press, 1964.

Simon, Herbert, *Administrative Behavior.* New York: Free Press, 1957.

Yauch, Wilbur A. *Helping Teachers Understand Principals.* New York: Appleton Century Crofts, 1957.

chapter 9

■ *The Teacher*

Conditions for Admittance into the System

The principal requirements for admittance into the system are legally defined by each of the several states. As was stated in Chapter 4, meeting the legal requirements for certification assures only that the teacher *may* be a candidate for a position—it in no way assures him that he will be admitted into the employ of any particular system.

The so-called "teacher shortage" has made possible a relative ease for most certified teachers to gain employment in some school systems. There are, too, school systems which place such a high value on keeping down expenditures for instructional services (that is, teacher salaries) that teachers with less than full certification can still find employment. The majority of teachers in some states still are without degrees. And there are school systems where less than fully certified teachers are employed simply because there were no certified applicants for position openings. Admittance to the system, then, is a function of not only the teacher but also the system.

The patterns of deployment of new teachers entering the field would seem to show that teachers seek employment in suburban school systems more than in urban systems; they tend to seek employment near an urban center, especially if it has a college or university where they might continue their study, rather than in a geographically isolated locale; and, obviously, they would seem to go where the better salaries are. Within these variables there are some conflicting conditions which cause teachers to make some choices. School systems near universities may have numerous applicants for employment from among experienced teachers who wish to do advanced graduate work. Because of the convenience of location, these systems may even be able to procure excellent teachers without offering a high salary. The geographically remote school system may have to offer a highly competitive salary schedule just to encourage applicants for position openings. There is a certain irony in the struggle of the remote school system. The high initial salary it offers may well attract especially desirable candidates for teaching positions but these are the same people who will probably aspire to further study in graduate schools or will be pirated away by a suburban district. The irony is made complete when one considers that the supervisory efforts in the remote district may have made a large contribution to the teacher's growth as a useful component in the system.

In recent years the National Education Association has compiled data which indicate the growing problem in the distribution among teaching specialties and at different grade levels of the new supply of teachers.[1] Present data indicate an oversupply of secondary teachers in certain areas and a commensurate undersupply of elementary teachers. The problem of distribution is acute at the secondary level with an oversupply of new teachers trained in the areas of speech, men's health and physical education, and the social sciences and an undersupply of teachers trained in the areas of mathematics, the physical sciences, English, and foreign languages. At the elementary level the problem would seem to be numerical—too few candidate teachers are preparing to teach at this level. A global view of teacher personnel procurement in the United States since the onset of World War II indicates that teacher preparation in general has not kept pace with the needs of the system.

School systems have attempted to counteract the shortage by searching through the general population to uncover (1) qualified graduates of earlier years ready to turn (or return) from other occupations to teaching; (2) housewives and mothers freed from other commitments since graduating from college with eligibility to become teachers; (3) housewives and mothers who formerly were teachers, now available to return to the classroom; (4) liberal arts college graduates without professional (or with only partial) preparation but willing to undertake full classroom responsibilities; (5) retirees from other occupations; and (6) a heterogeneous group of other persons to whom various kinds of emergency licenses were issued.[2]

However, most systems vigorously seek fully qualified professional teachers. The fully certified teacher today usually must have appreciably more formal education than the two years of normal school which would have qualified him for a full license to teach a

---

[1] NEA, *Research Bulletin*, XLIII (October 1965), pp. 72–76.
[2] *Ibid.*

few years ago. It is noteworthy that even with a continuing teacher shortage the requirements for full certification to teach at any level within the system are moving on a national scale toward no less than five years of collegiate and professional training.

The very fact that school systems are arranged into local school districts gives rise to another dimension of criteria used in selecting teachers for admittance into the system. The ethic of the school-community may well dictate how favorably the teacher will be looked upon as a candidate for a teaching position in the system. The ethic may be made explicit by the board of education, in which case the administrator charged with initiating teacher procurement will have been given guidelines regarding the types of personnel desired for the system. In the absence of guidelines the procuring officer will use his judgment—his perception of what the community wants—in selecting candidates he will recommend for employment.

Hopefully, the administrator charged with teacher recruitment will also consider what kinds of teachers the system *needs*. The latter consideration might predict that teachers who do *not* fit the local ethic are needed in the employ of the system. This is not to say that teachers will be employed who will set the school system in competition with the community ethic; rather, it acknowledges that teachers with differing backgrounds and beliefs might better provide perspective for the student components in the system and in a broader sense, for the whole school-community. The alert teacher who is a candidate for a position ought to be able to discern whether the system is seeking to employ only convergent teachers or whether divergent persons are desired to give the system a greater openness.

Some of the specific factors which might operate in selecting a teacher for admittance into the system include: religious preference; marital status; draft status; sex; race; physical appearance; and so on. It should be noted that in most states the law clearly denies the use of many of the aforementioned factors in selection of personnel for employment. However, to say that these factors do not operate in recruitment decisions would be to ignore the obvious.

Characteristics of Teachers

RESEARCH STUDIES

Why do people enter teaching? What are the characteristics of teachers? How are teachers motivated? In short, what is known about the persons comprising the teaching profession? The generalizations which follow attempt to describe the "average" teacher and all have a basis in legitimate research.

1. *The average teacher does not want to be a teacher!* Fifty-one per cent of beginning teachers in a large nationwide sample did not expect to be in the profession five years later—65 per cent for women, 26 per cent for men.[3] Within five years, 58 per cent of the women wanted to marry and have family responsibilities consuming their time instead of teaching. With the men, 51 per cent expected to be out of the classroom and into administrative or supervisory activities within five years. The majority of persons entering the teaching profession do not expect it to be permanent. What other profession must contend with such an attitude?

2. *Persons entering teaching are psychologically different from persons entering other professions.* Using an instrument called the Activities Index, John Gillis found that compared to persons entering other professions, teachers exhibit (at the .01 level of significance) the following characteristics:[4]

1. More cognitive organization.
2. More self-depreciation and devaluation.
3. More close, friendly relationships.
4. More deference to perceived superiors.
5. More love and protection of others.
6. More concern for detail, neatness, and arrangements.
7. More dependence upon others for love, protection, and assistance.
8. More intense emotional expression.
9. More preoccupation with self.
10. More erotic interests and expressions.
11. Less need to analyze, discuss, or reflect on social objects.
12. Less objectivity and more reliance upon perceptions and beliefs.
13. Less analytic and problem-solving needs.
14. Less assertive behavior with others.
15. Less spontaneous, impetuous behavior.
16. Less willingness to gamble or take risks.

From such findings, teachers have been defined as rather soft, compliant, compulsive, dependent, kowtowing, sex-starved creatures, and if the studies of IQ are correct, they "ain't too smart neither."

3. *The psychological make-up of teachers varies between the sexes.*[5] Research has shown that when compared with female

[3] Ward S. Mason, *The Beginning Teacher* (OE-23009) Washington, D.C.: U.S. Department of Health, Education and Welfare, 1961.

[4] John Gillis, "Personality Needs of Future Teachers," *Educational and Psychological Measurement*, XXIV, No. 3, 1964, pp. 589–600.

[5] Gillis, *op. cit.*

teachers the male teacher exhibits (at the .01 level of significance) the following characteristics:

1. More need to achieve.
2. More need to overcome failure and humiliation.
3. More need for personal power.
4. More aggression and hostility.
5. More desire to manipulate others.
6. More attention-seeking behavior.
7. Less willingness to gamble.

When compared with male teachers, the female teacher exhibits (at the .01 level of significance) the following traits:

1. More need to abase and self-criticize.
2. More need to be friendly and have friends.
3. More denial of hostility.
4. More willingness to submit to superiors.
5. More need to love and be loved.
6. More intense emotional expression.
7. More need for narcissistic and erotic behavior.

4. *The psychological make-up of teachers varies according to the grade or subject preference of the teachers.* Different kinds of teachers prefer different kinds of teaching activities. In a study by Karl Garrison the following differences were noted through the use of the Edwards Personal Preference Schedule:[6]

Women electing general secondary courses manifested significantly greater need for achievement than did prospective teachers of lower elementary, upper elementary, and nongeneral (business education, music, art, physical education) secondary education. Prospective women teachers of special education also showed a greater need for achievement than teachers of lower elementary, upper elementary, and nongeneral secondary.

Teachers from social science, language arts, and math/science all exhibited a greater need for achievement than did lower elementary teachers. The language arts and math/science teachers also manifested an achievement need significantly greater than those from upper elementary, business education, and physical education.

Lower elementary teachers exhibited a greater need for nurturance than any group except special education teachers; math/science teachers also showed a need for nurturance greater than those from social studies, upper elementary, language arts, business education, and home economics.

[6] Karl Garrison and Mary Scott, "A Comparison of the Personal Needs of College Students Preparing to Teach in Different Teaching Areas," *Educational and Psychological Measurement*, XXI, No. 4, 1961, pp. 955–964.

With regard to succorance, the greatest need was among upper elementary and the lowest among special education. Lower elementary teachers showed more need for succorance than secondary or special education teachers.

5. *The teachers' dependent needs are such that when the opportunity arises, they make a bee-line for mother and the safety of home.* In a recent sampling of Michigan teachers (n = 259), it was found that the teachers took their first jobs only 25 median miles from home and their current jobs were an average of 16 miles from home.[7] In terms of grade level, the secondary teachers started 50 miles away and moved closer whereas the brave elementary teachers started ten miles away and then moved closer. Teachers from the farm and the very large (50,000+) cities were more prone to head for home than those from medium size towns.

More amazing is the study of the true "homers." Fifteen per cent actually started in their home towns, and enough teachers joined them to bring the total to 26 per cent who were actually teaching in their home town. In addition, those who got to their home-town stayed there (88 per cent). Only 17 per cent of the teachers who started outside their home town stayed put.

Actually, most of what can be said categorically about characteristics of teachers is both self-evident and probably of little consequence in viewing teachers as a component group within the system. It is common knowledge that more women than men are to be found as teachers in the elementary grades; that patterns of attrition from the profession vary with the sex and age of the teacher and the system in which he was employed; and that anthropometric assessments show teachers to range in characteristics as broadly as the general population (an interesting aside is that teachers would seem to have a greater mean life expectancy than the general population).

Intensive concern with teacher characteristics requires that one become concerned with perception. Essentially, these characteristics, even the self-evident ones, devolve from how the teacher is seen by another person or how the teacher sees himself. Teacher characteristics are, then, what they would *seem* to be. What they really are becomes a moot point, although some characteristics have come to be accepted because many viewers or authoritative persons have agreed upon or designated particular characteristics as those of teachers. The latter point would seem to support this line of reasoning when one considers that some characteristics ascribed to teachers are found by those teachers to be repugnant.

[7] Jesse Soriano and James Heald, "Coops for Homing Pigeons," *Michigan Education Journal*, Vol. 43, No. 4, October 1, 1965, p. 27.

IMAGE REACTION

Often the result of this is that the teacher may attempt to alter the image he is conveying of himself. In recent years much has been written and said about teachers coming from middle-class homes and subscribing to middle-class values—and perhaps teaching middle-class values in the classroom. This middle-class orientation has been chided for teachers whose classrooms are populated in the main with children from lower-class homes. Class value differences between the teacher and the students have been cited as dysfunctional for the teaching-learning setting. If the teacher should agree with this reasoning then he might elect to engage in some alternate forms of behavior.

Nothing can be said as to how or whether he has changed his mind; attention must be focused on behavioral change because this is the only criterion on which characteristics can be based. The motives in this sort of behavioral adaptation might be highly professional—the primary concern might be the improvement of the teaching-learning situation. However, similar behavioral change might be evidenced by another teacher with entirely different motives, such as feeling the pressure to conform to what authoritative educators say teachers *ought* to be like. The latter teacher might well be one who would describe himself on a teacher-characteristics questionnaire as the kind of person he believes the author of the questionnaire had in mind as a "good" teacher with the "right" characteristics and value orientations.

A gross consideration of teacher characteristics within any given public school system would probably hinge on the balance between goals to perpetuate and maintain our social system and goals to liberate the student and enhance his being as a free-willing member of society. The balance between these goals is evident in an inspection of the behavior of human components within the system. It is uncomfortably easy, however, to cite "good" teacher characteristics as those evident in school systems where morale is high, pupil achievement is good, and, in general, the school-community is existing in a state of conviviality. The discomfort grows out of a concern with the ever-present possibility of confusing cause with effect.

Whatever "good" teacher characteristics are[8] they will have only a temporal validity, and then only for a given school system. Is it not possible that systems characterized by low morale, high teacher turnover, low pupil performance on standard achievement tests, and a heated dialogue between the school and community might have in their employ teachers with laudable characteristics? Is it

[8] See AASA, *Who's a Good Teacher?* (Washington: AASA, NEA, 1961).

not also possible that students in such systems may be acquisitive in other than the usually described manners and that their gains in potential for behavioral adaptation may be great?

At the risk of over-generalization certain observations might be made about possible teacher characteristics. The new teacher in the system is often faced with a choice in behavior between attempting to adopt the ethic of the system or letting his personal judgment and recent professional training guide his actions. The new teacher may have to choose between identifying with administrative or teacher components in the system. He may have to decide the extent to which he will align himself with particular individuals and groups within the school community. He will be faced in the classroom with resolving conflicts among his goals, goals of the system, and goals of students.

The teacher who is conscious of the rational aspects of those elements that characterize him will use his ability as a rational being to make these and other decisions. His personal integrity will then depend upon the extent to which he is able to behave in accord with the decisions he has made.

The Role of the Teacher in the System

The notion of role or role portrayal is inextricably tied with the problem of perception; the role to be portrayed is one which must be communicated. The role of the teacher in the system must be communicated by the system to its teachers; otherwise, the teacher is left to infer his role from observation of the systemic environment, or in desperation, when observations are befogged, to intuit what roles are to be portrayed.

EXPECTATIONS

No attempt is being made here to demean intuitive judgment; rather it is suggested that integral components of systems ought to have some defined role expectations if the system is to meet the criteria for integration. Because those in the system who explicate roles for both the teacher and for the system are human components, it might be anticipated that the several role expectations be considered before definitive statements for the roles of either are made. Definitive statements of role need not be necessarily prescriptive in the sense that role interpretation is diminished. These statements might well acknowledge the teacher as a professional component who, if the most is to be gained from his serving the system, should be expected to invoke his professional judgment in the portrayal of his role as a teacher in the system.

It is important for the system to recognize that all teachers probably do some things in common, hence there can be some common role expectation. But by far the most of what a teacher does differentiates him from the other teachers in the system. Although many of the differentiations are subtle, they are there. The existence of these differences in role should caution the system and its teachers when attempts are made to make more uniform the role of teachers. The fact that the teacher is a highly trained professional should in itself attest to the desirability of teachers engaging in role interpretation.

It must also be understood that the role of the teacher in the system is a function of how the teacher perceives himself in the larger environment, beyond the bounds of the system. This extension of role expectations for the teacher reflects his prior experiences in training institutions, family life, other social experiences, and possibly his expectations which have been the result of employment in other systems. Too, role expectations of the teacher will reflect what the teacher aspires to, both within the present system and possibly beyond this to his marital desires and hopes, concern with professional advancement through further study, and the meeting of other personal goals which may be only vague at the time. The role a teacher portrays at any given time within any given system is, then, a composite of prior experiences, perception of present observation, and the projection of future desires.

STUDENT CONTROL

Systems of public schools would seem to value somewhat highly teachers portraying roles which tend to elicit a controlling of students—roles which tend to support a climate in which the students observably demonstrate the kind of behavior held to be desirable by the society sponsoring the system. In a sense, it might be said that the system often has the same aspirations for teachers that it has for students. Components charged with the administration and supervision of the system would seem to give greater approval to teachers who choose to parallel their roles with the general role expectations of the system than to teachers who choose roles which tend to be divergent from systemic expectations.

Interestingly, in systems where student control is operating at a high level of efficiency, components are relatively free to give verbal support to a systemic environment in which controls might be looser or of lesser necessity. If this is true, systems which solicit for the teachers a strong controlling role with students may be the systems in which the desired control does not exist; they

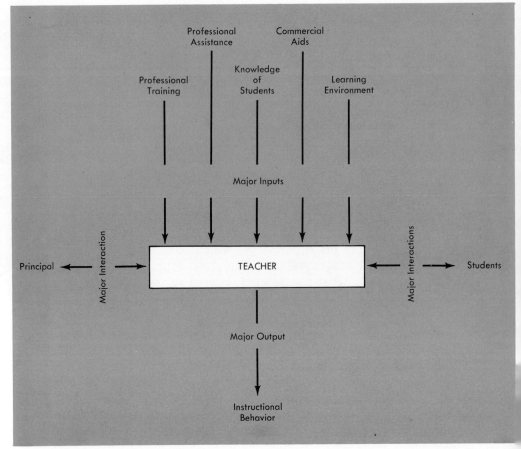

Figure 9-1. Conceptualization of the role of the teacher in a public school system.

may also be systems in which both teacher and student alienation are being bred at the expense of achieving goals for which the system purportedly exists.

The Task of the Teacher in the System

The teacher's primary task is that of environmental manipulation. This task is not only primary but also critical because the teacher has, in a sense, a captive audience. The teacher can do little to arrange the disposition of student components in the system. The student comes as he is and each brings with him his unique experiential background. It falls to the teacher to assess "where the student is" and to become aware of his experiential background. (See Figure 9-1.)

INCENTIVE AND MOTIVATION

The teacher cannot assure that learning will take place. Even when it would appear that learning has taken place, there is no assurance that the teacher actually evoked the learning. The position is taken here that the best the system can do is to provide appropriate *incentives* for learning. Certain incentives are provided by the system for all students, whereas other incentives are provided in individual classrooms or for individual students within the classroom by the teacher. These incentives are provided as the best estimates which professional components can make to enhance the possibility of learning. *Motivation,* on the other hand, is an internal or intrinsic element in learning. It enters the learning situation only as the individual learner chooses to invoke it. It is not, then, one of the tasks of the teacher to motivate students—*students must motivate themselves.*

Where the teacher feels confounded in his task it might be that too much attention has been given to what he thinks students *ought* to be interested in and too little to the existing interests of students or to the students' experiential backgrounds for the task being undertaken. Crudely put, the teacher may become so wrapped up in "teaching" something that he may overlook the student. Under these conditions the teacher is treating students as *homo automata,* denying all differences among students. In performing the task of communication he is still teaching some "thing" to students—not teaching students.

OTHER TASKS AND DUTIES

Attention has been given first to the essential and basic task of the teacher as he is intimately involved in facilitating student learning. However, mention must be made of the teachers' many tasks which are only peripheral to the teaching-learning situation. The teacher is commonly expected to perform a number of custodial tasks, which might range from record-keeping in the classroom to chaperoning student activities sponsored by the system. Although these tasks are peripheral to classroom teaching and learning, they bear an important relationship to the overall goals of the school system. Without adequate and accurate records there may be no source to which teachers might turn when information is desired on student accomplishment and potential. Where the school system sponsors activities for students at which teachers are expected to chaperone, the activities are seen as part of the curriculum of the school; conceivably it is through these activities that the school hopes to elicit attitudinal learnings in students.

There is a danger that the teacher will look upon as mundane all tasks which detract from teaching-contact time he has with students. If the goals of the system are to be accomplished, teachers must engage in both individual tasks and tasks which can only be accomplished cooperatively. Some of these tasks are schoolwide and require the teachers' collective support.

Myriad examples of variation in tasks for the teacher might be cited. If there is a trend, it probably is toward a further specialization of the teacher as a component in the system. Computers and teacher aids have reduced the number of clerical and custodial tasks being assigned teachers. The advent of team teaching has encouraged the use of teachers in tasks for which they are especially well trained and capable rather than assigning them tasks which cover a broad range of material in a variety of subject areas. Increasingly, time is being allotted teachers for planning, with the hope that more thorough planning and utilization of particular abilities will provide more effective teaching. The teacher of the near-future in the school system may well spend far fewer contact hours with students but will perform his tasks more effectively. He will probably be expected to know more about his students and what he teaches than ever before. The demands of these tasks will probably require that he become more of a professional teacher component in the system than ever before.

The Impact of Nonhuman Instruction on the Teacher

There would appear to be a certain anxiety among teachers when they consider nonhuman instructional devices. Concern has ranged from wondering whether such devices might put teachers out of work to serious questioning of whether these devices are as good as, let alone better than human teaching. Possibly the greatest source of concern are those teaching devices that do not require the teacher's presence. It should be noted, however, that no device exists at this time which can make rational decisions for the direction learning will take beyond the information on *specific* variables fed into the device. And, obviously, any feeding of information will have to be done by humans.

Teachers need to be concerned with nonhuman instruction so that they can determine where and when these devices could be used to improve instruction of students in general. It has long been recognized that multisensory perception on the part of the learner and multisensory approaches to teaching enhance the possibility that learning will take place. In the main, the teacher and nonhuman devices have been limited to use of sight and sound stimulation, with some use made of manipulation giving representations of size, shape, and texture. The commercial film industry has gone the school one better by experimenting with motion pictures which are accompanied by appropriate odors thus incorporating the sense of smell. The problem is not one necessarily of utilizing all the sensory mechanisms of the learner but rather of assessing which ones when used will best facilitate learning—which ones will sharpen the learning and predict a greater retention.

Critical questions which the teacher must ask include the following: Which devices ought I to use in presenting a particular concept or body of material? How must I prepare for the use of the devices selected, and what types of follow-up activities will be necessary? What relationships should exist between what is presented by devices and what I personally present? And, most important, how must I, and the students, adequately prepare for the effective use of any devices selected? Probably no greater misunderstanding and mismanagement has grown up over the use of nonhuman instructional devices than in this latter area. The unplanned use of these devices as clever gimmicks has often led to teachers souring on their worth and students being confounded by the presentation.

Once it has been decided that particular nonhuman instructional devices might enhance learning, and once the teacher has the confidence that he can effectively use the devices, he must then prepare the students for their use. It is probably here that the nonhuman instructional device has its greatest impact upon the teacher. He may be able to see the merit in its use in instruction, may have mastered the manipulation of the device, but what does he know about how this device will "interact" with students in the teaching-learning situation? If the device requires that he be involved in its use (for example, an overhead projector) he will have the chance to monitor student sensitivity and motivation. In this case he is a participant-observer in the teaching-learning setting and can "correct for" unanticipated difficulties. When a device is selected that does not require the teacher's presence, it is crucial that the student be adequately prepared for the instructional motif. In the latter case the information the teacher gets on what instruction actually took place is in the form of feedback, and since it comes *after* the instruction, the only correction which can be made would be in further use of the device. The literature of education is replete with both research and testimonials to the effect that a crucial element in using nonhuman instructional devices involves teaching the student how to be an effective consumer—how to learn efficiently through the use of these devices.

Two specific areas of concern should occupy the teacher when he plans learning activities to follow instruction by a nonhuman device. These concerns really are not greatly different than those he might have following his own presentation of material to students. But, there is one significant difference. He may know less of what has happened to the student during the nonhuman lesson than he would had he taught the lesson himself and been able to engage the students in discussion *during* the lesson. Student use of teaching machines might illustrate the case in point. The student in using a teaching machine may be, as a result of his progress in the lesson, redirected to material which will serve as a review in the event that he has encountered difficulty in the programmed lesson. The student may, on the other hand, be accelerated to more difficult or abstract material in the event that he is able to respond to the programmed material unerringly. The teacher must know what has happened to individual students and to class groups if he is to continue to teach after the nonhuman instruction and maintain continuity of the material being taught.

Nonhuman instructional devices do not release the teacher or lessen his responsibility. If anything, their use requires that he be even more keenly aware of what has happened. The accent in using nonhuman devices is upon enhancing the possibility of learning for the student not upon lightening the work load of the teacher. This is as it should be if the goals for the system are described in terms of the student.

The Teacher and Special Service Personnel

Because schools are principally concerned with the task of educating students, and because teachers spend probably more contact time with students than any other component in the system, teachers may get the mistaken notion that they are "going it alone." Little else could be farther from the truth. The generic idea of a *system* allows that all components contribute to and function in the system. Theoretically, a component which had no utility in the system would be dropped. Part of the problem with other components in the system may emanate from their being less visible in the scheme of things. Teacher components may further contribute to this problem by their refusal to recognize other components or their indolence in acknowledging the contributions other components make toward improving teaching and learning.

An inclusive list of special service personnel would be difficult to describe because the resources among public school systems vary. These components would usually include guidance workers, counsellors, health personnel, curriculum consultants, department heads or academic area consultants, special subject teachers, custodians, and persons, such as a school social worker, who might work between the system and the larger community. The titles assigned in the above enumeration are of little consequence; they really refer to domains in which other components than the teacher work to support the educational endeavors of the school system. Most of the components listed are within the system but often the system will employ or use personnel from without the system. The "outsiders" might come from the community in the form of a resource person who is especially able to illuminate a particular topic or a consultant from some distant point who is brought into the system to assist with a particular problem or project.

The role of special service personnel in any given system is amplified by the extent to which these persons contribute to the educational program and the degree to which teachers and administrators designate them as important components. The latter designation is often based simply on the extent to which these people are used.

In school systems where teachers are hired and then "turned loose" to teach what they purportedly are prepared for, special service personnel may not exist in large numbers or may just get lost in the shuffle of teachers going about their individual ways. Such schools do not meet even minimum criteria for a system. Articulate school systems not only employ a broad array of special service personnel but they also plan for the deployment and utilization of these persons in such a manner that they will best function within the system. Health service facilities of the school identify in students physical characteristics which ought to be brought to the attention of the parents for referral to a private physican. They also maintain records which permit the teacher to assess more accurately which students should be withheld from certain activities for health reasons—students for whom appropriate parallel activities might be arranged.

Guidance and counsellor personnel provide a service which the teacher and the student might use. The teacher is able through these services to inquire at some depth into the characteristics of his learners and the community and to gain a breadth of further information which will enable him to better plan his teaching-learning activities. The student, with direct or referred access to the counsellor, is able to gain assistance in understanding more fully the nature of his problems and to expand his range of choices in resolving his concerns. Guidance services maintain not only a compendium of information but also have the capacity to generate new information when it is necessary or desirable.

Curriculum personnel in the system arrange for and enable teachers at different "grade" levels and in different subject areas to meet together for planning and discussion purposes. Curricular components facilitate the teachers' understanding of what has been taught in the system prior to the level at which they are teaching and of what will be taught at succeeding higher levels within the system. Special service components in curriculum assure that there is the opportunity for sequential concept development within a discipline and also that activities might be arranged to support teaching in other disciplines. Curriculum workers frequently find that they must engage in research activities to generate required data.

Department heads, grade chairmen, and their ilk are often perceived as being administrative components in the system; however, they serve special service functions as they arrange that teachers are exposed to new materials and as they assist in the development of teaching methodology and the utilization of content material.

Special subject or special class teachers sponsor student activities which the regular teacher component might be ill-prepared to teach. Too, these teachers are often assigned to work with unique groups of students, thus lessening the range of types of students with which the regular teacher must work in the classroom. In a sense, the special teacher broadens the student experience in a manner not possible if reliance were placed entirely upon the regular teachers on the staff.

Custodial personnel in the system also serve as special components in that they facilitate the arrangement of the physical environment so that optimal learning and teaching might take place. The general appearance of the physical environment of the school may very much affect student perception of the school per se.

Social work personnel, although in the employ of the system, conduct their activities both within and without the system. In conjunction with the school system guidance services and other community agencies, social workers generate and prepare case materials and counsel many people in the hope that the best disposition of student problems may be found. The social worker is a clear example of system component who works, in the context of a larger system, with the components of several subsystems and by so doing improves the likelihood that the teacher will enjoy a greater success with more students in his classroom.

Members of the community may be brought into the system as special service components on a short-term basis. Possibly the local historian would be utilized by certain teachers to generate interest in local history and the people who had significant roles in that history. In the primary grades children often make trips to agencies of community government, such as fire and police stations. The lore presented by employees in these agencies is frequently more accurate than any teacher might be expected to have. Further, the student usually assigns a special credibility to information tendered by these persons—a greater credibility than what the teacher might be expected to elicit.

Yet another short-term component might be the consultant who comes into the system from some distance away. Possibly a team-teaching leader from another school system is invited to visit the system to discuss and demonstrate different approaches to planning and techniques of instruction. Theoretically, where teachers visit another system to see demonstrated techniques used in instruction, the demonstration becomes a peripheral component for the home system. The visiting teachers take in certain of what they see demonstrated and judge the relative merits of the techniques and materials in terms of what they are doing in their own classrooms. The relative influence on this "external" component is seen in the extent to which it breeds modification or adoption in the home system.

Increasingly, school systems are employing one other component who might be described under the heading of special service personnel. The research worker in the system is a nearly pure example of the service person. He is responsive to the needs of all of the components in the system and the system as a whole. His task is one of designing how needed data might be assembled, coordinating its collection, and providing for the dissemination of findings so that the outcomes will be understandable to other components in the system.

No system will function long at any level of efficiency unless a continual assessment is made of the utility of components. Tasks and roles of components may require modification; whole components may become dysfunctional for the system; and components may need to be added to the system. Components support the system, collectively, to the extent that they recognize the several contributions that each component can make to the efficient operation of the system and to improvement in the operation of each component in the system. As one or several components fail to recognize any other component in the system, the system and the nonrecognizing components fail to some extent in performing their appointed tasks.

Teacher-Student and Teacher-Community Relationships

It should be stated again that the system of public schools and all its components exist for the purpose of the education of youth. The teacher, then, is a service component of the system, and the student is the primary recipient component of the services rendered by the system. Although relationships might be fostered which tend to respond to the desires of many different components, including teachers, the primary relationships ought to be directed toward facilitating desired behavioral change in students.

The relationships between the teacher and students are the product of their experiential backgrounds. The teacher has the remembrance of what he thought school and teachers were like when he was a student; he knows what schools, teachers, and students are said to be like from his exposures in professional training courses; and he also has concern with what the system expects him to do in the classroom in the way of maintaining an appropriate order or decorum.

The student brings to the teacher-student relationship what is probably a different set of experiences. They are at least different in the sense that they have accrued over a lesser period of time and are seen through the eyes of a younger person. The student reacts to the image his parents have of the school and teachers. He also brings to this relationship certain notions which have been bred in his peer group. The relationship between the teacher and the student is surely colored by the success and failure which the student has had in school-related activities to date.

TEACHER-STUDENT

On the surface, the dialogue between the teacher and his students may evidence a clear communication of ideas. However, because of the possible differences in experiential background, the communication between the teacher and students (or for that matter, between the teacher and the community) may badly miss its intended mark. What is being communicated may be hopelessly misperceived by each party to the dialogue. Figure 9-2 demonstrates how this dialogue may confound communication.

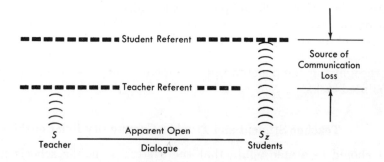

Legend: S's are parties to a dialogue or discussion; Referents are the contexts out of which each S is speaking. To the extent that the Referents are dissimilar or not understood by all S's the intended communication may be diminished.

Figure 9-2. A source of misperception in dialogue.

It falls to the teacher, then, at least because he has an age seniority and because he is charged with overseeing student behavioral change, to attempt the explication of his motives and those of the system. This explication necessarily should be directed toward assuring that the student will be able, with his experiential background, to understand what is being communicated. The teacher, in inquiring of student expectations, ought to be keenly aware of the possible referents used by the students. Neither the teacher nor the student may always agree with the referents being used in each case; however, to ignore differences in referents predicts that relationships will be generated which neither the students nor the teacher understands.

Where no direct attempts are made to establish relationships between teachers and students, the relationships which evolve will obtain as a consequence of "testing" by both components. The teacher will discover how far he can go in a variety of directions with students through initiating activities which cause students to respond to his direction until they become frustrated or react in some manner which the teacher finds not to be desirable. The converse is also true. Students will test teachers by initiating behavior which tends to describe the latitude the students will be given in behaving as they choose in particular activities. Not to attempt directly to establish expectancies on which teacher-student relationships might be built would appear to be no better than hoping that transfer of training will occur rather than teaching specifically for it.

TEACHER-COMMUNITY

The relationship of the teacher with the community is, in many respects, not unlike the teacher-student relationship. A significant difference might be that community members represent age peers of the teacher, and there is somehow the notion among the people of the community that *they* have hired the teacher to teach within the public school system. He is often seen as an extension of the school into the community. The community may expect him to reflect, both personally and professionally, what it believes the school ought to be like. Teachers sometimes have the suspicion that the Bill of Rights was written for everyone else—not for teachers. In the relationship between the community and teachers in the public schools there are what might be called blind aspirations on the part of both parties. The community members might be expected to hope that these teachers to whom their children are daily entrusted will support the community ethic in the classroom. The teacher might be equally hopeful that community members would support him in endeavors with their children which take exception to some of the local beliefs and aspirations.

Neither the teacher nor the community is necessarily wrong—each has a vested interest. Fortunately, that vestment of interest for both the professional teacher and the thoughtful community is in the best education for youth in the system. Figure 9-2 again applies. If an understood relationship is to exist between teachers and the community, there must be a mutual respect for the different referents from which each speaks.

A further facet of the relationship between the teacher and the community is the fact that members of the community have in common an earlier exposure to the public school system. Nearly all of them have known it as students. What is sometimes forgotten, even by teachers, is that it is not the *same* system they knew as students. Forgetting that the system has been displaced in time often leads to a condition where community members feel justified in being judgmental—often in areas where even professional judgment is difficult.

Again, the teacher and the system are challenged with the task of making clear to the community the referents from which the system and its teacher components operate. In developing a useful dialogue between the school system and the community it is not enough for teachers or the system to profess that they have only the "best" motives. The system has the responsibility to arrange activities so that the community can gain a reasonable understanding of *why* what is being done is good. Relationships based in the main upon testimonials tend to lose their persuasion as the school-community attempts to use these relationships as a foundation for the mutual support of education.

Problems and Issues

1. *What ought to be expected of teachers?* Clearly, the teacher is a crucial component in the public school systems. The system must therefore set some rather specific expectations for his performance as a professional component. There is only a limited knowledge of teacher characteristics; also, little is known of the nature of his impact upon the system. As with any system comprised of human components, the public school system must acknowledge the diverse nature of its teachers. But, to capitalize upon this component, the system must also attempt to understand the characteristics of its particular teachers. It must be asked whether the teachers are shaping the school system or the system the teachers. Where each is shaping the other to some degree, are the goals of education the principal motives for the behavior of both groups?

As the system, and particularly its administrative components, becomes more sensitive to the professional strengths and weaknesses of teachers in the system, then it becomes possible to engage in selective recruitment for needed personnel, to mount in-service programs for specific purposes, and to redeploy personnel in the system so as to gain a more efficient use of their services.

What is the responsibility of the teacher to assist the system and its other human components to know him better?—How do the personal expectations of the teacher impinge upon his professional role?—Are there things which ought *not* to be reasonably expected of teachers?—Who shall decide the expectations?

2. *What are some of the problems surrounding the community perception of the teacher?* Not only does the teacher see himself differently from time to time but others may perceive him in ways which he has never considered. The collective perception which the community has for the teacher is important to the school system and individual teachers. Where the community views the teacher as a person who is prudently engaging in a desirable venture, the system will often enjoy strong community support. When the teacher is perceived as engaging in behavior which is divergent from the desires of the community, pressure for change or non-support may be invoked by the community.

The community sees teachers collectively through the system, as individuals outside of school hours, and as the teacher of particular children when students talk of their daily experiences. For the community to "know" the teachers requires that both the system and individual teachers choose to make teachers more visible. What should the community know about the teachers in the school system?—How should this be communicated to the community?—What role should the school system play in supporting this venture?—Are there matters pertaining to teachers which are not the proper concern of the community?—In what ways might teachers assist the system in understanding and knowing them better?

3. *How can the teacher "become" if he is to be more than a position-holder in the system?* When a new component is added to a system there are a number of adjustments which have to be made. The other components must learn how to work with the new component. The system may have to make some adjustments to better use the new component. And, the new component also has some professional responsibilities. The teacher brings his training and other prior experiences to the system.

Although the system might be expected to assist him, it is his task to "become." It is he who must decide whether the effort is to be made to improve himself in those ways which will make his services in the system more valuable. The teacher component has the capacity to appreciate himself—to increase the extent to which he is an asset to the system.

What are some of the things which a teacher might do to improve himself and his potential for professional service in the system?—Are there specific ways in which the system might help the teacher "become"?—How might teachers assess whether they are becoming more valuable to the system?

Selected References

American Association of School Administrators. *Who's a Good Teacher?* Washington, D.C.: The Association, NEA, 1961.

Barzun, Jacques. *Teacher in America.* New York: Little Brown and Company, 1945.

Conant, James B. *The Education of American Teachers.* New York: McGraw-Hill Book Co., 1963.

Mason, Ward S. *The Beginning Teacher* (OE-23009). Washington, D.C.: United States Department of Health, Education and Welfare, 1961.

Woodring, Paul. *New Directions in Teacher Education.* New York: The Fund for the Advancement of Education, 1957.

Yauch, Wilbur A. *Helping Principals Understand Teachers.* New York: Appleton-Century-Crofts, 1957.

chapter 10

■ *The Student*

Characteristics of Students Entering the System

Characteristics, it has been said, depend greatly upon perception. Because students have been described as components in the system of public schools, the impression may be given that students are being perceived as less than human. Nothing could be less true. The fact that students are one among the several human components in the system gives rise to a concern for both the unique and the common characteristics which they portray for those who would view the system.

COMMON AND UNIQUE CHARACTERISTICS

Students have in common the fact that most of them represent a captive audience in the system. The law requires that they be in attendance within an educational system. All other human components in the system remain as systemic components at their own volition. The idea of this legal captivity of the student becomes more understandable when it is considered that *all* components in the system of public schools—for that matter, the system itself—purportedly exist to serve society through providing educational opportunity for its youth.

Students are unique as human components in the system in that they represent a strikingly different age group from other human components. Although they enter and leave the system each year (as do teachers for that matter) their tenure within the system is that time of life when they are preinitiates for adult society—that time when there is often a rebellion toward the adult group and its ethic and at the same time a seeking of acceptance from the adult group of behaviors directed toward supporting youth peer groups.

Role conflicts for students differ more in degree than they do in kind when compared with those faced by other human components in the system. One means of viewing this might be to consider the school system as an intervening condition. Teachers and administrators are employed components in the system but they also have out-of-system lives conditioned by their domestic hopes and aspirations. Students, too, have out-of-system lives and are conditioned by pressures and aspirations that may be seen by them to be grossly unrelated to their existence within the school system.

PURPOSE

Although the very existence of the system of public schools is rational only to the extent that it succeeds in modifying student behavior in desired ways, the student becomes a conscious participant in the process of changing his behavior only to the extent that he accepts the possibility that the school system can and should accomplish this task. In the absence of the student's understanding of why society has established this system and placed him within it, he becomes little more than one who "passes through" the system—giving little to it and certainly limiting what he is able to get from it.

One test of student characteristics might be to inquire whether students see the system of public schools as a "controlling" or "liberating" force. It might be suggested that students will evidence a heightened rebelliousness in rather direct ratio to the press of the system to sponsor a controlling environment. Conversely, the efforts of the system to expand the student's range of choices in terms of using knowledge and values might well foster his desire to increase his participation as an active supporter of systemic goals—goals which very much involve him.

The operation of the system has efficacy to the extent that it recognizes both the common and unique characteristics of student components. Obviously, these characteristics will vary from system to system and within any given system over a period of time. Since these characteristics are based upon the perceiver or perceivers, an important consideration for the system will be not only the frequency of assessing student characteristics but also the spread of differences in perception at any given time when the observations of several viewers are taken into consideration.

PERCEPTIONS

Concern in recent years with specific groups of students and ex-students (dropouts for example) has led to investigations which point toward learning more about how the student perceives himself. Pioneer studies in this area suggest that the student's view of himself may be quite different from that held by other human components in the system and persons from without.

The student perception of how teachers and administrators perceive him is probably most evident for him in their behavior as they interact with students within the system. The student must usually rely heavily upon present behavior of components with whom he interacts. Often the teachers and administrators rely too heavily upon what they have been told are the characteristics of students, or they may even narrow their preconceptions of students in terms of stereotypes which have evolved through years of experience with young people.

The dangers here should be quite clear. When characteristics of students are evolved from different reference bases, it becomes increasingly difficult to understand them in such a manner that interaction among human components in the system might be enhanced in accord with systemic goals. When matters of knowledge and its acquisition are intertwined with matters of values and attitude development, this mixing of dissimilar elements may impede the clear understanding of either.

Possibly the desirable approach for both teachers and students in seeking to better understand the behavior of one another would be for each to attempt to be as authentic as possible in his own behavior. This condition within the system would seem to depend upon a good deal of mutual trust; it would suggest that where human components "sense" they are not being understood in their behavior, they feel not only free to but feel obligated to verbalize as best they can the motives for their behavior.

Because humans seem to be endowed with certain frailties, the climate of authenticity within the system would need to assure that there are adequate protections for the humans involved. It is conceded that this climate is not life-like in the sense that there would be a concerted effort to reduce ego threat and any other impediment to the accomplishment of systemic goals. If it is accepted that the student and all other human components in the system also live in the world outside the school system, and that role expectations will vary for each of them within and without the system, then might it not be reasonable to move toward a climate within the system of public schools which would increase the probability that the goals of the system might be realized?

Problems of Observing the Student
Within the System

Because the student is both the "input" and the "output" of the system, techniques must be devised which will assure the most critical observations of student behavior. The goals of the system of public schools presume that the system should somehow operate to alter what would otherwise be only the natural development or evolvement of the student. Although there may be differences in the direction of behavioral change sought among different school systems, the only real assessment the school can make of movement toward goal accomplishment is through observation of behavioral change. It might be suggested that behavioral change in a desired direction is seen by the school as hopefully predictive of further change in that direction through the life of the student after he leaves the school system.

OBSERVING

Deportment of the student in the classroom, how he complies with the constraints set by the system, and paper and pencil evaluations of his achievement hardly exhaust the range of behavior available for observation. Nor need the teacher necessarily be limited to his personal observations of students in assessing behavioral change. It is difficult to know whether tradition or seeking easy avenues of assessment has led to the sterility of much recorded observation of student behavior. This sterility may be the result of preconceived notions held by teachers about students. Preconceived notions are dangerous only to the extent that they limit the use of the abilities to observe and profit from the observational experiences. In fact, training all human components in the system to engage in critical observation may require that they be exposed to some preconceived notions—at least those which involve our present understanding of how one might best be an observer.

Since human components within the system are constantly interacting, observations are made within the framework of participant observation—the observer, because he is an interacter, cannot remove himself and his influence from that which is being observed. Although this condition of the systemic environment may lessen the scientific accuracy of in-system observation, it is a necessary condition to such observation.

RECORDING

A further problem of student observation revolves around the type of record kept of observations made. Where the observer is the only person who will use the record, the major problem is probably only one of objectivity. Where, on the other hand, record of the observation will be used by several people, the record should be such that a minimum of interpretation is necessary. To the extent that the record contains subjective, evaluative judgments, the values held by the recorder or original observer must be known before the record can be useful to other readers. Such stigmatizing comments as, "John is not a good student—he's just like his brothers and sisters," are not only relatively useless entries in the records but may place the recorder or observing teacher in legal jeopardy.

Little of the record kept on a student is what might be called privileged information—that which need not be shared, even by court order. More importantly, it would appear that there is a trend toward making the school record of the student available to parents and guardians upon their request, with only the stipulation that the record be interpreted for the parent by a competent person in the employ of the school system. There is no assurance that the parent will understand the record. For that matter, there is no assurance that other teachers or administrators in the system will understand the record of student observations.

What has been the upshot of this? Those overly concerned with libel and slander have suggested that fewer records be kept and that less be said. Where the latter occurs there may be a prostituting of the assessment media used to determine whether the goals of the system are being met. In a sense it is being suggested that we record fewer observations of student behavioral change, thus limiting necessary systemic feedback mechanisms but assuring that we will be less vulnerable to attack from without. This is a posture of flight from professional responsibility.

Reviews of student records and methods employed in observing student behavior have led professional personnel in school systems to consider some of the moral-legal contradictions which they might face in their professional relationships with student components in the system. Consider the case of a school psychologist working with a student where the psychologist judges that his relationship and the progress made with the student are such that there would be an appreciable risk if the relationship were to be terminated at that point. The parents of the student notify the school that they want an immediate termination of the relationship between the psychologist and their child. The psychologist is notified that he is to terminate immediately his relationship with the student. Legally, parents can invoke such a right. However, conditions might be such that the school could exclude the student, thus making it incumbent that the parents place the child in another school or face action in the courts. The question being posed directs attention to the fact that there is no assurance that the parents will arrange for continuing psychological services for their child and in the opinion of the school psychologist this is necessary. The school psychologist is insubordinate if he refuses to terminate his relationship with the student. He violates his professional responsibility if he does terminate the relationship with no assurance that continued professional services will be provided. What should the school psychologist do? Of no less importance, what should the system have done in preparation for such an eventuality?

Observation of student behavioral change must be related to the goals of the system. When the direction of desired student behavioral change is identified, there can be established feedback mechanisms which are most appropriate to identify and delineate student behavior. It then must be decided what controls are necessary to make the information gained through feedback or observation most usable so that the system might institute needed adjustments.

Impact of the System upon the Student

Sensitive observation of student behavior permits the system to determine the degree to which it is moving toward goal accomplishment, but the system must also have the capacity to adjust or modify its environment in directions suggested by student observation and other influences from both within and without the system. Lacking this capacity for flexibility, the system of public schools provides only a relatively static environment through which the student merely "passes."

SOURCES OF INFLUENCE

The influences on the system—which in turn become influences on student components—obtain from a conglomeration of sources. Their conglomerate nature is based upon the sources not being always discrete. Often the people who serve as influencing agents belong to several groups, and each group represents a somewhat different vested interest. At any given time the public school system exists in a state of balance among the many potential influences directed toward it. Pressures from without the system might include current international concerns and range to some specific desire in the local school-community. From within the system, professional employees may be urging the system to respond to particular recommendations regarding curricular content or teacher-student ratio. Also from within the system there are the pressures exerted by student components to shape how the system will describe its relationship with students. The latter pressure may be subtle, difficult to observe—and it may well not be a fully developed point of view. But, it seems only reasonable to assume that the system which is not responsive to student desires can hope for only a marginal impact upon its students. The possible exceptions might be systems in which professional personnel planning the program for students have had unusually good fortune in intuiting what the students want or the systems where there exist a certain a priori student acceptance of the value of education per se and a trust that the system has only the highest motives in influencing students.

There is no contention here that students will necessarily know what is best for them—for that matter, the wise educator might question whether anyone has the vision to know what is "best." What is being contended is that the student recipient of systemic influence will be more responsive when he senses that there is some relationship between that influence and what he wants or what he is willing to accept as potentially good for him.

There is a great deal built into the given—that which is mandatory for the systemic environment in which the student exists. The length of the school year, the day, often the class period or the number of them; the particular teachers who will work with the student that year; the attendance unit to which the student is assigned; and sundry other factors are somewhat mechanically fixed if not set by law. However, even within these factors and certainly beyond them there is an immense flexibility available to the system. If this flexibility is to be used to improve the probability of desired behavioral change in students, then the system must set into operation monitoring subsystems which will predict *how* the available flexibility ought to be used.

One form of such a monitoring subsystem might include a continuing appraisal of how other systems have adapted their programs to better work toward goal accomplishment. Another might be arranging for information appearing in the literature to be directed to professional educators and regularly communicated within the system. These monitoring subsystems support the impact of the system upon the student in at least two ways. They tend to generate a better understanding of knowledge and value systems which should lead to the student seeing the systemic program as a thoughtfully organized venture rather than as some ad hoc abuse of his time. They should also permit a somewhat better reading of student motives and interests which might have applicability within their particular system.

Another format in which the system has impact upon the student is one where there is an extension of the notion that the student is but the recipient of information dispensed—often a system where values are taught by moral testimonial. The extended system envisions the student component as a true interacter. In such a system reliance is not placed fully upon subsystems which monitor student behavior, such as teacher observation; rather the student is an active participant in the day-to-day operation and evolvement of the system. The student gives to the system as well as receives from it. Where the student is seen as more than a recipient, the system has made a commitment that includes the risk that students will sometimes make choices with which there may be disagreement among other human components in the system or even in the school-community.

Accepting that risk allows the system to invest a certain faith in its student components. Students in such a system may become more responsible for the operation of the system and also for their own behavior, because they have a personal investment in decisions which will predict how the system is able to support activities directed toward serving their needs and those of society.

Essentially the difference being discussed is one between a system founded upon the premise of imposition in dealing with student components as opposed to a system which is aware of many available resources, including its students, upon which it might draw in its efforts to promote desired behavioral change in students. It is suggested that the student will be more receptive to the latter type of system.

Since no human component in the system is closer to the student than the teacher—at least no closer in terms of contact hours—the impact of the system upon the student is probably interpreted by him largely as he sees the teacher. Where intrasystem communications are weak the student may get the notion that the system is, in the main, comprised of a group of teachers with little in the way of common goals to commend them. Granting that there will be perceptible differences among teachers, there ought also to be some perceptible common strands which represent systemic direction.

It is possible that the system might at the administrative level have come to some considerable agreement on goals and yet failed to communicate this agreement among other components, especially teachers, who are working most closely with students. From without, such a system might be seen as one having a well-articulated goal structure. From within, the system goals may be seen as chaotic—having in common only those characteristics which have obtained as a result of chance.

Impact of the Student upon the System

If students are to have an impact on the system it is essential that there be recognition that students are components within the system. The foregoing statement may appear self-evident until one considers that school systems exist which seem to be designed to facilitate most the career lives of teachers, administrators, and so forth, to the end that concern with students gets lost in the shuffle.

Presuming a certain amount of goodness in systemic motives, there are still dangers. Students may be seen by the system in what might be described as a gross view—the stereotypic student. This view denies, of course, all that is known or suggested about individual differences. Yet students are quick to sense the teacher, the administrator, even the school system by whom they are seen collectively rather than as individuals with diverse goals and abilities.

There is an equal danger that the students group will be described overtly in terms of specific students who represent extremes in the continuum of characteristics for the student body. The student who scores an 800 on the CEEB is remembered and frequently referred to when statements are made about the student group. So is the student remembered who was a perennial burr in the side of the attendance officer and has since found his way into a penal institution. Both the exceptionally bright and the exceptionally dull are remembered and referred to. But what of all the rest? Specifically, what of all the individual students—components within the system—who have not distinguished themselves by their behavior either nobly or ignobly?

Each school system has a number of receptors through which it is possible for students to distinguish themselves—in a sense, to have impact upon the system. However, too often these receptors have evolved as a result of either what the system wants "out of" its student components or they are the result of constraints placed upon student behavior, in which case they evoke punitive results when used by students. Simply put, the systemic receptors are not always arranged to sense or monitor what students individually and collectively might wish to convey to the system.

Because in the main the machinery of most school systems would seem to be of adult manufacture, it is not unusual to anticipate that systemic receptors—specific means through which students might gain identity in the system—are geared to sorting out student behavior which is favorable or unfavorable according to the values of adult components who manage the system.

Systems which lack broad and sensitive receptor structures place their student components in the position of choosing among three courses of action as they seek to exert influence or have impact. Students can use the existing receptors; they can seek to induce the development of new receptors that might be more compatible with their desires to influence the system; or, students might choose to become "other-directed" and, hence, exert their influence—including that influence which might most productively have impact within the system—through other systems than the school or in the larger social environment. When student influence is exerted outside of the school system, the school may become dysfunctional as a medium through which students direct their effort toward being better understood.

The impact of the student upon the system may, then, be related to student self-perception of his value as a component in the system. The transmission of the notion that the student is a valuable component in the system is probably most directly handled by the teacher. The teacher who exudes an openness toward students is, in fact, creating the possibility that more and better communication might take place between the student and other systemic components. Often the teacher must start at a most rudimentary level in establishing the importance of the student in the system. It may be necessary to persuade the student that it is possible for him to learn, to participate usefully in the system. It may also be necessary to convince the student that his active involvement in systemic activities will improve the possibility of his success in the system and throughout the rest of his life.

The kinds of influences which the students might exert upon the system may not appear to adult systems components to be especially related to the goals of the system. Student influences may seem to be adolescent, tangential, even annoying. Conversely, students often see adult component influences as so much hokum. If student impact upon the system is to be fostered, then the initial influences tendered by students must at least be accepted as authentic—representing first attempts to communicate with and participate in the school system.

Criteria for Determining Behavioral Change

During the time that the student is a component within the system he will evidence some decided behavioral changes. Some of these changes he would probably have shown whether or not he had been in the system of public schools. Some behavioral changes may very well have been influenced by the student's having been in the school system. Yet other of these behavioral changes may be principally the result of his having been involved with the schools. The problem arises when we attempt to differentiate among the causal agents. School systems and their human components would seem to be ego-bearing structures in that there is often credit taken or ascribed to the system for "good" outcomes or behavioral change in students. Equally, it is not unusual to hear that deviant behavior of students is the fault of parentage, environment, or some cause unrelated to the school.

Unfortunately, the public school system has not yet reached that level of virtue where all undesired student behavioral change can be legitimately ascribed to external sources. In systems where less able students are required to undertake the study of material which they cannot understand, the systems may be engaged in sponsoring behavior which they do not want to evoke—behavior which is, however, not at all unusual for the student under the circumstances.

The problem for the system is one of attempting to isolate the kinds of activities in which discrete behavioral changes in students might reasonably be expected to occur. If the desired behavioral changes *do* occur, the system is moving toward the accomplishment of its goals. Whether the system was instrumental in the behavioral change becomes not only moot but also a concern of lesser consequence.

The school must also be concerned with relationships between activities both in and out of the system and with relationships between different behavioral changes. Although this is probably a highly individual thing, there are orders or hierarchies of change which might be anticipated. Specifically, attitudinal changes in students may be more difficult to effect. Yet, when these changes take place their impact may be evident over a considerable range of student activity. Whether it is a matter of social relationships or scholastic achievement on a standardized test, students will, at a given time, stand at varying points of development. Their rate of behavioral change, be it attitudinal or performance on a test, will also vary—both for the individual student and among students. The capacity for behavioral change in the student may become greater, with no overt sign that change is taking place (the student may appear to be on a plateau). Evidence of behavioral change may be given by the student outside the school system—possibly in the home or with his peers rather than in the classroom.

Students may engage in exploratory behavior, especially when it is not clear what kind of behavior is wanted as a result of school-sponsored activities under the supervision of teachers. Possibly the student will come up with alternate forms of behavior more appropriate for him than those behaviors expected by the system.

The criteria for behavioral change must, then, be specific enough that the system can identify activities which might be expected to foster change in the desired direction, yet they must be broad enough to allow for individual differences in interpretation and application. Although the system may believe it "knows" certain behavioral prerequisites for persistence and success in life, it must acknowledge that individual students will always be capable of proving the presumptiveness of the system wrong.

Statements of criteria for behavioral change might include discrete expectancies which the system imposes upon students, such as the requirement that students evidence by some means a certain facility in a subject before they will be permitted to undertake the

next higher level of study in that subject. These levels of expectation are not difficult to assign as long as the system recognizes
that any point of cut-off set is but an arbitrary point, determined
by best judgment but still subjective. The danger lies with coming
to rely too heavily upon such subjective limits and assessing student behavioral change more in terms of the limit set rather than
in terms of individual student accomplishment in the direction of
the desired behavioral change.

The teacher and the administrator in the school system must be
constantly aware of the changing capacity of individual students
for desired behavioral change if their assessments of students is to
have any base in rationality. The foregoing presumes that the
system, especially through the teacher, must make diligent and
continuous efforts to keep currently informed about student capacity for change—or, probable student growth toward goal accomplishment for the system.

Attitudinal change in student behavior is more difficult to monitor. There is the immediate risk of ascribing motives for behavior.
The student who seems to show a "good attitude" may be displaying
only what he has judged the teacher wants to see; he may have
learned how to adapt to systemic expectations. The teacher may
delude himself into describing the behavior of a student he likes
as "good behavior." Hence, also arises the problem of "halo-grad-
ing" of students. Teachers often fall prey to challenging the student to describe why he is behaving in a particular manner and
then evaluating the behavior in terms of the logic of the motives
cited by the student. This approach not only leaves little room for
emotive behavior but it also casts the student in a setting in which
the only acceptable defense is one which will be understandable to
the teacher.

School systems which have as their goal the liberation of the
student so that he might be better equipped to make choices and
which offer a broader range of options for his choice-making,
develop criteria for behavioral change which are oriented more
toward student needs and less toward systemic maintenance.

Although the school system may have broad criteria to be used
in assessing student behavioral change, it generally remains for
the teacher in the classroom to actually make the principal observations which will comprise that assessment. He will have his own
notions of how the established criteria should be interpreted, and
in the absence of system-wide criteria he will evolve his own.
Since in most systems there is a formal plan for advancing or
witholding student progress through the several stages or grades,
the teacher must find the means whereby he can balance the assessment of student facility with subject matter and student growth

in other behavioral areas which might bear a larger portent for his success in life.

Behavioral Change and Learning

Behavior and learning are taking place all the time. Some contend that it is not possible for there to be behavior without learning. The system of public schools has something of an advantage in that the primary behavior it seeks or sponsors for student components is learning. Since an enumeration of what *might* be learned would be endless, the task of the school in society is one of making more efficient certain learnings—especially those deemed useful to society. Figure 10-1 present a conceptualization of the student's role in the school system.

The most casual inquiry will show that students in the school system demonstrate an awareness of only an extremely small segment of what is currently known. It falls, then, to the school system not only to select and employ the most efficient methodologies

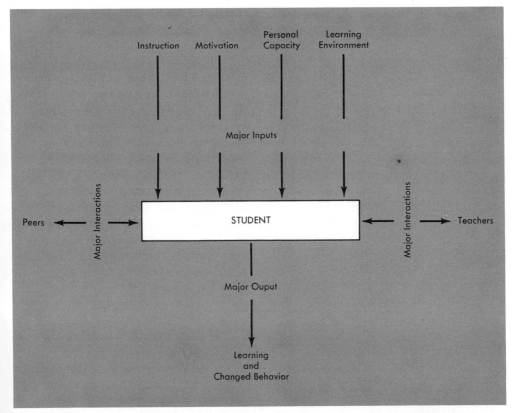

Figure 10-1. Conceptualization of the role of students in a public school system.

in teaching but also to select with great care what is to be taught from the larger fund of knowledge. Systemic choices in the area of finite knowledge may really be of lesser importance, since it can be predicted that much of what is current knowledge today will be repudiated or at best modified with conditioning statements.

The essence of learning as interpreted through behavioral change may lie with the facility the student develops in generating new knowledge or in describing differently that which he already knows. Facility in these two skills will be essential if the student is to be capable of problem solving.

What problems the student will face in school and later in life can only be guessed at, but these guesses have to be made or else the school system may be preparing the young to live with only the problems faced by their forebears. This suggests that concern with attitude development may be more important than funding the student with knowledge. The student's willingness or sense or urgency to face problems, make choices, and behave in accord with those choices may key the success of the school system in its efforts to induce desired behavioral change in students. The system has given the teacher the management of the learning setting. It is he who makes the decision as to whether the teaching-learning environment will be knowledge or attitude-centered or what ratio of the two will exist in the classroom.

Knowledge dissemination by the teacher—even knowledge acquisition by the student—may well occur at an astoundingly large rate, yet there may be no discernible behavioral change in students. The condition has to exist where it becomes important to the student that he *act* or behave in some productive manner so that there can be evidence at least of his potential for behavioral change based upon what has taken place in the classroom. If the student is to sense the need for this action, he must intuit or be taught why he should be motivated. Where the student sees no relevance for himself in what is being taught, he can hardly be expected to initiate behavior providing feedback for the teacher— the kind of feedback which says. "I can see the importance of this for me, this is what I would do, are there not other things I need to know about this," or some other indication that the student has undertaken an involvement, has chosen to participate in the teaching-learning environment.

The expressed urgency for the school system through the teacher to conduct learning activities so that there will be behavioral feedback on the part of the learner—the student component—is based upon the notion that there must be overt or observable behavior if the system is to be able to assess whether its program objectives are being met. In the individual classroom the teacher must be attentive to whether his observations of student behavior adequately identify the student's changing capacity as a learner. As teacher observation becomes more global in form, it becomes increasingly necessary to infer changes which may have taken place in the learner. Probably a wiser approach would be one of devising first the most sensitive and critical observations so that later inferences and global judgments might be more accurate.

Again, critical observations can be arranged for determining the extent to which the student component evidences a capacity to manipulate particular concepts. It can be determined, for instance, whether the student is able to select an appropriate mode of attack for a specific problem, whether he is able to select the most efficient mode among several appropriate modes, and whether he is able to resolve the problem through using the mode of attack selected. What becomes difficult to monitor is the development of value constructs which predict, in part, why individual students choose to attack or ignore particular problems. An important learning outcome from the standpoint of the school system might be that the student makes wise decisions in terms of which problems he chooses to attempt to resolve. The student's knowledge or capacity for problem resolution is of little consequence if he chooses not to consider the problem.

Learning, then, is related to desired behavioral change in at least two specific ways. The student must acquire the capacity for resolving problems—a capacity which involves knowledge acquisition—and he must be able to determine which problems he must choose to solve for both his own good and the good of society. In each case it would appear that the motivation of the student component in the system is essential if learning activities sponsored by the system are to be related effectively to desired behavioral change in students.

Although students in their early years in the school system may be interested more in the "here and now" of their lives, they typically become increasingly interested in the prospects for their initiation into the larger adult society as they grow older and have been longer in the system. The system, therefore, is challenged with providing the students with different rationales for undertaking particular learnings. The difference among rationales might be graduated in accordance with the age or, more importantly, with the changing interests of students. Particular learnings which the system envisions as important for the student in his adult life may have appropriate reasonableness for the student who is in his last year in the system. The importance of particular learnings for adult life may wholly lack reasonableness for the student in first grade. In either event learning activities sponsored by the school system may fail to evoke student motivation to participate and learn where the rationale for the learning is not understood and accepted by the student.

If the principal output of the system is student behavioral change then each component in the system must necessarily be concerned with assuring that the learning activities sponsored by the system bear some relationship to supporting the desired behavioral changes which the system attempts to evoke in students.

Problems and Issues

1. *How can goals for the system be translated into behavioral terms?* Goals for the system involve inducing desired behavioral change in students. The hope is that both the individual and the society will benefit. But, goals are aspirations. It is necessary for the system to have objectives, operational plans, if goals are to be worked toward. Attainment of objectives may be measured by assessing the incidence of desired behavioral change in student components. It is not enough that teachers understand what behavioral changes are desired. Student components must also know what these changes are. Further, the system increases its effectiveness as students are able to differentiate between high-priority behavioral change and what may be only suggested for consideration by the student.

The principal interpretor of systemic goals for the student is the teacher. His success in communication and persuasion may well predict the extent to which students recognize what their public school education is about. How does the school system generate objectives from its goals?—How does the teacher communicate systemic goals and objectives to students?—To what extent are teachers and students involved in the process of setting goals and objectives for the system?—By what means might the teacher determine whether students understand the goals and objectives of the system?

2. *What impact does the student have upon the system?* Hopefully, the student component and the system are more than a sometimes unwilling recipient and an arrangement for doling wisdom. The student is fully capable of identifying and initiating needed change in the system. He is also immature in some ways. There are understandings which, once acquired, may enable him to consider more thoughtfully his life and the prospects for his society.

The system provides a setting in which students might be given the opportunity to engage in some "risk-taking" in their behavior. To the extent that the system is custodial for students, to the extent that the system engages principally in dispensing to students, it refuses to acknowledge that the student has the capacity to *participate* in the system. Moreover, the system has an opportunity to learn from its students as it encourages their active engagement in the system.

How might the system improve itself by observing student behavior?—What might teachers do to improve the climate of the system so that students will feel freer to test behavior patterns?—In what ways might students productively participate in the management of the system?

3. *How might the different expectations for students be resolved?* The system must be concerned with resolving conflicting expectations for the student. Not only are there his own expectations and those of his parents, the community, and his peers, but there are also differential expectations among the several professional components of the system. The student frequently discovers that "authentic" behavior has little or no consistency if his many masters and audiences are to be pleased and to favor him.

Clearly, the school cannot fully control the expectations held for youth. But, the school system and its professional components can do much to moderate the differences in perception and expectation. The system can at least clarify what it expects of the student. The system can assist in assuring that teacher components do not hold unreasonable expectations for students. The student can aid himself by making known his expectations for himself and for the system.

What might the system do to draw into the open the several and diverse expectations held for students?—What are some expectations which might be unreasonable?—Are there expectations for the student which might be educationally unsound?—How can the teacher develop a dialogue with students which will enable all to better understand expectations?

Selected References

Haimowitz, Morris L., and Natalie R. Haimowitz, eds. *Human Development–Selected Readings.* New York: Thomas Y. Crowell Co., 1966.

Jersild, Arthur T. *Child Psychology,* 5th ed. Englewood Cliffs, N.J.: Prentice-Hall, 1960.

McNeil, Elton B. *The Concept of Human Development.* Belmont, Calif.: Wadsworth Publishing Co., 1966.

Remmers, H. H., and D. H. Radler. *The American Teenager.* New York: Charter Books, 1957.

Seidman, Jerome M., ed. *The Adolescent—A Book of Readings*, rev. ed. New York: Holt, Rinehart and Winston, 1960.

Stone, L. Joseph, and Joseph Church. *Childhood and Adolescence*. New York: Random House, 1957.

Strang, Ruth. *The Adolescent Views Himself*. New York: McGraw-Hill Book Co., 1957.

part IV

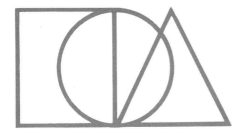

Areas of

Relationships

chapter 11

■ *Personnel Processes*

The nature of almost any system comprised primarily of human components is such that the decisions made concerning those components are among the most crucial to the success of the system. Without reasonable harmony among the various human elements, the system has little chance to be dynamic in search of its goals. Staid, conservative, and noncreative personnel procedures are likely to contribute to staid, conservative, and noncreative educational systems. Human relations and organizational morale are not problems of systems comprised of mechanical devices. But, in an American public school system, these factors must be considered in planning personnel programs geared to the accomplishment of systemic goals.

As with the planning of other components, the agent responsible for systems development must consistently assess his personnel decisions against the goals being sought. For example, if a superintendent, new to a public school system, were charged with developing a "new curriculum," this charge would undoubtedly affect the decisions he would make in the employment of new staff, in the deployment of his existing faculty, in professional improvement programs developed within his district, and in the manner and content of professional performance appraisal. In another district, where changing population patterns are reflected in a need to diminish college preparatory programs and to increase vocational education programs, the superintendent would again be faced with relating those needs to the personnel function of his office. Translation of educational needs into personnel requirements is the initial personnel decision.

Assessing Personnel Needs

The major personnel functions, including employment and dismissal, have been largely vested with boards of education in the various states. As a matter of practice, the boards have rather consistently charged the superintendent of schools with fulfilling personnel responsibilities, although they have retained the power to approve or to reject the decisions made in their behalf. Only in smaller, conservative districts have boards of education continued to engage in the practice of hiring teachers without the professional recommendation of their chief executive officer. Most systems have come to realize that the superintendent, as chief executive officer, must have some latitude of freedom if he is to discharge his responsibility for the development of an educational team capable of fulfilling the goals of the enterprise. He, then, is largely responsible for developing the processes by which teachers are (1) recruited, (2) employed, (3) assigned, (4) utilized, (5) improved, (6) appraised, and, in some cases, (7) rejected.

In seeking to discharge the personnel function, the superintendent must continually be concerned with the dynamic characteristics of his system. He comes to recognize that his organization has a limited tolerance for difference. If his selection of new employees is consistently outside of the organization's tolerance, he inevitably finds himself with morale problems. However, he is also cognizant of the fact that the addition of each new employee changes the tolerance level, and that he can thereby make evolutionary changes in the capacity of the organization to accept higher degrees of difference. On the other hand, he also recognizes that continued employment of people similar to those already in the system is a sure guarantee that the system will continue to remain as it has been or to progress only at the same rate that it has been capable of moving.

Personnel decisions are the most potent decisions a systems executive can make if either the direction or the rate of change is to be altered. Changes in the systems of human components are stimulated most by adding new components, changing the behavior of retained components, or through the rearrangement of the manner in which component interaction is accomplished. If additions, changes, and rearrangements are stimuli to systemic alteration, then the skill of the executive officer will be measured largely through his capacity to get appropriate organizational responses as end products of his personnel decisions. The magnitude of the problem is relieved or compounded in proportion to the commitment of the teaching profession to fulfilling its obligation to encourage young persons of high caliber to join the teaching profession. The capacity of the superintendent to select good teachers for a school system is directly related to the ratio of well-trained, qualified teachers available for the vacancies existing there. The manner in which the profession recruits bright young people to enter the field determines both the quality and the quantity of the assortment from which selection will ultimately be made. Data in Chapter 9 would indicate that schools will inherit the products of their professional recruitment.

Replacement problems are similar in mechanical and human component systems. In systems composed of mechanical components the loss of a crucial component prevents a function from being performed. Slow deterioration of the part slows down function accomplishment at an almost imperceptible rate. The loss or deterioration of a human component in a school system has a similar impact upon the power of the system to accomplish its goals.

The actual steps leading to the selection of one person over another will vary slightly from one system to another. In high quality systems where the assortment from which choices will be made is large, various kinds of screening devices will be employed in an attempt to secure the most qualified persons. In districts where the choices are very limited, the selection processes may be quite crude, for the superintendent may accept the necessity of hiring any applicant without regard to qualifications. Nevertheless, many of the steps leading to selection are common throughout all districts.

DETERMINATION OF NEEDS

In a static system, the determination of professional needs is exceedingly simple. When a second grade teacher resigns, retires, or goes on leave, a replacement is hired in the form of another second grade teacher; when an English teacher leaves, another English teacher is hired; and so on. In a dynamic system where inputs or goals are changing, the process is not quite as simple, for the superintendent must continually be aware of the kinds of things which must be accomplished and the manner in which the professional staff will make its contribution. Changes in the nature of class organization at either the elementary or secondary level may require new concepts of staff utilization; the particular kinds of competencies sought would not be apparent from a summary of the kinds of competencies being lost. Of immediate concern are problems of redeployment, retraining, and the development of inservice programs.

In mid-winter, the superintendent will normally make an assessment of the plans of his existing staff to return for the following school year. That assessment, when coupled with changes stimulated by shifts in goal priorities, provides information for the development of the long-range staffing plan. The plan is explicit in terms of the quantity of personnel required and the specific competencies being sought. The translation of this plan into a recruitment brochure is accomplished and submitted to agencies, such as university placement offices, with the request that the agency provide assistance in locating individuals with characteristics described in the specifications.

ASSESSING QUALIFICATIONS

There are those who would say that research has provided no answers to guide superintendents as to the kinds of people who will make "good teachers." Nevertheless, the superintendent is faced with the task of deciding which of several persons shall be offered employment within his school system. When given choices, he is not required to rely solely upon chance to make the most appropriate selection. For example, he starts with an image of the position to be filled in mind. The loss of a staff member in any system leaves a void the perimeter of which is never wholly known. However, the superintendent must become quite specific in defining the "shape" of capabilities being sought within the various applicants. An assessment of the tasks to be assigned and performed by the new teacher must be established before assessing the potential of the applicant to fulfill the requirements.

Policy and prejudice are also a part of the assessment process. For some characteristics the board of education of a school district or the state certification officers will have prescribed the minimum requirements for entrance into the educational system. Such things as the number of credit hours within the field to be taught and the number of credit hours within the field of education are items often prescribed by policy or law. Other items entering into the selection decision, however, are not so controlled. When the superintendent arbitrarily decides for or against a candidate on the basis of grade-point average, marital status, or the modulation of the applicant's voice, his decisions can only be subjective.

Regardless of the source of the criteria against which applicants will be ultimately judged, the employing official within the system must have access to information which can be compared to the criteria. Such information is normally gathered from (1) credentials, (2) letters of recommendation, (3) application blanks, (4) interviews, and, occasionally, (5) visitations.

The credentials filed by applicants with employment agencies and placement offices serve as good sources for gathering reasonably objective information about a candidate. As normally prepared, credentials provide information about the academic background of the applicant, including the kinds of preparation programs undergone, the kinds of certificates held, and other biographical and personal information. The credentials will also contain letters of recommendation from persons chosen by him. Telephone calls to past employers are also commonly used to assess the various potentials held by the prospective teacher.

In addition to these sources of information, application blanks are normally used by school systems to obtain a maximum amount of information. The application form will be designed to provide specific, objective, and subjective information about the candidate which is normally deemed important by the employing system. Included may be such things as the quantity and quality of work done in a major field of study; the kind of certification; work experiences other than teaching; addresses and telephone numbers of persons who can be contacted for recommendations; priority choices for subjects and grade levels to be taught; curricular activities which can be directed; statements about the availability of the applicant; the minimum salary acceptable; and often a handwriting sample is required. Occasionally, the applicant is asked to develop a short statement of educational philosophy which can be used in assessing how he might "fit" with other professional staff members.

The interview is normally the final step in the selection process, and it tends to be the most important single feature. It is the only point at which the candidate gets an opportunity to decide whether or not he wishes to participate in the system represented by the employing official. Concurrently, the employing official is attempting to assess the degree to which the applicant will be compatible and his capacity to contribute to the goals of the educational enterprise. Within the structure of the interview the employing official will normally attempt to fill information gaps left from the other sources. Personal characteristics and subjective judgments normally come to a focus within the interview setting.

As goals have become more complex and as the responsibility for implementation has been decentralized, many systems have involved persons other than the superintendent or a personnel director in the employment procedures. Building principals, charged with developing particular curricular programs and teachers, who may have unusual interaction requirements with the new component, are often involved in helping to assess the candidate's potential within the system.

The final process, visitation, is seldom employed except in those districts which have large personnel staffs and who receive applications from very large numbers of highly qualified persons. As a general rule, superintendents simply have not taken the time to go to other school districts to watch a teacher teach. In some districts, of course, visiting employers are not welcome. If the visited teacher is good and the district to be visited is desirous of retaining his services for the coming years, the feeling is somewhat understandable. Perhaps the most common visitation is done in districts that provide supervisory services for student teachers. In those districts, it is quite simple for employing officials to observe the potential teacher in a teaching situation without having to engage in activities which are sometimes viewed as piratical.

EMPLOYMENT OR REJECTION

At various stages throughout the selection process, provisions are made for the rejection of applicants. A study of application blanks and credentials may provide information sufficient to justify a rejection decision. Similarly, an analysis of the other documents and procedures utilized in assessment may also provide just cause for rejecting the applicant as having insufficient potential for meeting the qualifications sought by the employing system.

When employment is desirable and the candidate is willing, offers of positions are normally made by the superintendent of schools, with the implication that the employment is not legalized until formal action has been taken by the board of education. At duly called meetings of the board, the superintendent will provide information concerning the candidates he wishes the board to approve and upon a motion passed, the applicant becomes a working member of the system.

Assignment and Orientation

Following appointment, the new staff member is assigned to a position within the system where his potential for contributing to the accomplishment of systemic goals, at least as perceived by the employing official, has the best opportunity to be realized. The position involves a physical location and a professional responsibility. The new teacher is thus assigned to a building and, indeed, even a room within a building, but more importantly he is assigned to professional responsibility reflective of systemic expectations. Within his assigned room, he will ultimately perform assigned and unassigned tasks.

In an attempt to improve the efficiency, in goal-directed terms, of the activities to be pursued by the new teacher, orientation programs are normally developed. The orientation is general in that it must provide linkage to the total educational system and its goals, and it is specific in that it must be directed toward the understanding of more "local" subsystems as represented by the various buildings, classes, and subject matter under the purview of the teacher.

Orientation programs are normally designed to provide the initiatory interactions between the new component and the existing members of the system. The interactions may be designed as both professional and social, but they are organized to provide for the rapid acceptance and integration of the new teacher into the operation of the total enterprise. Because of the necessity of the components working together in harmony, the initial contacts tend to be very important and as such are generally programmed by responsible agents within the system.

A second function of orientation programs is to inform the new teacher about the various practices and policies within the school district and to provide an introduction to the administration of the system. A new teacher, bogged down with routine and the myriad details which must be mastered as a new member of a system, cannot provide a maximum contribution to the system's operation. As a result, attempts are made in orientation programs to appraise the new member of those items which are of crucial import as he undertakes his new duties. Items of lesser import are normally delayed until a later date.

Some aspects of orientation programs are not directed only at the new members of the system. Some kinds of activities require that the older membership be actively "reoriented." When major new goals are accepted, when organizational changes are initiated, or when major adjustments are made in operational methods, it becomes imperative that all human components, new and old, participate in orientation processes. The smooth transition from one method of operation to another or the acceptance of new goals by all components can be accomplished only when the entire membership relates the new aspects to their particular sphere of operation. Thus the internalization of new responsibilities becomes an additional function of orientation programs.

The final function served by orientation procedures is concerned with short-range, annual objectives. After acceptance through internalization of the long-range systemic goals, human components within an operational system need further to accept, and internalize, the objectives by which the goals will be met. Educational goals tend to be broad-range and idealistic in terms of their rapid accomplishment. As a result, more specific short-range objectives must be chosen which have the potential of directing the organization in a step by step fashion toward the goals. Short-range steps are specific and are directed at action programs. It has been said that a man cannot walk a mile without taking the first step. The objectives are analogous to the individual step and tend to be small enough that the components are not overwhelmed by the magnitude of required involvement.

Appraising and Evaluating

One of the more difficult interpersonal relationships which occurs in the course of operating a public school system is that between supervisor and teacher. Appraising, evaluating, or rating a particular teacher's competence is not normally a favorite pastime of an administrator. Nevertheless, legal and professional expectations require that the task of appraising be accomplished.

EVALUATION—WHY?

Not the least of the many reasons why an evaluation should be made of the effectiveness of a teacher within a public school system is that society expects it to be done. Society has become conditioned to the concept of continuous evaluation, and the public schools played no small part in the conditioning process when they instituted the report card concept. In addition, the workaday world to which the membership of the society belongs keeps a continuous evaluation program on its membership. That same society comes to expect that its teachers will be going through similar processes. The local telephone workers are under an evaluation program, the post office employees undergo periodic civil service evaluations, stores and businesses have promotional policies based upon the degree to which an employee has contributed to promoting the goals of that organization, the military is conditioned to periodic fitness reports, and even the universities have their committees on rank and salary. Rightly or wrongly, society can see no reason why the work of a teacher should proceed in an unevaluated fashion.

The second major reason for evaluation also resides with society. Communities not only expect teachers to be evaluated, but they have the economic right to demand that an adequate job of evaluating the effectiveness of teachers be done on a periodic basis. From a legal standpoint, the local school district has almost unlimited power to establish the kind of school system that it wants to create for its children so long as the community confines the operation of the school within the law as established by federal and state constitutions. That power, along with the parochialism of homogeneous communities throughout the country, permits a society to make some rather specific curricular demands upon the educational system. If, for example, a community wanted a particular kind of economics taught because it held that a particular kind of economics embodied the kinds of precepts the community wanted their children to accept, who is to stop them? And much more dangerously, if they demand that the schools inculcate their brand of economics, the teacher who holds to the concept of academic freedom for himself and his students loses a great deal of support. The supervisor, if he is a supporter of academic freedom, finds himself in a difficult dilemma when the community is demanding that he get into the classroom to see that the "true" economics is, in fact, being taught by all teachers in the system.

Communities do have some rights to establish curriculums. They also have some responsibilities in understanding that the children to be educated will be crippled to the extent that provincial concepts of what constitutes an adequate education hold sway. Most administrators, teachers, and supervisors accept as a professional responsibility the leading of such communities away from such provincialism toward enlightment.

A third reason for evaluating the work of a teacher is a little more tangential. Behavior is related to expectation. If this be the case, then only good could come from having teachers know that the community and its educational representatives have certain expectations as to what constitutes appropriate teaching behavior. Evaluations and appraisals under such circumstances tend to be centered around the manner in which a particular teacher meets the expectations of excellence.

A fourth reason—the improvement of instruction—for evaluating effectiveness of teaching staffs seems to be the most important. Establishment of the degree to which professional expectations are met is only a first step in helping teachers toward goals of self-improvement. It seems inappropriate to launch a program of professional improvement without first establishing the existing status of professionalism. An analogy may be found in the case of a man who wakens in the middle of Grand Central Station surrounded by the time tables of all the railroads in the country. Unless he can establish that he is in Grand Central Station of New York City, he has no hope of getting home *even though he knows where he wants to go.* The routes to a particular end vary according to the point of origin, and it should be one purpose of evaluation programs to establish those points.

The final reason for establishing appraisal and evaluation procedures are more practical and more often accepted as the reasons that make evaluation legitimate. To make a personnel decision concerning promotion, dismissal, the granting of tenure, or the awarding of additional salary increments, the administrator responsible for carrying the organization forward must have an assessment of the individual components under his employ. The degree to which these components are serving their respective roles in the accomplishment of systemic goals is the most legitimate outcome of evaluation processes, and the data thus collected are essential in the establishment of the personnel decisions. Both society and the professions have a right to expect that personnel decisions will be based upon a conscientious and professional assessment of the systemic worth and potential of each professional component under consideration.

EVALUATION—WHAT?

Given that instructional programs need continual improvement, and given that improvement begins with evaluation, what is it then that needs to be evaluated? It is precisely the "what" to be evaluated that has proven to be the most consistent stumbling block to the establishment of professional salary schedules based upon assessments of competence. Nevertheless, a determination must be made as to what is important in the performance of professional duties.

It is suggested here that the "what" should be largely determined by the profession involved, namely, the teachers. Patients, for example, would be less than adequate in determining the excellence of a particular dentist. Dentists actively involved in the business of dentistry are the ones who know the requirements for good dental practice. It seems self-evident that those who are actively involved in the business of teaching are the ones who should best judge the requirements of good teaching practice.

Teachers within local school districts are capable of describing, in behavioral terms, what constitutes good teaching. Obviously, teaching behaviors which contribute toward goal accomplishments should be honored by the profession. Other kinds of behaviors, however, must be given consideration. In those states having strong professional practices acts, rather explicit definitions of appropriate behavior are available. Similar statements developed by local communities would be helpful in unifying the professional components of a teaching staff around the goals toward which they are required to direct their professional efforts.

The administrator with supervisory responsibilities may also find himself with a related dilemma. Given professional statements about what constitutes acceptable behavior, and given a responsibility for improving the teaching capacity of his staff, he must face the question of how much poor teaching can be afforded in districts before he gives up his therapeutic activities designed to salvage the less-than-good teacher. Likewise, he must decide at which point the teacher is to be rejected as unacceptable in terms of his capacity to contribute toward the accomplishment of systemic goals. There would seem to be no way for the chief executive officer of a public school system to remove the element of subjectivity from a specific assessment that a given teacher's behavior is inconsistent with that considered desirable within the context of the system's operation.

EVALUATION—HOW?

Within American public school systems the evaluation of teacher competence is normally accomplished in one of three ways: (1) through the utilization of supervisors in a staff relationship, or (2) through the utilization of building principals in a line relation, or (3) through self-evaluation. The profession has come to accept, largely through the efforts of the Association for Supervision and Curriculum Development, the concept that supervision for the purpose of instructional improvement can best come from specialists who operate without the power to promote, dismiss, or affect the salary of the teacher being supervised. As a result, the concept of supervisors outside of the administrative structure has expanded greatly over the past few years.

When an assessment of a teacher's competence has been judged as relevant to a decision to promote, to dismiss, to retain on a tenure status, or to increase the salary for merit reasons, that judgement has normally been made by a line officer in the form of a building principal or the superintendent of schools. Through this procedure, society has some guarantee that its standards of teaching behavior are being met. This does not imply that the responsible administrative officer is responsive only to society in the discharge of this particular duty. He is, of course, a member of the same profession represented by his teaching staff, and as such, his assessments of competencies for the same four purposes must, of necessity, incorporate a personal and professional bias outside of those represented in the system's society. He also must view himself as a protector of the profession and when behavior is outside the limits deemed appropriate by the profession, the responsible administrator is as likely to take corrective action as if the stimulus had come from the society.

The manner in which evaluations are conducted does not differ markedly as a result of the nature of the supervisor. Both the staff supervisor and the line supervisor are likely to rely upon such methods as classroom observations, assessments of nonclassroom behavior, peer evaluations, and professional introspection as legitimate ways to assess the quality of the individual teacher's contribution to the system. It should be remembered that the manner in which professional employees are evaluated is only a means to an end. In each case, the means provide data which may be used in comparing teaching behavior with that which has been established as standard.

No discussion of issues involved in evaluating and appraising the work of personnel would be complete without some consideration of the differences between organizations staffed primarily with professional personnel and those staffed primarily with nonprofessional personnel. The history of the American labor movement has been replete with example of labor-management problems surrounding the issue of the supervision of employees. Nevertheless, labor-oriented organizations have incorporated into their systems far more legal constraints and legal definitions about how the supervisory act shall be performed and the relationship between supervisor and employee. Such has not been the case in organizations comprised primarily of professional persons.

American teachers have consistently sought to associate themselves, by analogy and any other means, with the other professions found within American society. In the attempted association, they have correctly witnessed that most other professionals operate without a hierarchically arranged authority structure. In addition, teachers have felt responsible for the improvement of their professional capacities. They have elected to return to school and to engage in other scholarly endeavors designed to improve their own professional competencies.

Teachers are engaged in the process of education and are gainfully employed by a quasi-public corporation; as a result, they are in a position somewhat different from other professionals. The educational corporation has a board of control serving as its employers, and as a result, some restrictions, whether desirable or not, are placed upon employee behavior. In more recent years the teaching profession has attempted to improve the ends toward which evaluation programs have been directed. As a result more enlightened state organizations of teachers have passed professional practices acts. In essence, these acts are attempts by the teachers to place much of the appraisal of professional behaviors within the area of responsibility encompassed by the teachers themselves. If successful, teachers will move yet another step closer to the unrestrained professionalism they so urgently desire. Responsibility for the conduct of the membership will, therefore, be vested within peer groups rather than superimposed by an administrative hierarchy.

Rejection and Retention

Following every appraisal activity, a decision is ultimately made to retain or to reject the person being appraised. Superintendents in many states are no longer free to make unilateral decisions about the desirability of arbitrarily dismissing a member of the teaching staff. The teaching profession, as a reaction to the indiscriminate dismissal of teachers by superintendents and boards of education committed to keeping local expenses at a minimum, have won teacher tenure laws in many states. Such laws normally provide that a teacher may not be dismissed without just and specified causes, that the superintendent and the board, in following a dismissal procedure, will be required to proceed in specified steps, that the teacher under threat of dismissal shall have a right to a hearing, and that the teacher shall have a right to and a procedure for an appeal of dismissal action. In most cases, the teacher tenure acts have provided a probationary period during which time the behavior of the prospective tenured teacher may be observed, evaluated, and improved. Restraints levied against the arbitrary dismissal of a teacher by boards of education are normally invoked only after a probationary period.

Rejection of a teacher as undesirable under tenure legislation has had two specific consequences. First, the superintendent and principals within a local school system have been forced to increase their concern over supervisory and appraisal kinds of activities, and secondly, the procedures under which a teacher may be justifiably dismissed have been regularized. In the first case, principals and superintendents have become more concerned about the career aspects of a given teacher's professional life, and under the latter the teachers have been guaranteed some rights which were being withheld in some of the unenlightened school systems.

It has been argued that the combination of professional practices acts and teacher tenure legislation can be a potent force for the development of a stronger educational profession. The teacher tenure acts will provide teachers with protection against unscrupulous and capricious boards of education whose arbitrary actions have deterred the attainment of professional status, particularly through denial of academic freedom. On the other hand, the professional practices acts can serve to guarantee society that the behaviors engaged in by the members of the profession are appropriate to the accomplishment of the goals of American public education.

The Personnel Subsystem

Figure 11-1 graphically portrays the relationship among various aspects of the personnel process. As illustrated, the process that brings new teachers into the educational system is a continuous one. It provides for initiating them into the ongoing operations of the system, for their improvement while members of the system, and for adding additional membership when changing goals require it.

The personnel subsystem is only one part of the public school system. However, of all subsystems it holds the greatest potential for accomplishing the goals of the system. Other subsystems are important and are goal contributors, but only through the behaviors of the human components does a school district become a dynamic educational system.

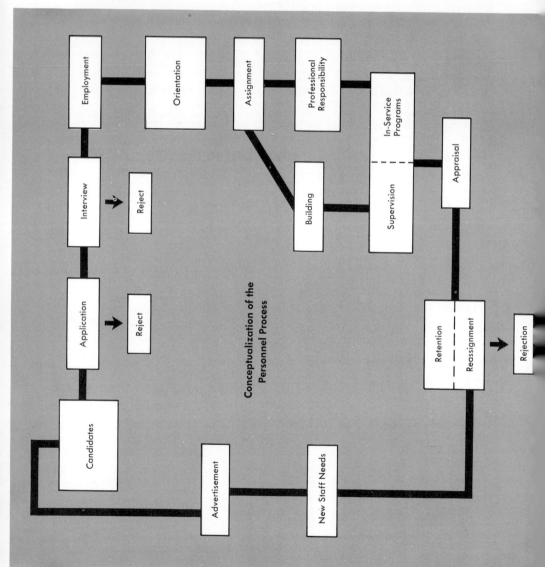

Figure 11-1. The personnel processes.

The interactions of administrators and teachers engaged in personnel processes are superseded in systemic importance only by the teacher-pupil interactions in the teaching-learning process. In large measure, the success of the latter is predicated upon the efficacy of the former.

Problems and Issues

1. *In what way should teachers participate in teacher selection procedures?* The knowledge bases of decisions concerning how a potential teacher "fits" into the local system differ among administrators and teachers. Their relative proximity to the teaching position is different. Their perspectives on the importance of subject matter competence and a teaching style may also be different. Certainly their relative perceptions of the professional environment in which the potential teacher will find himself is different.

Teachers and administrators also have differing responsibilities to the system. In the process of teacher selection, the final decision, to appoint or not to appoint, legally resides with the board of education. The superintendent normally makes recommendations to the board concerning the desirability of appointment. The superintendent's method of preparing his recommendations varies greatly from district to district. As he prepares should he receive recommendations from teachers?—Should teachers "interview?"— How should building principals be involved?—What kinds of arrangements can be made for candidates to visit with classroom teachers?

2. *By what means can professional educators attain and preserve academic freedom?* The right to seek and to teach the truth as they interpret it has long been the teachers' most fundamental professional demand. Their professional expectations, however, are not always met, and they sometimes find themselves with less than complete freedom. The question of "ownership" of the public school system sometimes rears its head with the perceived owners —the local community—sometimes overextending themselves in a zealous effort to mold the system after their own desire.

Not all infringements on freedom come from the local level. Statewide curriculums sometimes dictate that teachers teach a particular subject matter to include certain state-prescribed "truths." Thus, teachers are sometimes told to "teach this or that" and administrators to "supervise this or that." Even their teaching method sometimes comes under attack when a community feels its children are being given too much freedom or are being too restricted. When a teacher's freedom comes under attack, how shall he react?—How shall he seek redress?—How can he change his environment?—What resources are at his command?—How can the system protect him?—What are legitimate limits to a teacher's freedom?

3. *How should teachers participate in evaluation activities?* Many states and almost all local districts demand that an evaluation be made of each teacher's effectiveness. The responsibility for accomplishing such evaluation is normally vested in administrative officers. Administrators, however, do not have exclusive power to subjectively assess a particular teachers competency. As a member of a group outside of the teachers, he is not privy to much information which legitimately might be used in making judgments of competence.

In some districts, utilizing team teaching, it is quite easy for peers to observe the teaching effectiveness of another team member. Informal judgments are unconsciously made even though formal evaluations are not accomplished. A very real problem also remains in differences between teachers as to the role which they wish their peers to play in formal or informal evaluation procedures. Given the necessity for making an evaluation, what part should peers play?—What dangers are involved?—Can dangers be overcome?— What weight should peer evaluations have?

Selected References

American Association of School Administrators. *Staff Relations in School Administration*. 33rd Yearbook. Washington, D.C.: AASA, 1955.

Castetter, William. *Administering the School Personnel Program*. New York: Macmillan, 1962.

Chandler, B. J., and Paul Petty. *Personnel Management and School Administration*. Yonkers, N.Y.: World Book Co., 1955.

Elsbree, Willard, and E. Edmund Reutter, Jr. *Principals of Staff Personnel Administration in Public Schools*. New York: Teachers College, Columbia University, 1959.

Elsbree, Willard, and E. Edmund Reutter, Jr. *Staff Personnel in Public Schools*. Englewood Cliffs, N.J.: Prentice-Hall, 1954.

Kindred, Leslie, and Prince Woodward. *Staff Welfare Practices in the Public Schools*. Washington, D.C.: Center for Applied Research in Education, 1963.

Moore, Harold. *The Administration of Public School Personnel*. New York: Center for Applied Research in Education, 1966.

Steffensen, James. *Staff Personnel Administration*. Washington; U.S.O.E. and U.S.G.P.O., 1963.

Van Zwoll, James. *School Personnel Administration*. New York: Meredith Publishing Co., 1964.

chapter 12

■ *Instructional*

Improvement

Assessing What the Teacher Brings to the System

Unquestionably, the most important thing the teacher brings to the system is himself. This is probably best evidenced by the persistent concern recruiters of teachers give to the candidate as a person, supporting the view that what is taught and how it is taught cannot be divorced from the person who is engaged in teaching.

In spite of this great concern, little systematic assessment of the teacher as a person is made in the process of recruiting professional components for the public school system. Those persons engaged in recruitment, selection, and deployment of professional personnel would seem to rely more upon some mystique—most assuredly an off-the-cuff, subjective judgment—in determining the characteristics of the teacher as a person. Possibly this has become a mark of pride among recruiters. It is not uncommon to hear a recruiter, often an administrator in the system, say "I can tell after a few minutes in the interview with a candidate teacher whether he will be able to get along with kids—whether he will be an effective teacher." What is bothersome—even tragic—here is that the assumption may be that there is "a type" of person or that there is "a way" to teach which is uniquely effective.

Excepting extreme variations in personal characteristics, and even this is not always true, studies of teacher characteristics would seem to indicate that there is no "type" or "way" that can be distinguished as uniquely desirable. Essentially, within the school system, there is an interaction between many types of teachers, types of students and the many types of instructional motifs which might be appropriate under particular circumstances.

Too often selection of teachers for the system is really based upon judging whether the individuals selected will "fit" the be-havioral mold adopted within the system. Where this obtains, it should be clear to the candidate teacher that the decision has been made in that particular system that there is in fact "a way"—a particular way with the exclusion of all others—to teach.

More enlightened systems may appear through their recruiters to be engaged in the same kinds of judgments. But, the motives may be very different. In these systems there may be an honest effort in recruiting to select *different* types of teachers who may employ a wide diversity of instructional approaches in the classroom. In these systems the decision may have been made that it is wise to have different types of teachers and that there is functional utility in varying instructional procedure in the classroom.

The public school system that hopes to exist as a microcosmic representation of the larger society will often seek teachers from different geographic regions in the United States and will solicit for exchange teachers from abroad to make even wider the cultural exposure available to student components. Teachers will be sought from a range of social class backgrounds. In short, teachers will be selected because they are different and because they represent the larger cross-cultural setting.

The teacher also brings to the system what has been his par-ticular formal training for the profession. He may also bring his prior experience as a teacher or related experiences and a well-developed competence in instructional methods. The first-year teacher probably brings to the system a recent and intensive ex-posure to the latest thinking in his content area. Each new teacher has probably brought to the system certain assets upon which the system and its several professional components should surely plan to capitalize. It need not be unusual, for instance, to have a first-year teacher providing leadership in discussion of content (what is to be taught) in an inservice program conducted by the system for its professional components.

The new teacher also brings to the system an attitude toward the profession—a set of unique dispositions which describe the nature of his career commitment. The common error made by recruiters is to see or project this disposition of the candidate for a teaching position only in terms of the local school system. In fact, the candi-date teacher may have developed no "feel" for the local school system. His orientation may be directed much more toward the particular disciplines in which he has been trained or, possibly, toward the profession in general rather than a particular district in which he might seek employment. The candidate teacher is usually not locally oriented at the time he seeks employment in a local school system. His local orientation will result from such factors as the extent to which he is able to see himself appropriately involved in the professional activities of the system and the extent to which the other components in the system and the school-community tend to encourage his active participation in the affairs of both the school and the community.

Assessing What the System
Offers the Teacher

Systems will vary in their desirability, depending upon the needs and desires of particular candidate teachers. In terms of the instructional program, a system which has adopted rather rigid modes of operation—the kind of system in which the new teacher does what others have been doing—may be most appealing to the teacher who does not wish to innovate or who would rather be told what to do and how to do it rather than exercise his professional discretion. This same system might be repugnant to the new teacher who wants to "try his wares" in the classroom with students.

In a sense, the candidate teacher may make the same mistake often made by administrators in recruiting teachers. He may seek employment in a system where he will "fit." He may be looking for convenience in the sense that he will feel more comfortable working with like-minded people and practicing his profession in ways which he has come to look upon as familiar. On the other hand, the candidate teacher may be moved to seek a position in a system where there is a real challenge to conduct the process of education. In this latter system the principal thing commending the position of teacher is the inherent challenge to undertake successfully the professional task of teaching. Peace Corps and VISTA workers might typify the kind of individual who would seek the challenging public school system.

Surely, there is no shortage of public school systems in which a challenge exists for the teacher. The candidate must ask himself, What kind of challenge do I seek? One system may maintain a resources and teacher planning center; another system may offer little or no time for planning during the regular school day, let alone space or resources for this activity. In each case the school system is providing a challenge. The teacher who has time and facilities is challenged to develop his instructional prowess through the use of what the system has provided. The teacher who has not this time or the resources is challenged to find or create (innovate) instructional techniques to improve his professional performance. It should be noted that in each system the improvement of instruction is being sought. The difference is that in one system there is formal support through the provision of time, space, and resources, whereas in the other system (often as a result of inadequate fiscal support for the system) the teacher must rely more upon his wits —his verve for the challenge—to engage in instructional improvement.

The provisions of Public Law 89-10 are making large amounts of money available in those systems where there are identifiable groups of children who have been deprived in one manner or another. However, the press of large numbers of students, full teaching days, and marginal facilities may have a special portent for in-service instructional improvement both in these school systems and in institutions where teachers for these systems are being trained.

School systems in which instructional improvement is really desired (and since improvement usually predicts some change, this cannot apply equally to all school systems) must look to their professional components for guidance. This is especially true where choices have to be made as a result of budgetary limitations upon the system (and although it applies differentially, it does apply to probably all school systems). It is often cited that when teachers are provided a "free period" or "planning period" during the school day, the time is used most frequently for social intercourse and the consumption of coffee. Although the public relations "image" of teachers using time during the school day in this manner may be less than wholly desirable, is it not entirely possible that improved instruction does result from teachers having the opportunity to relax? To some physiological and psychological types, the opportunity to unwind may be more productive of instructional improvement than reading an article in a professional journal during that time released from teaching in the school day.

One other thing, then, that the system offers the teacher is the extent to which he will be recognized as a person as well as a professional. The school system which describes its teachers as employees—the system in which the community feels that the teachers are "local employees"—may have depersonalized its notion of the teacher to the extent that professionals in the school system get the idea that they are subsisting rather than living in the school-community. At the worst, teachers and administrators may be given the impression by the community that they are really privileged to be in the employ of the local school system.

Personal and professional recognition of teachers and administrators by the school-community should encourage teachers to suggest what might be wise choices in supporting instructional improvement. There is, too, the simple humanistic observation that where professionals are also accepted as community citizens, they would seem to be more willing to both initiate their own improvement and to be more responsive to systemic efforts to enable this improvement.

Little mention has been made of the "hardware" which a system may offer teachers. The physical environment for teaching may have been thoughtfully arranged, there may be excellent support facilities, the students may even be cleaner of body than those in some neighboring school system; however, it is still contended that the principal offering the system has for the teacher is how the system and its school-community desires to accept the teacher as a person and the extent to which he is given discretion in his professional activities.

Establishing Goals for Instruction

It might be expected that goals for instruction in the public school system would be one thing on which there was considerable agreement. The instructional process may be described as the media used to communicate whatever content has been selected for presentation to students. It is hoped that the content presented will lead to desired behavioral change in students and also that teaching methods used will assure that there is a broad understanding among the students of the content presented. The goal of instruction, then, is to "get through" to the most students in a manner which gives the content meaning for them, thus maximizing the possibility of desirable behavioral changes.

There are three principal variables which operate in establishing the instructional goals in the public school system: (1) the physical or environmental setting of the system dictates some limitations for instructional goals; for example, overcrowded conditions with abbreviated teacher-student contact time; (2) the personal characteristics and professional competencies of teachers also predict the goals to some extent, for example, the female teaching staff members may be strongly oriented toward their domestic roles as wives and mothers or toward moonlighting jobs for additional income, whereas in the classroom the lecture method of instruction may predominate as a matter of habit or because it is the method with which the teacher feels comfortable; and (3) further, the student components have an impact upon the instructional goals for the system; for example, differences among students allow that particular modes of instruction will be more effective with some students than with others, and students also become accustomed to particular instructional techniques and may be resistant to variations in presentation for which they have not been prepared.

Certain of the limitations upon instructional goals may be overcome in the system through adapting facilities and in-service programs for the professional components, whereas others may be beyond the "reach" of the system, in which case they must be accepted as part of the given when the instructional goals for the school system are set.

Where all of the three principal variables affecting instructional goals are not considered, there is the risk that the goals will be set with primary or sole consideration being given to only how the professional components are disposed. And, in this there is, of course, the risk that teachers and administrators might be myopic —might fail to give adequate consideration to the other variables which affect the instructional goals for the system.

It is unlikely that instructional goals of any worth can be set for the school system without first giving consideration to the broader goals of the system and of the society. These broader goals will probably predict *what* ought to be taught rather than *how* the appropriate content should be presented to students. Once appropriate content has been decided upon for presentation, it again is imperative that the instructional methods used be those best suited to the content. The criterion measure to be applied here is, Does the mode of presentation (instructional method) selected reasonably assure that the content will get through with maximum meaning to most students?

The ordering of goals then begins with the broadest goals, from which are then selected the goals for observance by the system. Secondly, once systemic goals have been set, appropriate content is decided upon. Only after these stages in goal-setting have taken place is the system ready to establish instructional goals.

Refining Instruction to Meet Goals

NEED FOR REFINING

Implicit in the process of refinement is an understanding of what is being done. Since instruction is, in essence, communication, refinement of instructional goals very much involves an understanding of the communication process. How do teachers know whether the content being presented to students is getting through with maximum efficiency? Some overt approaches which are not without merit might include attempts at testing student understanding of content presented and asking students whether the presentation of content was clear to them. The only problem with relying upon such techniques is the difficulty in accounting for what might be called latent learning—the beginning of student understanding, which even he may not recognize and which will probably not be clearly evident in his responses to test items. It is equally unrealistic to expect that a student can react to the clarity of a presentation of content if he has not had exposure to other instructional modes against which he might judge the particular one used.

Both the teacher and the student profit from the refinement of instruction where different techniques are used. The teacher is able to assess his talent in using various modes of instruction; his professional training should assist him in being sensitive to the students' reception of the different techniques. The student who is given the opportunity to engage in learning under a variety of content stimuli becomes more flexible in adapting to different learning settings; he also becomes more sophisticated in his ability to compare the relative worth of the several instructional techniques being employed.

Since the primary goal of the school system is to evoke desired behavioral change in students, the instructional methods used in the school might be specifically designed to give incentive for students to react to what is being presented. Although it is only an imperfect measure, the student response to the content and its method of presentation is still the best sign to use in attempting to refine instruction.

Supporting Refinements

Instructional improvement to meet systemic goals requires a strong commitment from the system—more specifically, the board of education and the professional administrative components in the system. Even a cursory look at instructional methods will disclose that, apart from the differences among teachers, certain content and student reaction to the teaching methodologies dictate that such things as large and small group instruction and multi-sensory stimulation are especially useful in particular circumstances. The fiscal implications alone are immense for the system. The audiovisual budget may have to be enlarged, flexible teaching space may have to be sought in buildings which have interior bearing walls, and teachers who discover that there is more than "one way" may be sorely in need of intensive in-service and formal preparation to enable their successful use of some of the "new" modes of instruction which they have discovered. Professional personnel with specific competencies may have to be employed to provide logistical support for the system that has chosen to undertake instruction in many different ways. Present personnel in the system may find themselves performing tasks which have become obsolescent in the system. Regular staff members may have to be redeployed, and others may have to decide whether, even with retraining, they can continue to contribute to the goals of the system.

As the board of education and professional staff members consider these problems, they may choose to throw up their hands in favor of continuing to keep school as it was in the past. Refinement of instruction has a snowballing effect which is difficult to stop once it is started.

Where the refinement of instructional goals has been deemed important, it is crucial that an explication of the goals reach through the professional components in the system to the students. Instructional goals which do not make sense or cannot be understood by the student leave him unaware of the rationale and wholly dependent upon his faith in the decisions made by professional components in the system. Both teachers and students ought to understand that there are some discernible differences between "short-term" and "long-range" goals for instruction—that the efficacy of certain methods used in the classroom will not always be immediately apparent.

Great care needs to be taken also to assure that testing programs adopted by the school and sensitive teacher observation of student behavior are related to both the content presented and the methods of instruction used. If there is no congruence between instrument and objectives, there is always the danger that testing and observation will disclose weaknesses and strengths in the program, based upon what was not taught and using methods of instruction which were not employed.

Personnel Involved in Supervision of Instruction

Directly or indirectly, all professional components in the school system are involved in the supervision of instruction. If it is remembered that the curriculum includes *all* those activities which the system sponsors for students, then all professional personnel in the system engage in supervision—either of their own activity or of the activities of subordinate components. The most obvious supervisory relationship is that between the teacher and the administrator (the subordinate and the superordinate within the system). It is the administrator who must make such decisions as whether to recommend a teacher for a tenure appointment, whether to reassign a teacher so that he and, especially, the students will profit most from the relationship, and whether to recommend a change in the instructional techniques to be employed in the classroom.

It is extremely difficult for instructional supervision to take place where the supervisor does not have a "live" contact with the instructional setting. Surely, the principal in an attendance unit within the system can review the lesson plan of a teacher and can reflect upon the techniques outlined for presentation of the lesson.

The director of pupil personnel services can, in a like manner, read the written plan of a school counselor who has proposed the format for a student interview and make some judgments regarding the merits of the techniques suggested for the interview session. But, in each case, there is a lack of "action–reaction," there is no real feel for how the instructional technique was employed with students and there is also no feedback on how students responded to the techniques.

Although administrators in the system are usually charged with passing judgment upon the instructional methods employed by professional personnel working directly with student components, it is really the professional personnel who must supervise their own instruction. The professional component is there all the time he is in contact with student components, whereas administrative supervision can only take place on a most occasional basis.

The board of education is legally obligated to also be concerned with supervising instruction. Through the chief school officer— the top of the hierarchy among the professional components in the system—the board is accountable for sponsoring and endorsing appropriate instruction in the system. It is important to note that the involvement of the board of education in supervising instruction is not direct. Usually, the board might be expected to act upon the promoting of the professional staff and with the recommendation of the chief school officer for the district.

In most states there are at least suggested syllabuses for the content of the program offered in public school systems. Although these syllabuses do not often treat instructional methodology extensively, the suggested content to some extent makes particular methods more applicable than others. In this sense, the state engages in some supervision of instruction. States which are particularly active in education may also use field supervisors who monitor instruction in individual school systems. The increased use of state and nationwide examinations and the portent for making comparative judgments of educational programs may also predicate which techniques of instruction are selected for use.

Parents and other patrons of the school system in the community are often overlooked as supervisors of instruction. Concern with their judgments arises mainly when pressure is brought to bear upon the system to start using some widely publicized method or cease and desist in the use of a technique to which the citizens have taken exception for some reason. Although citizen supervision of instruction—largely through hearsay evidence—carries no mandate for action in the legal sense, the pressures which can be brought to bear upon the public school system are such that the citizenry cannot be ignored.

In the last analysis, the decision to supervise instruction is one which must be made by the teacher. The system can provide many forms of assistance in improving technique, but without the willingness of the teacher, without his commitment to the urgency for refinement of teaching methodology, there cannot be very much hope for those efforts at supervision imposed within the system.

Techniques Used in Teacher-Administrator Instructional Improvement

RESPONSIBILITY FOR SUPERVISION

The administrator in the public school system has as his principal purpose facilitating those activities which are sponsored by the school and are directed toward accomplishing the goals of the system. The relationship between the administrator and the teacher is one in which the administrator supervises instruction while the teacher engages in instruction. It might be expected, then, that the supervision provided by the administrator would, in fact, facilitate instruction and would lead to its improvement.

Although the titles of positions vary, the teacher cannot help but recognize that the person designated to facilitate the improvement of his instruction is the same person who is his superior in the hierarchy and who will probably pass an initial judgment on his competency to teach in that system. Once this is understood it can be observed that there is a great deal of waste motion and effort made to convince teachers that supervisors are their friends, that they have no punitive intentions. As professional components in the system, teachers and administrators ought to be able to agree that superiors are charged by the system with judging the performance of subordinates and that this is a natural and legitimate phenomenon in a hierachical organization of people such as a public school system. Further, teachers and administrators ought to be able to agree without too much difficulty that the system in which they hold positions exists primarily for students and that the performance of all professional components in the system is ultimately judged in terms of how well students are served in terms of the goals of the system. This means, of course, that the system does not exist to serve the convenience of either administrators or teachers and that the relationships between these professional components may be strained from time to time. But, since *each* component is important to the successful functioning of the system, teachers and administrators must choose to work together if they really support the goals of the system in which they have chosen to be employed. A lesser commitment on the part of professional components in the system can only be described as selfishness, which is dysfunctional in terms of systemic goals.

TECHNIQUES OF INSTRUCTION

Instructional improvement can be sought by the administrator through arranging for teachers to visit one another in the system and to observe in other school systems. Demonstration teaching lessons might be presented to portray particular techniques of instruction. Media specialists might demonstrate the various uses of equipment available to the teachers. Although teachers will observe techniques being used or demonstrated, they may resist chatting among themselves about how they engage in the act of teaching. Teachers ought to be encouraged to observe presentation technique as well as content. This is especially important when the demonstration lesson is in an alien discipline where the observing teacher may become infatuated with the content and less attentive to instructional techniques being used. Teachers need also to discuss and observe in similar and dissimilar grade levels and content areas. The array of observations should indicate that there is the need for articulation and continuity of teaching method as well as content if the program of the system is to have meaning to the students.

The administrator must plan for an observation in the classroom. He needs to review what is to be taught during the visit. He needs to know what are the goals for the unit of teaching and the characteristics of the students in the class. He needs also to remember that his physical presence in the classroom may appreciably alter the relationship which normally exists between the teacher and the students. The administrator should be as alert to the behavior of students during the lesson as he is to the behavior of the teacher— judgment of instructional outcomes is based upon student, not teacher, behavioral change.

The advent of what has been called team-teaching makes necessary collaborative agreement upon goals, content, and the teaching methods to be used by the several teachers who will share in the presentation of a segment of the content of the program. Even within team-teaching as a broad technique, particular approaches will vary. A team-taught unit might include a large group lecture describing, for example, a physical law and then be followed by several small group sessions devoted to discussion of how the particular law can be observed and how it is applied. Yet another team approach might use a series of special teachers (for example, music, art, and so on) who would give breadth to a unit in a course in Spanish. The latter approach intends to reinforce the humanistic dimension in the formal study of language.

The use of flexible space and different-size student groups has made it incumbent upon teachers to be mutually reinforcing of techniques used so that students will find a continuity in presentation style as well as gain an appreciation for the variations in techniques used.

ADMINISTRATIVE ROLE

It is most important in instructional supervision that the administrator not miscast his role. He is *not* (with few exceptions) competent to present himself as a content or subject matter supervisor. The administrator engaged in instructional supervision might better devote his attention to the teaching-learning environment—to *how* things are happening—rather than a superficial and often ill-understood assessment of the content being presented. The administrator is constantly trapped in this dilemma by having to work with architects, lawyers, engineers, and teachers in many areas of specialization. He cannot be all things to all people. He should not try to be.

Another error which the administrator might avoid is that of discussing instructional improvement with a teacher in terms of what the administrator or some other teacher did in the classroom. Again, the "here and now" problem arises. The only experience common to both administrator and teacher is that time when the administrator observed the teacher during a presentation in the classroom. Discussion of improvement in technique ought to be clearly related to the observed experience. Since the teacher has probably used his discretion in making the presentation, it might be wise for the administrator to invite the teacher to explain why he chose those particular instructional techniques.

Although the administrator may believe that he knows of "better" instructional modes, he might remember that the teacher may know better his own capabilities and the students to whom he is presenting the lesson. An instructional technique cannot be better per se. It is only better to the extent that it improves communication of the content material while taking into consideration both the teacher and the students.

The administrator often does not have the time to make as frequent visits as he might wish in the classroom. For this reason, it seems imperative that some record be kept of the observations which are made. The record provides normative data for the administrator. A series of recorded observations provides ipsative data for the teacher. Although the observed classroom does not provide a fully natural setting, a video tape of the observed lesson would provide the kind of record which could be reviewed by the teacher and the administrator, assuring that attention might be centered upon that particular lesson. Where the administrator must rely upon his notes or his memory, much of what was observed may be lost. Too, attempting to make a record during an observation can severely distract the observer from what is happening in the classroom. Video tape recordings are not inexpensive, but they may be a realistic expenditure for the public school system since approximately 70 per cent of the budget for the system is usually committed to providing instructional services. It seems unfortunate that so much should be spent on instruction in the system while often so little time or money is budgeted for observing and recording the effectiveness of this activity.

There is a good deal of sentiment among some administrators that the classroom is the castle of the teacher and that the administrator should not "appear" in the classroom unless the teacher first has extended an invitation. Sometimes this sentiment is described as the administrator respecting the professional prerogatives of the teacher. In any event it ignores the administrator's responsibility for what happens in the classroom. Where the administrator waits to be invited or offers assistance only to those who seek it, it may be discovered that he is spending a disproportionate amount of time doing the wrong things with the wrong teachers. Those who invite the administrator to observe in their classrooms are often the teachers who least need assistance in refining their instructional techniques. It might be that the teacher who does not invite observation—the teacher who may be exceedingly proud of his instructional talents—is the one who is most in need of observation and assistance. It is desirable for teachers to be receptive to observation and desirous of help in improving their instruction in the classroom. However, where rapport between administrator and teacher has not been built, or where it is not good, this does not in any way reduce the importance and the urgency for the administrator to fulfill his obligation to the system (and as a professional) to supervise the instruction given by classroom teachers.

Appraisal of Instruction

Criteria for appraisal of instruction are again being treated because of a particularly complex problem which arises in the assessment of instruction. It has been said that the primary criterion to be applied is whether instruction communicates best the content being taught. And it has been noted that the mode of instruction depends upon the characteristics of the content, the teacher, and the students to whom the material is to be presented. It has also been noted that the administrator has a responsibility in the public school system to supervise classroom instruction.

What has not been treated is that the classroom teacher may be the person best able to determine what instructional techniques should be employed in presenting particular content material to certain groups of students. Unless the public school system has extended considerable discretion to its teachers, the teachers may have the impression that it is the responsibility of the system to determine which instructional techniques are to be used in the classroom and that this is not an area of professional responsibility for the teacher.

Where instruction is to be judged, one criterion for this assessment must be the *qualifications* of the professional components who will make these judgments. It is not being asked whether administrative personnel should judge classroom instruction—this is clearly one of their present responsibilities. It is being asked whether they are competent to make such judgments. Might not peers of the teacher be better able to assess his instructional performance? Is this not part of the essence of becoming a profession? If teachers are asked to strive toward making teaching a profession, should they not be encouraged to assume responsibility for their own policing—in this case, assessing the excellence of their own instructional performances in the classroom?

Collegiate training institutions which prepare teachers cannot be expected to develop a teacher receptivity to instructional supervision unless it can be clearly shown that the supervision to be given will be a competent assessment of the worth of instructional performance. Teachers can, however, be encouraged to become more responsible for their own performance, and this surely can be supported on professional grounds.

Where the administrator is asked to observe and judge the performance of a teacher in a situation where the teacher may himself be better qualified to judge the performance, there can only be a lessening in the stature of the administrator in the eyes of the professional teaching staff of the system. Since the matter of administrative responsibility for teacher performance cannot easily be gotten around, it might be suggested that the administrators in the system rely more upon teacher advisement—that is, involve more teachers in observing instruction—in reaching decisions on the quality of that performance in instruction.

Problems and Issues

1. *How should teacher effectiveness be assessed?* If the system is to function effectively, there must be assessment of the performances of every component in the system. The act of teaching or instruction is a behavioral act. With varying degrees of accuracy

this behavior is observable. Traditionally, the effectiveness of teacher components is determined by administrative personnel. Increasingly, teachers have been questioning whether administrative components are capable of making accurate assessments. Possibly a more serious concern is the extent to which the criteria used in judging the teacher's performance are stipulated in behavioral terms.

Both teachers and administrators are professional components and most administrators have been teachers. However, once a teacher becomes an administrator, his tasks become quite different. Because administrators have been held responsible for assessment, often, at least unconsciously, the criteria are theirs. Attempts to involve teachers in the development of criteria for assessment have not been especially productive. Nor have teachers been particularly pleased with attempts to rate each other.

What are some of the specific behavioral criteria which should be used in teacher assessment?—By whom should the assessment be conducted?—If several components should be involved, which components, and what roles should each play?—Does the board of education have a proper role in teacher assessment?—What teacher behaviors ought not to be included in assessments?

2. *How can the supervisor assist instructional personnel?* The system employs supervisory personnel for the purpose of up-grading instruction. Teacher components often look upon supervisors as foremen. The supervisor is frequently a *persona non grata* among teachers. It is often suspected by teachers that supervisors assist in evaluating teacher performance.

What is occasionally forgotten by teachers is that supervisory personnel are not generic ogres. They, as teachers, have been employed by the system to aid in better accomplishing the tasks of the system. There is little likelihood that the supervisor can assist instructional improvement without the willingness of teachers.

The supervisor must have credibility among teachers if the component is to be effective. Possibly the greatest resistance among teachers grows from a feeling that the supervisor does not really know—he does not know the students and he is not intimately involved with day-to-day instruction. And, there is always the possibility that the supervisor is seen more as an administrator than as a teacher.

Need the supervisor be an adversary for the teacher?—What are some of the ways in which supervisory personnel can be of unique assistance to teachers?—How might teachers better communicate with supervisors?—Are there elements of the instructional programs which should remain solely at the discretion of the teacher?

3. *Should the supervisor be in a "line" or "staff" position?* The
school system will tend to deploy personnel in a manner which it
believes will be most effective for accomplishing the objectives
which have been set for the system. Whether supervisors are "line"
or "staff" is of lesser consequence than the manner of teacher
acceptance of supervisory personnel.

Where the position is line, the supervisor has clear authority and
may stipulate that particular procedures be used by teachers. The
staff position requires that the supervisor act by persuasion in
dealing with teacher components. A crucial consideration for
teachers is their perception of how the system has chosen to
designate supervisors. The choice of the system dictates its perception of the relationship the system has with its teachers.

Teachers who sense that the school system is actively concerned
with improving instructional performance may profit from supervision. Teachers who suspect ulterior motives in supervisors or the
system in general may be immune to assistance.

How can the teacher work effectively with a "line" supervisor?—
What ought to be the conditions of the relationship between the
teacher and the supervisor?—What forms of persuasion might the
staff supervisor use with teachers?—What should be the role of the
principal in instructional improvement?

Selected References

Bruner, Jerome S. *The Process of Education.* Cambridge, Mass.:
Harvard University Press, 1960.

Bruner, Jerome S. *Toward a General Theory of Instruction.* Cambridge, Mass.: Belknap Press, 1966.

Burton, William H., and Leo J. Brueckner. *Supervision a Social Process,* 3rd ed. New York: Appleton-Century-Crofts, 1955.

Harris, Ben M. *Supervisory Behavior in Education.* Englewood Cliffs,
N.J.: Prentice-Hall, 1963.

Leeper, Robert R., ed. *Role of Supervisor and Curriculum Director
in a Climate of Change.* Washington, D.C.: Association for
Supervision and Curriculum Development, 1965.

MacDonald, James B., and Robert R. Leeper, eds. *Theories of Instruction.* Washington, D.C.: Association for Supervision and
Curriculum Development, 1965.

National Society for the Study of Education. *Theories of Learning
and Instruction.* 1964 Yearbook, Part I. Chicago: University
of Chicago Press, 1964.

Shulman, Lee S., and Evan R. Keislar, eds. *Learning by Discovery.*
Chicago: Rand, McNally and Company, 1966.

chapter 13

■ *Curriculum Development*

Assessing the Potential of Components in the System

Systems gain efficiency as their components contribute to systemic goals. It is essential, therefore, to assess what are the potentialities of the components which comprise the system. The assessment has a dual importance: to know how best to use existing components, and to determine what additional components might be needed to better serve systemic goals.

One aspect of component potential involves the knowledge of content which professional personnel have at their disposal for use in the system. By content the reference intends to distinguish between *what* is to be taught as contrasted with *how* teaching is to be conducted. Although the two cannot be wholly separated, content refers, in the main, to what is to be taught.

Initially, the content knowledge of the new teacher in the system might be assessed through reviewing the transcript of studies formally undertaken at the university. About the best that can be said of this kind of assessment is that the teacher probably has some understanding of, or at least has had an exposure to, the principal ideas usually presented in those courses listed on the transcript. Vague as this assessment is, it surely is more concrete than the assessment of that fund of knowledge from which an experienced teacher might draw. Actual assessment involves arranging for teachers, to demonstrate their understanding of the subject matter. Of course a further problem obtains at this point. Who is to judge or assess the extent of that knowledge once it is demonstrated?

Assessment of content potential among professional components in the public school system requires that there be components in the system who are "content specialists"—persons who are keenly aware of the array of knowledge which has been generated in a specific discipline. The so-called knowledge explosion probably makes it incumbent upon the school system to employ several of these specialists; it is unlikely that any one teacher, and most assuredly no single administrator, could keep abreast of current knowledge in the several disciplines represented in the broad curricular offerings of the system.

Determination of content potential of components predicts how the professional personnel of the system might best be deployed—which teachers might best present particular material—and also provides a rationale for future teacher procurement and in-service training for presently employed teachers.

The thoughtfully organized public school system has extended its thinking from goals for the system to content of the educational program, so that the goals might be realized or worked toward. Unfortunately, in some school systems (and the word "system" is used loosely here) the goals would seem to permit an educational program where teachers haphazardly present what they know, hence the "program" of the school becomes the probably unrelated presentations by the teachers. Professional systemic goals are only rarely the result of chance. The intention in assessing content potential of professional components in the system is to procure and deploy teachers with particular knowledge in such a manner that systemic goals will be served.

The line of reasoning is also used that any fully certified teacher is competent to teach. But it must be asked, competent to teach what? Both teachers and preparation programs vary. It behooves the system to make every reasonable effort to determine whether a teacher being considered for employment has, in fact, the knowledge expected of him by the system. In the event that the system decides that it wants this particular candidate teacher as a person, then the system must be willing to assume the responsibility for continuing the education of this teacher if he does not possess the requisite command of the content. School systems consider this latter point most thoughtfully in their recruitment of teachers. The logic here might be that it is more difficult to change a person than it is to increase the fund of understanding or knowledge which the person might need in the classroom.

The content potential of a teacher may be as much related to his willingness to acquire new knowledge and his capacity for this acquisition as it is to the presumed fund of knowledge which he brings to the system from his prior formal training and experiences. Assessing such matters as "willingness" and "capacity" is at best a subjective task, with some small objectivity being possible in determining capacity. However, what is the incidence of school systems making forthright attempts at assessing either of these characteristics in teachers who are candidates for positions in the system? Where it is said that the "teacher shortage" is such that we (the system) will take whatever teachers we are able to get, it is being conceded that professional components are really a rather undifferentiated group and that they can be injected in the system almost indiscriminately without danger of aborting systemic goals. In such public school systems the goals often become an enumeration of the "good" things which have happened when a hazy and superficial retrospective view is taken of the many experiences and activities sponsored by the system and conducted by the sundry professional staff members.

Collaboration in Vertical and Horizontal Planning

Collaboration in planning requires that more than one person be involved. The notions of vertical and horizontal refer respectively to grades kindergarten through twelve, or their equivalent in an ungraded system, and to the several professional components who offer instruction at one grade level or in the same subject. Taken broadly, this kind of planning involves all professional components in the system and it applies especially to teachers.

Using this form of planning, the content of the curriculums for the system presumes that all professional components are aware of and concerned with the broad goals of the school system and that discrete content areas will be clearly supportive of these larger goals. This kind of planning should not be construed as or confused with arranging a "lock-step" curriculum for the system. Rather, this form of planning acknowledges the importance of components engaged in curricular design being keenly aware of what they are collectively seeking in terms of student behavioral change. Then each teacher may, through his presentations, be able to support (reinforce) what other teachers are doing with a full recognition that his presentation of content material has been preceded by and will be followed by other material which, when taken together should appear to the teachers, and, more importantly, to the students, as having some logic of development and continuity. In short, it ought to make sense in terms of systemic goals.

Although it is possible for teachers to come to an understanding of systemic goals, especially in terms of student behavioral outcomes, it may be less reasonable to expect that each teacher is able to sort out how his fellow teachers in their grade or subject specialties are working toward accomplishing these goals. The very proliferation of jargon in each subject may make the process of communication more awkward. There is, too, the thesis that teachers may be disposed to feel that their grade level or their subject field is really making the major contribution. Hence, there may be generated a certain detachment from grade levels or other alien disciplines. If left to themselves, teachers might find appreciable difficulty in planning the curriculum of the school system so that each of its several elements supports the remainder of the program.

If the curriculum of the public school system is to make any sense, then a language for communication must be accepted by all professional components if they are to collaborate in planning. It is trite to say that this language should be the simplest possible. What is really important is that all components agree on what is to be meant by the particular language chosen. Once professional components in the public school system can agree upon what they mean when they speak, it is then possible that truly collaborative planning can take place.

Because what is planned will be used with student components and will also be interpreted for the board of education, probably the language used in describing what is to be presented (the curriculum) should also be understandable to these groups. Often the persons most responsible for assuring that clear language be used in planning are the subject matter specialists and curriculum coordinators for the system. Where they fail initially at this task, there can be little hope for success by classroom teachers at different grade levels and representing training in diverse disciplines.

VERTICAL ARTICULATION

Where professional components in the system are the principal planners, it might be expected that attention will be given first to vertical articulation of the curriculum—the ordering of presentation through the grades of material in a particular discipline. This may be especially true where teachers are cosmopolitan in their orientation, where they see themselves as first teachers of a subject and only secondly as teachers in the local public school system at a particular grade level.

A problem which arises here involves the student perception of articulation. The student, at any level within the system, sees not only the development of material in a particular discipline but also that in the several other disciplines to which he is exposed daily. As a result of this regular multiple exposure, he may become more sensitive than the teacher to the horizontal relationships; he may constantly be attempting to see the relationships among the several disciplines as they are being presented to him at one time. It is the student who has the daily exposure to multidisciplinary materials, not the teacher.

There is, of course, an exception—the teacher in the elementary grades. Since he teaches "common branch" subjects, both he and his students have the daily exposure to multiple disciplines. It is possible, however, that, while the students may be seeking some "sense" in the relationships among the several disciplines, the elementary teacher may be rather oblivious to the relationships among disciplines. His perception may be one of spelling AND arithmetic AND reading and so on, rather than an understanding that materials from separate disciplines are subsets of a larger system—the curriculum—which involves many interrelationships.

It is conceivable that students will *respond* to material presented in the classroom in such a manner that they are observing the relationships among disciplines whereas the teacher may ignore or redirect student responses so that they might apply more directly to a specific discipline out of which the teacher has chosen material for presentation. Under these circumstances horizontal articulation of the curricular offerings of the system, while being supported by the students' responses, is concurrently being punished by the teacher. It is unlikely that even the attendant student frustration will overcome the refusal of teachers to intentionally plan and teach for an understanding of multidisciplinary relationships. Again, the question must be asked regarding systemic goals: What desired behavioral changes in students are being sought by the presentation of curricular materials using particular modes of instruction?

Vertical articulation—the sequential development of material within a discipline—depends very much upon the trust that teachers extend to one another. Too often in school systems intermediate grade teachers "assume" that certain things just "have not been covered" or that the coverage was inadequate in lower grades; hence, initial work at the present grade level may involve a reteaching of what already has been presented. There is no argument with reteaching discovered to be necessary through the administration of diagnostic tests or the review of earlier learnings for proper purposes of reinforcement or drawing new and more subtle relationships; the quarrel lies with a usually faulty assumption that teachers at prior grade levels have not "done the job." It should be remembered that *forgetting* is one of the natural consequences of time. Obviously, there is a keen advantage where teachers K-12 are able to collaboratively plan what will be taught at each of the several grade levels within a discipline. It falls to the subject specialists and curriculum coordinators to determine whether teachers at each grade level are "getting the job done."

Variation in Subsystem Sets

Within the public school system there will usually be found a number of subsystems. These take the form of sets in that they may appear to operate rather independently of the larger system; they may seem to be self-sustaining internal units. Once the larger system has made provisions for such needed elements as personnel, space, operating funds, and acknowledgement that the subsystem is a part of the larger system, it is then possible that the subsystem may initiate and sustain its activities without special concern for the larger system or the broader goals for the youth being served.

An example of this might be one segment of the fine arts program of the school, such as music. Although there may be a verbal support for the broad goals of the school system, personnel in music teaching may develop a type of insularity which causes a myopic focus among its professional staff. The teachers of music may increasingly be concerned only with music education goals for pupils. This may be especially true where the larger system has not recognized to the satisfaction of the professional staff in music that desired behavioral change in students includes behaviors which are responsive to the fine arts.

Although the example may appear to be overdrawn, it is reasonable to assume that subsystems evolve and develop within the larger system especially where their internal solidarity is necessary if they are to survive. Conversely, where the larger system acknowledges the importance of programs (potential subsystem sets), there may be a lesser need for the militant development of a self-sustaining organization within the system since the system itself has by its acknowledgement given it appreciable guarantees for acceptance.

Overacceptance can also promote the development of variation in subsystems. This may especially be true where the acceptance devolves from outside the public school system. In such a case there might be a strong acceptance in the community for the interscholastic athletic program of the public school. The public school system may acquiesce in this support in the larger sense, but some real frictions may develop with other curricular programs of the school. Although the athletic program might choose to "go it alone" with the support it has, it will probably elect to make overtures to other programs in the system so that it can also enjoy internal acceptance. The approaches open to a program having external, but lacking internal, acceptance are many. It may choose to emulate other programs offered by the school. It may raise the academic requirements for student participation in its several activities.

Professional personnel in the athletic department may dress and act like the teachers in the traditional academic departments.

In each case of variation cited above, the subsystem is reacting to acceptance or rejection from one or several sources in a manner really no different from that which might be expected of the larger school system as it seeks to maintain its position in the community and the larger society. The sadness may lie in each potential subsystem not realizing that it is important as a component part of the larger school system *because it is different*. Each separate program in the curriculum serves a unique function, at the same time serving the broad goals of the school. Each separate program also has the ability to support other programs in the curriculum. The separate programs, when taken alone, do little to realize systemic goals.

Although it might be expected that each separate subsystem will "carry its weight" in the curriculum of the school, the separate programs should not have to "earn their wings"; rather it is the responsibility of the system to acknowledge and support each of the several programs which comprise the curriculum. It seems unrealistic to expect that the system would fail to support a program which it has chosen to include in the system.

The Need for Supporting Structures of Time, Personnel, and Facilities

The curricular program of the school system is by itself inanimate. Its viability in terms of systemic goals comes from the support it receives and must have if it is to be anything more than a paper plan. The three principal media which enable the transmission of the curriculum to student components are time, personnel, and facilities.

These supporting structures are not catalysts; rather they are very much a part of the reaction which is taking place within the system as student behavioral change is sought. The student is constantly reacting to his environment and while he is in school that environment which may impress him includes both animate and inanimate elements. The elements of the student's school environment are viable or have animation for his *as he perceives them*— the generic animation of these elements has lesser consequences for systemic goals.

TIME

The structure of time is important to curricular considerations of the school system because it is a fundamental dimension of existence. No matter what configuration of stimuli is planned for presentation to students, its inclusion requires time. Too often, the only time planned is that which is judged necessary for the classroom presentation of particular material. This might come close to sufficing if it were true that no planning was necessary and it could be assured that all students would grasp with equal ease what was presented. In reality, the classroom presentation may consume only a very small amount of the teacher's time devoted to the curriculum. The teacher's time is also needed to prepare resource units, to select aids which might make the presentation clearer, to assess relationships which might exist with other portions of the curriculum to which the student will be exposed at approximately the same time, to decide upon the tools of evaluation which will be used with and after the presentation, and, of course, to provide a buffer of time which might be necessary to deal with "unforeseen" developments during the presentation of the lesson.

The time made available within a school system is also dependent upon other supporting structures. The presentation of certain curricular material might require that an extended block of time be used to assist the continuity of the presentation. Time for planning may require that a particular group of teachers be free from other assignments to plan together. The work load of supporting personnel may dictate the amount of time it will take to complete the clerical tasks associated with preparation of curricular presentations.

When teachers are free to meet for planning, there be a place for them to meet. Further, it may be necessary that they meet in a particular place so that resource facilities of the system might be used in the planning. Failure to coordinate these supporting structures obviously makes the systemic curriculum less efficient; it also causes teachers to rely upon ad hoc adjustments, which may lessen the thoughtfulness and thoroughness of their preparation and presentation.

PERSONNEL

Personnel is a supporting structure for curriculum. Unless it is felt that all teacher components in the system can plan and present curricular materials equally well, there is the problem of determining who among the professional staff are best qualified to conduct particular teaching activities. Both professional and nonprofessional personnel are intimately involved in supporting the curriculum of the system. Particular teachers possess competencies which make them uniquely suited to serve as resource persons or leaders in team teaching units. Clerical and custodial personnel are necessary to assure that paper work is completed and that building space is "set up" for the presentation which the teacher will give.

Not only is the problem of coordination of these people complex but also it must be remembered that these people are all engaged in present tasks while others are being planned. Clearly, it is unrealistic to expect that the needed coordination can be accomplished by anyone in the system other than components with designated responsibilities for coordination.

Since the curriculum of the school system is the medium of exchange in attempting to evoke desired behavioral change in students, all personnel in the system ought to have some understanding of how each human component supports the undertaking. As a particular person senses that he lacks a relationship to the program of the system or feels that his contribution is losing its effectiveness, the system must re-evaluate the tasks and roles of its human components. Changing social and individual needs predict that no system can remain static for very long and still hope to efficiently serve the student population.

FACILITIES

It has often been said that given the choice between good facilities and good teaching; good teaching would unquestionably be the wiser choice. The public school systems in America are fortunate in theat they do not often have to make the choice; most systems possess both. Facilities, do, however, assist or deter the planning and presentation of the curriculum of the school. The word most commonly heard in association with "good" school facilities is *flexibility*. Essentially, flexibility in facilities is valuable to the extent that what is to be presented and the mode of presentation are changing. Since there is no clear understanding of a "best," way to plan for or present the curriculum of the system to students, it might be expected that different arrangements for these activities will continue to be tried. Where the curriculum of the school is set by administrative edict, or where the facilities in which the system is housed are narrowly conceived, the flexibility in use of facilities presents a real challenge to teachers. In this sense the school system which provides a teacher a recitation room with fixed seating is, in fact, prescribing the limits within which he will be able to adapt his presentations to the nature of the material and the particular characteristics of the students groups he will instruct.

The physical facilities of a school system not only provide space in which teaching and learning might take place but they also represent, potentially, part of what may be learned. Learning (hopefully, the acquisition of materials presented which results in desired behavioral change) does not just "take place" in an environment; depending upon the learner, the environment is part of that which has been learned. The physical facilities in which learning has taken place may provide cues for the learner which will prompt his recall. The physical environment may extend the sensory dimensions of what has been learned.

It is the teachers who will finally decide how planning curricular activities is to be accomplished and it is the students who will finally decide how (or whether) they will learn. It therefore behooves the school system to carefully assess the curriculum of the present and what might reasonably be predicted for the future, at the same time providing for facilities which will accommodate the differences among both teachers and students.

Initiating and Refining the Curriculum

Certain elements of what will comprise the curriculum of the school system already exists. It might be said that the broad environment within which the school exists is a "given." From this standpoint, the student selects independently what he will react to (what will prompt his changing behavior), whether or not the school acknowledges or supports the existence of the environment. The school-founded curriculum can only add to, supplement, or explicate the larger natural environment. This phenomenon is probably best evident in the development of curriculums in the primary grades where the materials presented would seem to devolve from the "known world" of the student and then progress to expanding understanding of broader geographic, temporal, and abstract domains.

DEVELOPMENT

Initiation of the curriculum for the school system must take into account what the system has decided is important—particular elements or concepts which the system believes should be included in the curriculum. The system must also take into account what students would seem to be interested in—the aspects of the broad environment which command and deserve their attention and the probing questions they have about "unknowns" in their world. Curriculums which ignore a mature consideration of what ought to be taught tend to result in the presentation of materials which happen to appear in adopted textbooks, materials which have captured the momentary fancy of teachers or materials to which students choose to be responsive at the moment. Conversely, curriculums which are only the embodiment of state syllabuses, systemic adult planning, or the desires of the community patrons may result in presentations which capture little of the imaginations of students. Such curriculums are based only accidentally upon what might be their interests.

All school systems are somewhat trapped by their heritage. Traditionally, certain materials have been taught at particular grade levels, the state has probably "suggested" at least an outline course of study, teachers and patrons in the school-community have developed certain predispositions about the scope and sequence of what should comprise the curriculum, and textbooks which have persisted in adoption through the years have colored these predilections.

If these frailties in the organization of the school system (or, for that matter, any organization of society) can be accepted, then some of the more intriguing possibilities in curriculum initiation might be considered. At the outset it should be conceded that much of what has been taught probably has value and should in some manner continue to be taught.

But of greater importance are the possibilities which exist during the time of initiation. This is a time when not a great deal is known about this relative worth. The inclusion of one concept and the exclusion of another is, in a sense, "up for grabs." This is a time when hard facts and persuasion are employed (and, sometimes in a ratio which is badly out of balance). Mainly, it is a time of excitement because no one really knows but everyone is anxious to find out. It is also a time of danger. It is a time when the contagion of ideas can be confused with that which has been tested and found to be sound. There is the risk that initiating curricular efforts will be swept into and inextricably mixed with other elements of the curriculum which have been carefully tested and refined. This risk is especially great where the exploratory ideas of one system are adopted by another school system—adopted without concern for their appropriateness or feasibility in the system.

CURRICULAR CHANGE

Refining curriculum probably is not nearly as exciting as engaging in initiatory activities. It is, however, essential if the resultant curriculum is to provide the system with concepts for presentation to students which will better evoke the desired behavior. The very necessary tedium of curricular refinement may be one of the principal reasons for so much curriculum regularly offered in the schools being unrelated to systemic goals—often, even internally unrelated, as concept after concept is presented to students in some haphazard manner.

It probably should never be asked "how much" refinement of curriculum is necessary. Viable school systems are constantly at work refining their offerings, although this may require that particular segments of the curriculum remain relatively constant for short periods of time. The act of refinement requires that attention be given to the goals of the system, the presenting components (teachers), and the recipient components (students). The principal assumption is that whatever is being presented to students can be improved and that there is always the possibility that it can be replaced by other material for presentation which might accomplish the task better. The process of refinement probably is best accomplished when evaluative tools are decided upon *before* the first experimental presentations take place. Additional tools may be used as presentation of the material dictates the need for other or more sensitive measures of whether the concepts being presented are meeting the criteria set.

One of the last things to be considered when curricular presentations seem to be failing to meet expectations in terms of student behavioral change is that the teachers presenting the material may not be up to the task. This may be the result of lack of familiarity with the material being presented, the choice of inappropriate modes of presentation, or any one of a host of other variables which may make the efforts of the teacher dysfunctional. It is entirely possible that the curriculum of a particular school system might be "up-graded" beyond the capacity of the professional teaching staff to cope with its presentation in the classroom. Although it usually is recognized (but not always) that students have limits beyond which they cannot reasonably be expected to cope, this same assumption is not often extended to teachers.

A further caution which should be suggested involves guarding against the application of a criterion of refinement which acknowledges that when the teacher comes to feel comfortable in presenting the material and secure in the methods of presentation employed, adequate refinement has taken place. This type of criterion says nothing about impact upon the student; rather what is being measured is the ease which the teacher finds in dealing with the material.

Curriculum refinement must persistently be measured against criteria which test whether what is being done improves the possibility of accomplishing the goals of the system. The implications of what is being done at one grade level or in one course are manifest for many of the other activities being conducted by the system. It is even possible that curricular revision in one discipline may effect only a moderate improvement in the program for that discipline while making a marked contribution to the success potential of what is being done in another discipline or at other grade levels. Initiation and refinement should never be viewed in a lesser context than that of the whole system—and probably that view is too narrow.

The Role of the Specialist

The specialist in curriculum is seen as a professional component in the school system who has particular competencies and skills in *one* discipline or area of the curricular offering of the school. He may feel that his discipline is the most important among the several comprising the curriculum of the system. He often is interested more in what those in other disciplines can do to support his efforts than what he might do to reinforce the efforts of others. Nevertheless, he is an essential component in the total school system.

The specialist is the de facto leader of those who present material in his area of concentration. It is easier to describe this component in the secondary school of the system; however, he also may be a specialist in the common branch subjects in a system where the primary and intermediate grades are taught in self-contained classrooms. The specialist has an expertise in the content of the discipline or grade level. He is not an administrator. His leadership devolves from the fact that in his discipline he is the most knowledgeable person available within the system. His expertise *may* extend beyond content to include an understanding of desirable modes of presentation; however, this need not necessarily be the case.

The specialist is a resource person for other teachers. Although he may be a teacher himself, his principal contribution to the system may be the assistance he is able to provide other teachers who are regularly engaged in teaching. For this reason school systems tend to relieve the specialist from at least some of his teaching load. If he is to be effective he must be free to visit the classrooms of other teachers; to meet, during the day, for purposes of planning; to visit other school systems; to attend conferences and seminars; and generally to be available as his assistance is needed rather than committed to a daily full-load of classroom presentations.

It may be possible to separate specialists into two categories: those who are convinced that what they know is "right" and insist upon supporting this predetermined content, and those who are not at all sure of what is "right" (although they probably have predispositions) and are willing to at least listen to the thinking of others. The latter group might also be typified by a receptivity to experimentation in both curricular offerings and mode of presentation. In some respects, the system itself predicts what will be the character of the curriculum specialist. In school systems where the curriculum is perceived as "closed" the specialist is faced not with making decisions but with continuing to interpret to teachers the decisions which already have been made. In this sense he is less a resource person and more a moderator of what has been decided.

Not only must the specialist be aware of what is "new" in his discipline or at particular grade levels but he must also be in a position to continue to defend those elements in the discipline which he believes should persist in the face of suggested changes. There must be a continuing defense of what is being done unless the line of reasoning is to be, "we will continue this curricular pattern because this is what we have decided to do," or "this is what we have been doing."

The specialist is also confronted with the problem of "what is good for students and for the society at large"—and, especially, for the future of each. His position on what should be offered in a discipline may not be a popular one. His power of persuasion will, in part, predict the success of his desires when the board of education for the system makes decisions regarding what will be the general curricular offering of the school system.

Specialists may come to be seen as prima donnas in the public school system. They have obvious and often narrow vested interests. However, systems which lack these professional components representing the several disciplines also lack the necessary vigor of interchange among disciplines and grade levels which enables wiser decisions to be made for the curriculum of the whole system.

The Role of the Coordinator

The coordinator of curriculum is also a specialist. It might be said that he specializes in being a generalist since his task is to arrange for the operations of professional personnel in the several disciplines and at several grade levels. The coordinator is usually not a content specialist in one of the disciplines offered as part of the curriculum. He may or may not be especially knowledgeable concerning which modes of presentation are particularly useful. He is an administrator. His administrative efforts will predict to a large extent the successful vertical and horizontal articulation of the curriculum.

It is the coordinator who works with specialists, department chairmen, grade chairmen, and teachers (but to a lesser extent with the teachers) in attempting to exact a desirable balance among disciplines in what will be presented to student components in the system. While the discipline or grade level specialist may and probably does do some teaching to maintain his familiarity with both students and the content of his discipline, the coordinator probably has no greater exposure to the regular classroom setting than occasional classroom visitations.

The forte of the coordinator lies with his skill in human relations and a clear understanding of the larger goals of the school system. It is he who must stimulate the initiation of curricular experimentation with a tempering of thoughtful evaluation. As he considers the continuity of the program for a student at any given year in the system, he must also consider the relation of that year in the continuum of those which the student will spend in the public school.

The coordinator, knowing that different students learn at different rates (and, for each student, at different rates depending upon the discipline), must arrange that what is undertaken in one year provides internal reinforcement and at the same time the necessary variety to avoid boredom. He must arrange the curriculum of the system so that there are not significant gaps which might tend to reduce the impact upon students of what has been taught in an earlier year. A glaring example of this problem is evident in systems which engaged in "experimenting" with FLES programs and found that foreign language instruction in the early grades lost much of its impact when there were several intermediate grades in which no language curriculum was offered.

The coordinator is an administrator in the system because he is responsible, in the last analysis, for seeing that the curricular offering of the system is congruent with systemic goals. This is not a matter of persuasion. Although teachers and specialists in particular disciplines may provide strong rationales for their positions, decisions must be made in terms of systemic goals. In this setting it is obvious that the coordinator will not please all the professional components with whom he works. But that is not the point. The system does not exist for the "pleasure" of its employees. What is important is that curricular decisions affecting the entire system be the wisest decisions, so that each discipline which constitutes a subset in the larger system is able to make an important contribution to encouraging desired behavioral change in student components.

The coordinator is, then, a politician. His careful analysis of the professional staff members with whom he works will suggest the different approaches he will use in dealing with these people. The coordinator who is a "win-lose" type of person will probably be grossly dissatisfied with his position since most of the decisions arising from his activities will be compromises. If he is to live with himself he must come to realize that often compromise decisions are really the best decisions. However, where reasonable compromise is not possible or where vested interests threaten movement toward systemic goals, the coordinator has a clear responsibility to the system.

Problems and Issues

1. *How may an educational system provide continuity for its curricular program?* The rate at which teachers enter and leave a school system provides distinct advantages and disadvantages for those responsible for curriculum planning. The curriculum coordinator always finds that the subsystem through which he must facilitate curriculum revision is a dynamic one in that the professional components are almost always in a state of flux. The students refuse to remain immobile while the curriculum reacts with them.

The entire educational system must retain a balance somewhere between a state of immobility which precludes organizational viability and systemic excitation which stimulates movement in all directions at once. Curricular progress should be orderly and well planned. It should proceed with the tasks of educational accomplishment while simultaneously evolving new processes ready to meet new needs before they arrive. Given the dynamic nature of the curriculum planning process, how can continuity be retained?—How shall evolution proceed?—When is revolution justified?—With what community, professional, and student impact?

2. *How should instructional supervision and curriculum decisions be related within the educational system?* Each curriculum decision has an ultimate impact upon instruction. The acquisition of new materials or new procedures for securing audiovisual equipment both have an effect upon the manner in which instruction is facilitated. Instruction is expected to be the professional and end-product of curriculum, just as learning is expected to be the end-product of instruction.

The supervision of instruction, whether by line administrators or staff specialists, proceeds from the assumption that instruction can be changed and improved. However, supervision may also be undertaken for other reasons, including preparation for tenure, dismissal, or promotion decisions. Finally, the community holds expectations that supervision will be accomplished to provide a means for checking on the desirability of the experiences students receive under each and every teacher. Given the task of curriculum planning and execution and the multiple expectations for supervision, how shall they relate?—Who shall determine the relationship?—What roles shall teachers, administrators, and school board members play?

3. *How should the curriculum specialist be used within the system?* The employment of the first curriculum coordinator or the

shift to organizational hierarchy involving department heads with supervisory and curricular functions has a strange impact upon systemic components. When the specialist is employed, he normally assumes some duties and conducts some activities that were previously in the domain of the building principal. When a peer is elevated to a department headship, the teacher often perceives that someone else is being given recognition as a person more competent than he. In either case, the new appointee must carry a potential for psychological conflict with his very appointment.

After initial problems are overcome, the system must provide for the functioning of the specialist. If the system is kept closed, he has no hope for making progress in the instructional program. How can the system meet the specialist's needs?—How can teachers help? —How can he help himself?—What environmental and systemic conditions are most conducive to improving instructional change through a curriculum specialist?

Selected References

Association for Supervision and Curriculum Development. *Research for Curriculum Improvement,* 1957 Yearbook. Washington, D.C.: The Association, 1957.

Bloom, Benjamin S. *Stability and Changes in Human Characteristics.* New York: John Wiley and Sons, 1964.

Cay, Donald F. *Curriculum: Design for Learning.* Indianapolis: Bobbs-Merrill, 1966.

Ford, G. W., and Lawrence Pugno, eds. *The Structure of Knowledge and the Curriculum.* Chicago: Rand, McNally, 1964.

Goodlad, John I. *School Curriculum Reform in the United States.* New York: The Fund for the Advancement of Education, 1964.

Heath, Robert W., ed. *New Curricula.* New York: Harper and Row, 1964.

Peddiwell, J. Abner, *et al. The Saber-Toothed Curriculum.* New York: McGraw-Hill Book Co., 1939.

Pritzkow, Philo. *Dynamics of Curriculum Development.* Englewood Cliffs, N.J.: Prentice-Hall, Inc., 1959.

Stratemeyer, Florence, Harnden Forkner, and Margaret McKim. *Developing a Curriculum for Modern Living.* New York: Teachers College, Columbia University, 1947.

Unruh, Glenys G., ed. *New Curriculum Developments.* Washington, D.C.: Association for Supervision and Curriculum Development, 1965.

chapter 14

■ Policy Development, Interpretation, and Implementation

The Formal Policy of the System

Ideally, the policy of the board of education should represent the best description of systemic goals and the format of the system for their accomplishment. Historically, most policies of the school system have been set at the local district level. The policy-making powers of the local board are, of course, moderated by certain conditions established at higher governmental levels. Federal and state constitutions, regulations of the state commissioner of education, judicial decisions, and statutory law all operate as constraints upon the local board of education. Essentially, these higher authorities mandate what shall or shall not be done. Mandated responsibilities of the board are often described by such words as "the board shall have the *power* to . . . and, it shall be the *duty* of the board to . . ." This means that the board of education can do (it has been given the power) and also it must do (it is required that the duty be performed) those things which are specifically enumerated.

Higher authority also describes for the local board of education certain areas in which there has been given discretionary power—power for the board to act if it should choose to. Beyond specific constraints, the board may exercise its discretion freely so long as it does not violate existing law or regulations. This latter point is crucial when it is considered how extensive are the discretionary powers of the local board of education should it choose to use them. It is this power which permits the board to describe how the local school system will function. The board's description is its formal policy.

The formal policy of the board can evolve two ways. The board can prepare and codify its policy. Or the board can ignore codification of formal policy, in which case the actions of the board as recorded in its official minutes become the formal policy. The latter approach to policy often results from the board not wishing to be restricted in the action it takes. Without codified formal policy, the actions of the board may be frought with inconsistencies, so that neither the board nor other components in the system can consistently predict how the board will act in regard to a particular problem.

Formal policy does not mean that there should be a last and final word. It need not have the character of dictum. It does, however, intend that there be necessary guidelines for those who operate the system as components within it and that the system be described in such a manner that its goals and operations are understandable both to components within and people without the school system.

Good policy is not so specific that it removes the possibility of interpretation by the professional components charged with putting it into practice. Specific direction for the operation of the system is often in the form of rules and regulations developed in the system by professional personnel; these are a logical outgrowth of board policy.

Although the board alone can legally set policy for the school system, there are no restrictions upon the board to limit its seeking the advisement of other components in the system. For that matter, in most school-communities it is expected that policy, whether codified or evident only in the actions of the board, at least be reflective of the community ethic. Frequently friction arises when board policy represents the community ethic at the expense of reasonable concern with the desires of the professional employees within the school system. System-wide policy based only or disproportionately upon nonprofessional advisement refutes the notion that intra-system feedback can enhance desirable policy formulation. Policy which is imposed upon professional components by lay boards of education tends to reduce the productivity of interpretation by professionals and stifles the development of feedback within the system.

A functional advantage of codified formal policy lies with the opportunity to review what have been the prior actions of the board and to involve broadly both the community and systemic components in setting policy which will best facilitate the operation of the school system. Codified policy usually has a provision for the review of present policy in the event that it should become not workable. One criterion for good policy might be that it is clear, yet flexible enough that it need not be frequently altered. Changes in rules and regulations for the system often can avert the need for policy change.

Codified policy for the school system must be based upon an

agreed philosophy—agreed in the sense that the board members concur among themselves that particular philosophical tenets will guide their actions in policy decisions. Even broader than policy, the statement of philosophy describes what the board "believes in." The assumption here is that the board will make policy decisions in terms of what is good for the school system and that its decisions will transcend, hopefully, personal considerations and individual value orientations. The philosophy of the board should set the tone for policy development in the same manner that policy becomes the guideline for operating procedures used in the school system. It might be expected, then, that the description of the system and its operation would be consistent with the stated philosophy for the system.

The stated philosophy for the school system might include reference to the belief that students differ from one another. Board policy might recognize individual differences among students by stating that there shall be sponsored within the school system separate programs for students of varying ability. Regulations of the system might set arbitrary limits to be used in assigning student components to particular groups for activities in the system. Teachers in the system might, then, find it incumbent to devise lessons and assignments which recognize the differing capacities among students. The outcome of a philosophical acceptance that students differ ought to be evident in the classroom where teachers and students are interacting. Clearly, students ought to be engaged in such a way that their differences are acknowledged in the day-to-day operation of the system.

Boards of education will differ in the discrete areas selected for formal policy adoption. Commonly, such areas as bylaws and internal operation of the board, administration, staff and pupil personnel, instructional program, auxiliary services, business management, and school-community relations are outlined with formal policy. It is important, however, that there be policy concerning the several components which comprise the school system. The formal policy not only establishes the range of interaction expected among components in the system but it also sets discretionary limits within which professional personnel may interpret policy. In a sense, formal policy liberates professional employees to use their judgment in making wise decisions for the education of students within the system.

The formal policy of the board of education is important to teachers and administrators for at least one other reason. Board policy, unless it is capricious or arbitrary, has the cloak of law in the system. It is insubordinate for an employee in the system to act in violation of board policy. The board has no legal obligation to inform its employees of existing policy or policy changes. Although a moral responsibility might exist for the board to keep its employees informed, the legal responsibility to become and keep informed falls to each individual employee within the system.

The Informal Policy of the System

The informal policy of the system is probably much more observable than the formal policy. By its very nature, informal policy is not the written policy of the system. It may be, however, the policy by which components operate or behave in the system. Commonly, informal policy is the result of components interpreting formal policy and then translating their interpretation into behavior. Informal policy has a powerful impact upon the system in that where it comes to be agreed upon behavior, it may well supersede formal policy. Where the ethic for behavior within the system comes to be based upon such informal policy, less attention may be given to formal policy, hence the antecedents or first sources of interpretation may become obscure.

Informal policy in the system may develop through two means. The formal policy of the system may be broadly worded with little attendant direction for implementation—there may not be explicit rules and regulations which assist interpretation. Under these circumstances the interpretation of formal policy becomes the informal policy of the system, and it tends to persist and be reinforced to the extent that the board of education chooses to acquiesce in the interpretations made and their resultant behavior by systemic components. Informal policy may also develop within the system as a result of too many rules and regulations that tend to strangle the professional components in their afforts to interpret formal policy. In this case informal policy emerges as behavior designed to circumvent rules and regulations with which professional components disagree or which appear to be dysfunctional for the system. This latter form of development of informal policy presumes that professional components sense a certain uselessness in attempts to alter existing rules and regulations of formal policy.

Plainly, informal policy which emerges as a result of professional components being allowed to interpret policy, rules, and regulations is functional for the public school system only to the extent that the board of education and professional components extend a mutual trust that interpretations made are motivated by a concern for the best interests of the system and the achieving of systemic goals. It is equally obvious that all informal policy is not based upon mutual trust. For that matter, much informal policy may be bred in a system largely as a result of seeking convenience of operation.

The problem here is that convenience is often seen as convenience for an individual or for several components in the system rather than as reflecting an improvement in the operation of the system as a whole. The upshot of behavior which seeks to satisfy individual convenience may be behavior among systemic components which does not best serve the system.

Where informal policy is planned for and fostered in the system it must be expected that the action will not always be consistent. Although this negates the notion of policy per se, informal policy might be construed as the creation of latitude for decision-making by professional components so that individual decisions will be made based upon the merits of each case. This type of informal policy acknowledges the value of professional judgment and suggests that although behavior may be inconsistent, each decision is made with a separate set of facts being considered. While the primary concern remains with systemic goals, it may be *necessary* that individual decisions treat components differentially within the system. Although it may be policy to treat student components equally—to provide equal opportunities—it may be necessary to spend more time with and invest more money in the activities sponsored for some students in order for them to really have a semblance of equal opportunity.

It is important too, to note that informal policy, because it is not really policy at all, has no legal base. Since informal policy grows from interpreting formal policy, the interpreter takes a certain risk in assuming that his decisions fall within the legal intention of the formal policy. Legally, where the board of education for the system sponsors or supports policy interpretation, it is saying that this is first an area of discretionary judgment for the board and secondly that it solicits the interpretation of professional components.

If the public schools are described literally as systems, then there may well be no legitimate rationale for informal policy within each system. The very notion of informal policy suggests that the system has failed to provide adequately for such things as suitable formal policy, workable rules and regulations, descriptions of how systemic components shall interact within the system, and possibly most important, a communications network which would enable components to be sensitive to changing needs and attitudes.

One of the generic elements of a system is that it is operationally predictable; components within the system have specific purposes in terms of systemic goals. The existence of informal policy in the system reduces the predictability of systemic outcomes. Informal policies tend to increase the factor of chance in relationships among components, especially teachers and administrators. Likewise, informal policies may tend to increase the element of chance as a factor determining how well the system serves student components and society in general. However, one advantage remains. Informal policy may facilitate change faster than formal policy and its modification might allow.

Internal and External Communications Networks

Policy for social institutions is representative of that society only to the extent that elements of the societal structure can be heard and are heeded by those who make the policy. The system of public schools is somewhat unique in that it is a lay social institution operated by professional components. Although the broad goals of the society and the professional components within the system are normally congruent, specific objectives for the two groups may widely differ. One task for the board of education of the system is to establish a broad network of communication both within the system and outside it and then to adjudicate the positions of the two groups.

A first step in establishing a communication network is to decide what kind of communication is desired. There is little doubt that certain members of society and societal groups will wish to advise the board of education on all matters. Often, too, professional components will offer advisement which may be only remotely related to their professional role. The board of education for the system may choose to listen to any and all advisement; it may tend to listen only to that advice which comes from power groups (for example, leading citizens or long-tenured teachers); or it may so construct its communication network that recognition is given to the unique capacities of certain groups for particular types of advisement. In fairness to the politics or operating a public school system in society it must be conceded that members of power groups may often possess, by their very membership in such groups, the capacity to wield some control over the board of education. However, the board of education should recognize that communication from professional components in the system regarding such matters as teaching methodology has probably greater credibility than advisement from a lay group on the same topic.

An obvious second step after the board of education has decided what kind of communication it desires to have with particular groups is to begin action to make clear its decision. Two principal avenues are open to the board of education. It can solicit communication from internal and external groups, based upon its decision regarding what the groups have the reasonable capacity to communicate. Also, through its policies, rules, and regulations the board can stipulate areas in which it will assign greater credibility to communication from particular groups.

This filtration plan for board advisement presumes that the decisions of the board of education should be based upon the most competent advisement. It denies that on all matters the voice of every man and any group should carry equivalent weight in influencing the decisions of the board.

It is often said that people who have a hand in deciding policy will tend more to support that policy. Conversely, policy which is imposed will tend to receive greater scrutiny from those on whom it is imposed. Here, the board of education has a real problem. If it shows insight in establishing a sensitive communication network, it will be the regular recipient of a great deal of useful advisement. But, the board must take pains to assure that its advisors understand that they are just that—advisors. Only the board of education for the system can make policy.

Groups which have a strong vested interest in their advisement being communicated to the board of education may become disenchanted in the event that the board decision goes against their advice. Disenchantment may lead to shrinkage in the communication network. Worse yet, the board may find that vested-interest groups will circumvent the board of education in seeking to get their way, or should these groups exist within the system they may choose to ignore the policy decision and operate independently. In the case of vested-interest groups seeking to circumvent the board of education, our system of government provides legal means whereby the action of the board may be set aside. There are also legitimate means by which these groups may press for legislation which might make mandatory the action of the board of education where before the board could exercise its discretion. Chapter 15 will discuss specific instances where states have passed enabling legislation so that certain things may be negotiated between the board and professional components in the system.

Should teachers or administrators within the system choose to ignore a board decision on policy, the board of education is legally obligated to insist upon compliance. Surely, the board might elect to further evaluate the wisdom of its decision (especially since it is a lay board acting on professional advisement) ; however, until the decision is changed, professional components who ignore the decision are operating illegally and, in the minds of the authors, unprofessionally.

The breadth of the board communication network within the system would seem self-evident; it should extend to all components of the system. This would include administrators, teachers, pupils, and all supporting personnel of the system. The external network of communication for the public school system may be less self-evident. Often it is felt that this network is limited to the school-community. It is unlikely that any board of education can make sensitive policy decisions today if it has limited its external communication to the local community. Boards of education must be aware of current thinking at the state, national, and international levels if our society and the needs of its individual members are to be served by the public schools. Possibly the greatest danger lies with the board coming to depend upon most that information and those sources of communication which are most conveniently available. The physical or operational distance between the board and certain sources of communication should not predicate the worth of the information which might be communicated. To the extent that the board of education becomes a "local" board in its communication network, it also becomes insular and provincial. Board policy decisions based upon isolationist advisement may even fail to assure that the school system is assisting the students to live successfully in the local community in future years, to say nothing of his chances in the outside world.

Monitoring Policy Interpretation

A policy decision alone can hardly be expected to evoke uniform change in the operation of the school system. Where the board of education is concerned with feedback—information on behavior—on how policy is being interpreted, it might do well to help in setting the stage for policy interpretation.

The board, with the advisement of professional components, might prepare or endorse an operations manual—a document which translates policy into the behavior expected of administrators in the system. And, in the case of both teachers and administrators, job specifications would outline both tasks and roles expected of these components. Clarifying the behavioral expectations which the board has for those who will carry out its policy reduces the element of chance and lessens the likelihood of differential interpretation when such is not desired. Further, by specifying the interpretation desired and the behavior to be evoked under certain conditions, it establishes, by implication, the areas in which it is expected that professional components will exercise their discretionary judgment. It also acknowledges that the board supports their exercises of this judgment so long as it is not arbitrary or capricious.

The board must clearly establish which policies are to be open for interpretation as opposed to those for which it has prescribed the behavior expected from professional components. Anything less than this clear differentiation is dysfunctional for the board and, ultimately, for the system. There would appear to be little sense in employing professionals in the system if they are to be given little or no discretion in the use of their judgment.

Where expectations for behavior are too fully explicated by the board, teachers and administrators may become complacent; they may decide to do only what is expected of them, thus reducing their potential impact upon the system. Or, where board expectations and the judgment of professional components differ, friction may occur in the system. Where board discretion is extended to professional components, recognizing their capacity for prudent judgment, the board has chosen to "live with" the more frequent occurrence of behavior, which may not always be predictable. While it repudiates the desired predictability of a system, board tolerance for differential behavior—individual interpretation of policy—among teachers and administrators acknowledges the uniqueness of a system operated by professionals.

The board of education must also recognize that there tends to be a proliferation of rules and regulations in the hierarchy of the system. The board may set certain regulations for teachers and administrators, then administrators in the system may add to the list of regulations, so that the teacher, also a professional component, may be hemmed in by rules and regulations more than the board realizes. If discretionary limits are to be functional, it must be assured that they extend to all professional components in the system.

Although the board of education may choose to recognize teachers and administrators as professionals and thus extend to them appropriate discretion, it must be especially cautious in monitoring interpretation of policy not to hastily assess or pass judgment upon behavior exhibited in the use of discretion extended. Such hasty judgment on the part of the board can only connote to teachers and administrators the bad faith in extending discretion and recognizing professional competence. Surely, the board of education for the system must make policy and is legally responsible for how policy is interpreted within the system. However, thoughtful negotiation between the board and professional employees of appropriate areas for discretionary judgment should reduce the need for the board to "watch-dog" the system.

Effecting Policy Change

There is probably not a great deal of difference between what a board might do to generate policy and what it might do to effect change in policy. There is, however, one significant exception.

Where policy has existed, the board has had the opportunity to monitor or observe how effective the policy has been in practice. Where policy has been codified for formal adoption by the board, there is the increased opportunity to observe effectiveness in a systematic manner.

The public school system which has developed good policy will not often need to effect policy change. As has been noted, adjustments for changing needs and conditions within the system can often be resolved through the alteration of rules and regulations. Problems arise when it becomes clear that changes in rules and regulations exceed or deviate too markedly from the policy upon which they are based or when the rationale for existing policy becomes no longer functional for the system. It should also be noted that the perceived need for policy change may emanate from either too loose or too tight a control upon how the policy shall be interpreted within the system. In this case there may, in fact, be little or no need for policy change. What may be needed is a clarification from the board of education concerning the range of interpretation to be encouraged among professional components in the system.

Since the policy of the system is one of the fundamental tenets which will predicate the operation of the system, it is important in policy change to re-evaluate not only what has led to the perceived need for policy change but also the original rationale for the present policy. Simply put, change or alteration in policy should primarily be aimed at improving the operation of the system. Since the public schools are a service system in society, policy for the system has its first obligation to systemic good in general. Policy which favors individual components in the system must be regarded as a secondary consideration. But, even in this there is a logical inconsistency in that students are components in the system and are the principal reason for the existence of public schools. Policy which is good for the system, then, must also ultimately be good for the students in the system.

The rationale for both policy development and policy change must then, be grounded in what is good for students in the system. Unfortunately, too often policy would seem to be the product of pressure from outside the public school system (to hold taxes down, for example) and from within the system (to convenience teachers and administrators, sometimes in manners only peripherally related to the education of students). The student has no adult voice in policy formulation or change. Although the board of education may be most sensitive to the needs of students in the system, the fact remains that it tends to be most responsive to adult pressures in the school-community.

If the rationale for policy is to be based upon student needs—systemic needs—then it must be the choice of adults to exert pressure for action based upon these needs. This is not merely altruism or selflessness if public education is seen as also being an investment in the human capital of the society.

Possibly one reason policy is too little related to students and the goals of the system is that it is difficult to know what is good for students, especially what will be good for them in the future. Somehow it seems easier to set policy which will reduce pressure on the system being exerted by the adult world—pressure which is loud and clear, and often is related more to the adult group than to its children.

Appraising the Outcomes of Policy

The most fundamental outcome of policy is the behavioral change which takes place in students. Since the public school system is a large operation and is probably bureaucratic in structure, there is the constant danger that appraisal will be made of the system in terms of how smoothly the system operates. Smoothness is usually seen in terms of components in the system behaving in such a way that "waves are not made." Where there are no waves, where the system is seen as a "tight ship," appraisal really has been focussed upon the effectiveness of the bureaucratic structure rather than the goals of the system. However, it must be remembered that an effective bureaucracy is not an educational goal; it is rather an organizational objective.

Surely it is easier and more convenient to appraise policy outcomes in terms of fairly finite aspects of the system. Data can be collected which describe the rate of teacher turnover, the incidence of advanced study being undertaken by teacher components, improvement in teacher-student ratios, and the introduction of new curriculums into the system. As important as these data may be to an understanding of the overall effectiveness of the school system, none of these data necessarily point to the efficacy of policy in producing desired behavioral change in students.

Although it may be a human frailty to shy away from attempting to appraise something as nebulous as desired behavioral change in students, the task must be undertaken because this is the principal goal of the school system. Another problem in policy appraisal in terms of student behavioral change may emanate from policy for the school system being quite unrelated to student behavior. The evolution of the policy may have established it as being related more to systemic operation than to systemic goals, assuming that "good" systemic operation will necessarily lead to the accomplishment of desired systemic goals.

The disposition to appraise policy for the system through the use of finite or "hard" data may lead to a condition where present policy is lauded because the data collected and the criteria used in evaluating policy take the form of self-fulfilling hypotheses. As an example, it may be systemic policy to maintain a specific student-teacher ratio, or to strive for a reduction in the ratio. Data may be collected which indicate that the ratio is being maintained or being reduced. So far, the policy is "good" if it is assumed that the ratio set or reducing the ratio is seen as desirable, and this must be conceded; otherwise it is unlikely that the policy would exist. But, in this mode of appraisal what has been done to attest that maintaining a fixed ratio or reducing the ratio has had a desirable impact upon changing student behavior? Nothing. The error is one of assessing whether policy has been carried out rather than assessing the worth of policy in terms of systemic goals.

Since the system really has control over manipulating student activities only while he is in the system, appraisal of policy outcomes must necessarily deal largely with student behavior during that time when the system can still have an impact upon his behavior. Specifically, it must be asked whether policy and its interpretation by professional components in the system are eliciting desired behavioral change. There is a need then to define a developmental scale of behavioral changes which might be anticipated or expected among student components in the system. The scale might be broadly worded, taking into account individual differences and unanticipated events in the environment external to the system which might have an effect upon students. Again, finite measures in such a developmental scale would be the easiest to ascertain (the level of student achievement in particular academic areas might be assessed through appropriate testing). But rather than becoming wholly dependent upon such measures, the scale might include, for example, a number of attitudinal expectancies which are more difficult to observe; the scale of student development might include the expectation that student components evidence a willingness or desire to cope with problems and to consider some of the choices which might lead to their resolution. Although it is extremely difficult to test willingness or desire, such a judgment may well be critically important in assessing systemic policy.

It should be obvious at this point that the board of education cannot sit in judgment of its policy unless it has become keenly aware of what are the behavioral changes taking place among student components in the system. This kind of awareness makes it necessary for professional components in the system to be sensitive to all forms of student behavioral change and that there be some formal channels through which the observations of the teachers and administrators can reach the board.

Although appraisal of systemic policy will take place among professional components all the time—after all, they are carrying out the policy—unless the dispositions of those who are implementing policy are made known to those who are making policy, efforts at realistic appraisal are fruitless. Appraisal of policy outcomes by components at varying levels within the system may lead to policy being seen as having only a relative worth. The worth of a specific policy probably would be established by its congruence with the goals of specific components. Granting that no policy is likely to please equally all components in the system, efforts still should be made to make rational existing policy, at least in terms of systemic goals. There is probably no better time to make policy rational than when it is originally codified or when it is revised.

Revising Policy

Policy revision takes place in the public school system most commonly under one of two conditions. Present policy may come under fire from within the system or from without in the larger school-community. Although less frequent, policy revision may also come about because the school system has chosen to evaluate policy regularly. This kind of evaluation might indicate whether present policy is meeting immediate needs and whether it seems visionary enough to anticipate future directions.

The formality of revising policy, in the legal sense, hardly requires illumination. The board of education for the system is free to form or revise its policy so long as it does not violate higher authority (statutory or constitutional) or is arbitrary or capricious. In a sense, the formal revision of policy serves only to "get on the books" the altered intentions of the board of education. Effecting the policy revision is very much another matter. It is for this very reason that effecting policy change was discussed before appraising outcomes and revision of policy.

Revision of policy signifies a major change in the direction of the system. Again, it should be noted that frequently asked questions can be resolved within the system through the establishment of rules and regulations. It is not the function of policy to ritualize the day-to-day operation of the public school system. Policy sets broad directions and as such might be seen as a liberating rather than as a restricting element for systemic components.

Since policy change or revision signifies a major redirecting of the system, it seems reasonable to suggest that appropriate advisement from many sources might be sought before revision is completed. Remembering that the public school system is a societal institution operated by professional components should suggest the range of advisement which might be considered by the board of education before settling upon revision.

The essence of policy revision within a systemic setting is the extent to which the policy is communicated to the several components within the system. If it is presumed that proper advisement has taken place and that the revision in policy is in keeping with systemic goals, then there ought to be grounds for explicating the revision. This does not mean that policy revision will make sense to all components within the system or to interested parties in the school-community. It will make more sense to some than to others. Its defense in an ultimate sense lies with its relationship to systemic goals. Hence, it may require that individual components subordinate their personal desires and dispositions in favor of more pervasive goals.

The board of education is not really required to justify policy revision, but if it is concerned with implementation of the revised policy, it may well need to assist in creating the climate within the system for acceptance of the policy change. It is too idealistic to assume that advisement from systemic components will assure acceptance of policy change, especially since the advice given will not always be apparent in policy revision. Equally, it is naïve to expect that persons with other or vested interests will accept policy revision in good faith—faith that the board of education has only the highest motives and best intentions. But, in the last analysis, those who fundamentally disagree with a revision in policy must accept it as a matter of faith. This really should not disturb professional components or members of the school-community too much since in our form of government most policy decisions are made by lay groups (legislators and so on) and then implemented for the public welfare by persons with special competencies.

The checks-and-balances control on policy setting and policy revision is exerted by the school-community in its selection of persons to serve on the board of education. It is also exerted by the state through the legislature to the extent that mandated duties are extended to local boards of education. Since boards have discretionary power—policy-making power—only to the extent that they are not limited by law, legislators extend or reduce the range of this power as a function of the faith they have in boards of education to make prudent use of the powers given.

Policy revision, then, and for that matter, policy itself, must, to persist, tread (or waver) between that which has come to be acceptable as a part of the larger heritage within which the school system exists and the best guesses as to what the future will probably hold and demand for youth.

Problems and Issues

1. *How can the board of education develop con*, *unication networks which will assure accurate feedback?* The directions which the school system will take are initially the result of board action. Where this action is thoughtful, it is necessary that the board have recent and precise information. Much of this information is in the form of hard data which are being collected continuously. Other information is "soft." Soft information might include the attitudinal dispositions of components within the system and other people in the school-community.

The board of education is a trustee body for the state, is composed of lay citizens, and does not meet frequently. The problem of communication is enlarged by the fact that data are generated from so many sources. Some persons may choose to go to one of the professional components in the school system, whereas others might contact an individual board member.

Once the board of education has taken action, it is essential that there be a monitoring subsystem so that the impact of the board's action may be assessed. It is through this monitoring process that the board is able to evaluate the effectiveness and worth of its efforts.

How can teachers improve communication within the system?— How does information filter through the system to and from the board of education?—Which components in the system have responsibility for interpreting board policy?—How might the board of education determine whether it is receiving accurate information?

2. *What problems exist in putting into operation the policy of the board of education?* The school system gains viability as operating procedures are devised in keeping with the board's policy. It would be a relatively simple matter if one person were to set the operating procedure and all other components would dutifully follow it. However, such is not the case. It is necessary to recognize that many systemic components are professionals. If the system is fully to profit from its professional components, these people must be given enough discretion in their choice of behavior to insure that they can adjust their behavior patterns and those of their students to meet specific circumstances.

Administrators frequently seek the counsel of teachers and supervisory personnel before they outline operating procedures. Occasionally, the system will even seek the advisement of students—the ultimate recipients of systemic planning.

It is important that board policy be broad enough for professional discretion yet specific enough that its intent will not be lost in interpretation.

What problems exist for the teacher as he attempts to translate operating procedure into student behavioral terms?—What are some specific procedures which should be left to the discretion of individual teachers?—What kinds of information should administrators seek from teachers before operating procedures are established?

3. *How can the system monitor policy enforcement?* Board policy is an extension of both a public trust and a mandate from the public to the professionals in the system to act. Usually, the board has at least a legal if not a moral responsibility to determine whether its policy is serving as a guide for systemic activities.

A major element in the enforcement of policy is the extent to which the board of education trusts its professional components—the administrators and teachers. As there is less trust, the board may attempt to devise policy which requires little interpretation; policy which already has implicit operating procedures. This type of policy is not only demeaning of professionals in the systems but it also removes the chance for teachers and administrators to use their judgment.

Professional components can assist in the resolution of this problem by engaging in frequent reporting to the board. These reports are, in effect, feedback which describe how the staff has translated board policy into specific behaviors.

What kinds of student and teacher behavior might be used as evidence in reporting to the board of education?—What kinds of behavior might be difficult to report?—By what means might the board monitor the enforcement of its policy?—Are there matters of policy for the system which should be left to the professional components?

Selected References

Campbell, Roald F., Luvern L. Cunningham, and Roderick F. McPhee. *The Organization and Control of American Schools.* Columbus, Ohio: Charles F. Merrill Books, Inc., 1965.

Davies, Daniel R., and Elwood L. Prestwood. *Practical School Board Procedures.* New York: Chartwell House Inc., 1953.

Gross, Neal. *Who Runs Our Schools?* New York: John Wiley and Sons, 1958.

Reeves, Charles E. *School Boards, Their Status, Functions and Activi-ties.* Englewood Cliffs, N.J.: Prentice-Hall, Inc., 1954.

Rezny, Arthur A., ed. *Legal Problems of School Boards.* Cincinnati, Ohio: W. H. Anderson Co., 1966.

Smith, Max S., and Ray W. Smittle. *The Board of Education and Educational Policy Development.* Clawson, Mich.: Oakland Education Press, 1954.

Tuttle, Edward. *School Board Leadership in America.* Danville, Ill.: Interstate Printers and Publishers, 1963.

Walton, John. *Administration and Policy-Making in Education.* Balti-more: Johns Hopkins Press, 1959.

chapter 15

■ *Salaries and Negotiations*

School administrators, teachers, and boards of education have always recognized that the education of children is the overriding goal toward which their energy should be primarily directed. As a result, much of every school system's method of operation is reflective of the desires of professionals and lay persons to provide environments most conducive to goal accomplishment. However, not all of a teacher's professional life can be so altruistically oriented. Teachers have the same basic personal needs as any other population segment, and as a result within the educational system there resides potential for noneducational goals to come in conflict. More often than not, the conflict will center around the desire of teachers to achieve professional status and the salaries accompanying that status and the community's desire to obtain the best possible educational program at the least possible cost. When a community fails to see the relationship between quality and its price, the potential for conflict is magnified.

Although the personal concern of teachers may be closely related to salary matters, other conditions of employment are important to them. The number of classes which they can teach, the number of students with which they come in contact during the day, the amount of time provided for professional preparation and conferences, the amount of community support, and other elements within the teaching environment are important to teachers and from time to time provide the rallying points for concerted professional action.

Because large numbers of conservative school districts have traditionally placed monetary costs above the accomplishment of educational goals, teachers have, in the recent past, begun to organize themselves into bargaining units capable of bringing new and additional pressures to bear upon the board of education as the community's representatives. Encouragement to local teachers groups has come from national and state educational associations and from unions who have actively sought teacher membership. Additional support has come from state legislatures who have passed permissive or mandatory legislation to cover the process by which teachers and boards of education shall reach agreement on problems of mutual concern. The potential for conflict is great, and the general area of salaries and negotiations may well become the largest internal force for changing the shape of public education.

Salaries

The most common type of salary schedule employed in school systems at the present is one which employs monetary rewards for additional experience and for improved educational backgrounds. Such a salary schedule is based upon the assumption, subjectively arrived at, that each additional year of experience a teacher brings to the classroom setting is a positive force which makes him better able to accomplish the goals of the system. An additional assumption, subjectively arrived at, involves advanced preparation. It is assumed that a teacher who increases his educational background will have more to give to children, and as a result, salary schedules tend to reflect the assumption by granting increased monetary rewards for advanced preparation.

The total reward in this type of salary schedule, as indicated in Table 15-1 tends to be a summation of a starting salary, fixed by the board of education, plus the additional rewards for added experience (b) and added educational background (a). Thus a teacher's salary at any given point in time could be determined by adding to the starting salary the number of b increments for past years of experience and the number of a increments for each additional year of graduate study.

Historically, boards of education have found the above type of salary schedule convenient to their purpose. The two variable elements a and b could be easily determined and when given a fixed dollar equivalent the administration was prepared to create accurate budgets. Likewise, teachers found it convenient to have their salaries advance on the basis of longevity and academic background, neither of which required a judgment on the part of the board of education or the administrative staff. To boards of education interested in saving dollars, the above type of schedule has an appeal because a change of starting salary is received equally by all persons within the system. Thus a board of education knows

Table 15-1.   Typical Teachers' Salary Schedule

Experience	B.A.	M.A.	M.A. + 30
0	Starting Salary (SS)	$SS + a$	$SS + a$
1	$SS + b$	$SS + b + a$	$SS + b + 2a$
2	$SS + 2b$	$SS + 2b + a$	$SS + 2b + 2a$
3	$SS + 3b$	$SS + 3b + a$	$SS + 3b + 2a$
4	$SS + 4b$	$SS + 4b + a$	$SS + 4b + 2a$
5	$SS + 5b$	$SS + 5b + a$	$SS + 5b + 2a$
6	$SS + 6b$	$SS + 6b + a$	$SS + 6b + 2a$
7	$SS + 7b$	$SS + 7b + a$	$SS + 7b + 2a$
8	$SS + 8b$	$SS + 8b + a$	$SS + 8b + 2a$
9	$SS + 9b$	$SS + 9b + a$	$SS + 9b + 2a$
10	$SS + 10b$	$SS + 10b + a$	$SS + 10b + 2a$

$a =$ dollar award granted for each additional year of graduate study above the bachelor's degree.
$b =$ dollar award granted for each additional year of experience.
With a starting salary of $6,200 plus experience increments (b) of $250 plus additional degree increments (a) of $300, a hypothetical teacher with a Master's degree and six years of experience would receive:

SS	$6,200
$+ 6b$	1,500
$+ a$	300
	$8,000

that a raise in starting salary of $500 for a staff of twenty teachers will require additional resources in the amount of $10,000.

INDEXED SALARIES

Teachers, particularly older ones, have long expressed dissatisfaction with a salary schedule which sees fit to reward persons new to a staff at the same rate received by older, "proven" teachers. The type of salary illustrated in Table 15-1 guarantees that every person regardless of his length of service in the system receives the same additional amounts when starting salaries are increased. Older teachers have maintained, and perhaps rightfully so, that if a salary of $8,000 reflects a worth to the system greater than a salary of $6,000, then any raises in the total salary program should be reflected in the same kinds of proportions. As a result, indexed salary systems have become more and more common. Two kinds of indexed systems have developed—the simple index and the compound index.

In a simple index system, fixed percentages of the starting salary are added to the starting salary. Normally the percentages are added for increased experiences and for improved educational backgrounds as reflected in advanced degrees. The simple index differs from the previous salary schedule in that increments to the starting salary are percentages of that salary instead of fixed dollar amounts. Thus, when a change is made in the starting salary those persons with the most experience and the best academic backgrounds receive larger incremental gains than the younger teachers with less adequate preparation.

Compound indexed salary schedules increase at a rate which compounds for each change in experience or educational background. Table 15-2 illustrates a simple index which calls for dollar increases each year equal to five percent of the starting salary.

Table 15-2. Typical Simple Indexed Teachers' Salary Schedule

Experience	B.A.	M.A.	M.A. + 30
0	Starting Salary (SS)	SS + .05SS	SS + .10SS
1	SS + .05SS	SS + .10SS	SS + .15SS
2	SS + .10SS	SS + .15SS	SS + .20SS
3	SS + .15SS	SS + .20SS	SS + .25SS
4	SS + .20SS	SS + .25SS	SS + .30SS
5	SS + .25SS	SS + .30SS	SS + .35SS
6	SS + .30SS	SS + .35SS	SS + .40SS
7	SS + .35SS	SS + .40SS	SS + .45SS
8	SS + .40SS	SS + .45SS	SS + .50SS
9	SS + .45SS	SS + .50SS	SS + .55SS
10	SS + .50SS	SS + .55SS	SS + .60SS

With a starting salary of $6,200, a hypothetical teacher with six years of experience and a master's degree would receive:

$$
\begin{array}{lr}
SS & \$6,200 \\
+ .35SS & 2,170 \\
\hline
& \$8,370
\end{array}
$$

Similar increases are granted for additional degrees. The salary schedule illustrated in Table 15-3 also assumes a 5 percent increase but in this case the increase is compounded from year to year. The assumption in the compound index illustrated is that the teacher with nine years of experience is 5 percent more effective than the teacher with eight years of experience, and so on. Such an assumption results in a mathematical formula quite different from that of the simple index. Notice that the compounding process for a person with a bachelor's degree and nine years of experience results in an incremental difference of over 10 percent in favor of the compound index over the simple index (.552 v. .45).

It is obvious that the compounded index is advantageous to the teacher because it accelerates the rate at which maximum salaries can be earned. Both the simple and compound index systems are predicated on the same two assumptions discussed for the simple salary schedule illustrated in Table 15-1; namely, both assume that a teacher increases in worth to the employing community from year to year and that each additional graduate degree or its equivalent contributes toward his improved effectiveness.

Table 15-3.   Typical Compounded Index Teachers' Salary Schedule

Experience	B.A.	M.A.	M.A. + 30
0	Starting Salary (SS)	SS + .05SS	SS + .103SS
1	SS + .05SS	SS + .103SS	SS + .158SS
2	SS + .103SS	SS + .158SS	SS + .216SS
3	SS + .158SS	SS + .216SS	SS + .277SS
4	SS + .216SS	SS + .277SS	SS + .341SS
5	SS + .277SS	SS + .341SS	SS + .408SS
6	SS + .341SS	SS + .408SS	SS + .478SS
7	SS + .408SS	SS + .478SS	SS + .552SS
8	SS + .478SS	SS + .552SS	SS + .630SS
9	SS + .552SS	SS + .630SS	SS + .712SS
10	SS + .630SS	SS + .712SS	SS + .797SS

With a starting salary of $6,200, a hypothetical teacher with six years of experience and a Master's degree would receive:

$$
\begin{array}{lr}
SS & \$6,200 \\
+ .408SS & 2,530 \\
\hline
& \$8,730
\end{array}
$$

MERIT SALARIES

Another and far more uncommon method of paying teachers is found in districts employing merit salary programs. In such districts attempts are made to relate the professional contributions of the teacher to the worth of those contributions to the system. Merit salary programs have been singularly unsuccessful in those school districts where boards of education or superintendents have attempted to impose such salary programs upon their teachers. In those systems where professional teachers have been largely involved in the process of determining both the content and the process of the evaluation aspect of the program, merit salary programs have been far more successful.

Systems sucessfully using merit salary programs have found that the process of arriving at the various criteria for judging a teacher's effectiveness has been healthy for the system. Determination of criteria and the development of a process for evaluation require that all components of the system engage in professional dialogues over long periods of time concerning their central purpose. Evaluations of effectiveness are inevitably centered upon performance of duties in a behavioral fashion reflective of professional judgments about the relative merits of such behavior.

Merit salary programs obviously assume that a dollar value can be placed upon human behaviors and that fair and adequate judgments of the behavior can be made. The success of merit salary ventures is much greater in those districts where the system is attempting to *reward* teachers for professional service than it is in systems where the merit provisions are conceived as a means to hold down public expenditures. The capacity of merit programs to stimulate and encourage professional practices is moot.

Negotiations

To this point in the discussion of the manner in which a school district organizes itself to achieve its goals, stress has been laid upon the necessity for establishing harmonious, mutually helpful relationships in terms of goal accomplishment. In the very recent past, however, a new element has entered into the functioning of American public schools which by its very nature focuses upon differences between those charged with governing the affairs of public school systems and the teachers employed within the system. The introduction of the concept of negotiations between the two bodies has temporarily, and perhaps permanently, polarized some components within the system. The acceptance, on the part of teachers' organizations, of the labor-management model has been devisive and has tended to magnify the differences existing between administrators and teachers.

THE CHANGING TEACHER COMPONENT

For years, the teaching staff of American public school systems was composed primarily of persons characterized as "little old ladies" who "dearly love children." Many changes have recently been made within the teaching population: More young men have entered the field of teaching; the average age of teachers has markedly declined; more married women than ever before are engaged in teaching; and all of these changes have resulted in a teaching population much more sensitive to the environmental changes surrounding it. No longer are teachers satisfied with being the lowest paid professional group. No longer are they willing to accept the typical rations doled out by conservative boards of education. No longer will they accept treatment which is perceived as subprofessional. The "group personality" has undergone massive transformation. In many cases, the transformation has been largely bewildering to the public accustomed to the acquiescent "old maid" who so often comprised the teaching corps.

Another factor contributing to the changing behavior being exhibited by teaching groups has resulted from changes in the nature of their work. The past two decades have seen massive strides made in the reduction of the number of small, inefficient school districts. One-room rural schools are disappearing. The consolidation of school districts has resulted in increasing their size and simultaneously increasing the impersonal nature of the operation. Teachers are no longer as easily identified nor are they as subject to the subtle pressures of the local church, the local women's club and the local athletic boosters. Increasing size and its attendant anonymity have made teaching groups more prone to flex their muscles without fear of retribution. The increasing number of states which have adopted tenure laws to protect teachers from the vagaries of unprofessional school boards has also served as a strengthening factor in the bargaining position of the teacher.

The professional environment of the teacher has also undergone massive transformation. Within the past decade, increased competition has arisen between the teacher groups represented in the National Education Association and the American Federation of Teachers. The union organization, the AFT, has enjoyed great success in the major cities across the country. Their success has in no small measure been related to their capacity to achieve the kinds of economic objectives which teachers have long sought. Teachers within metropolitan areas could not help but observe the effectiveness of the bargaining done by the union organizations. The National Education Association, cognizant of the inroads made by the unions and the appeal which union successes were having for members of the teaching profession, elected to introduce corresponding pressure tactics in order to survive.

The struggle between the National Education Association and the teacher unions has largely centered over the organization of local teacher bargaining units. Competition within the local environment has done much to encourage the teacher to engage in intersystem political behavior undreamed of ten years ago. Terms like collective bargaining, strikes, sanctions, and professional negotiations were not common to the teacher's vocabulary prior to the onset of the movement.

Both of the organizations committed to representing teachers' groups have launched massive information campaigns which have stirred the desire on the part of teachers to change their lot. The economic injustices between various wage earning groups is constantly pointed out, and teachers find themselves with increasing hours of work, increasingly long school years, increasing requirements for summer study, and increasing economic demands brought about by families living in an affluent society. Simultaneously, teachers are made aware that the growth of their financial capacities is not keeping pace with those of other groups.

THE CHANGING BOARD OF EDUCATION

Just as teachers and groups of teachers have undergone transformation as a result of new thinking about their economic and professional status, so have boards of education been forced to undergo an analysis of the role which they are to play in the operation of public school systems. Boards in states where professional negotiations are underway find themselves bewildered when teachers are no longer automatically accepting the kinds of salaries and fringe benefits being offered to them. As with the teaching groups, the increasing size of public school systems has also changed the political ground rules for school boards. The kinds of pressures which were effective when the teacher was a neighbor are found to be no longer effective when the teacher lives and teaches in another community.

The board of education also finds itself in a position of being responsible for financing a public school system from tax receipts. Following World War II, the rate at which tax requirements at state and local levels have increased has been phenomenal. As a result, boards of education find themselves representing a community very much concerned with operating educational systems at the lowest possible cost. Such a goal is obviously antagonistic to the goals of teachers seeking better and better salaries.

THE NATURE OF THE PRESSURES

The pressure upon local boards of education being fostered in an era of professional negotiations varies widely from state to state. In some states, such as Michigan, boards of education are *required* to participate in bargaining with agents determined by the teachers. Bargaining must be in good faith on terms of salary and working conditions. Both Michigan and Connecticut statutes require that upon request of either party, written agreements shall be executed. In other states, Alaska and Wisconsin, for example, boards of education may enter into bargaining agreements with the local teachers' organization. Finally, in North Carolina, Texas, and Virginia, for example, it is illegal for boards of education to enter into bargaining agreements with any organization of public employees. States in the last category, are finding pressures from state and national teacher's organizations to change the restrictive laws and to ultimately permit and perhaps require that collective bargaining take place.

The nature of the typical teacher's individual contract is important in the strategy which teacher's groups sometimes employ with boards of education. Most teachers' contracts expire in the spring. If such contracts are not renewed under conditions acceptable to the teachers, they may refuse to enter into the contract. As a result, with the opening of school in September teachers may be without contracts and as such may elect not to begin the school year in their professional roles. Boards of education have little recourse because the teachers are neither striking nor breaking a contract in force. Thus, the element of time has been used by teacher bargaining units to increase the attention being made to their demands. In some states, tenure with attendant *continuing* contracts may pose different legal problems. Boards of education find that pressures to enter into contractual agreements with teachers increase as the opening day of school draws nigh.

The local school community is also a source of very real and abiding pressure upon boards of education. Communities are bewildered and confused with the antagonistic behaviors exhibited by teachers who had been docile for many years. Many communities have failed to accept the realities of the times, which are dictating that the power of the teaching profession shall be increasingly felt throughout the public school systems. In some communities, more than bewilderment has resulted. Because most school districts are fiscally dependent upon tax referendums, monies to finance new contractual agreements must be voted for by the population at large. As a result, some communities have had the opportunity to vote down the fiscal resources required to finance contracts which exceeded the desire of a community to pay for educational services.

In many cases, boards of education have been able to finance demands made upon them by the teachers' bargaining unit through reallocating the financial resources available to them. Thus, with a fixed income, boards of education have found it possible to redistribute the expenditure of that income so as to meet the financial demands of the teaching group. Such a change in expenditure is normally done at the expense of some noneducational program or through reducing the expenditures allocated for various kinds of equipment and supplies. In other communities, the newly available federal funds have provided a cushion for boards to help defray the cost of programs being negotiated by the bargaining units. Boards of education have also found other new pressures. In those states where negotiating agreements have operated under the aegis of labor legislation, boards of education have found themselves responsible for conducting bargaining in good faith. Reluctant boards of education who have attempted to delay the progress of the negotiations movement have sometimes been charged either in the courts or by labor mediation boards with unfair labor practices. Such orders may represent new pressures upon boards of education which have removed the boards from the rather isolated roles they once played.

Another kind of pressure has also been developed by the National Education Association. When local boards of education, or indeed even state educational agencies, have refused to create conditions of employment deemed as professional by the local membership, the national agency has been invited to investigate the operant conditions. When investigation has upheld the contention of the local teachers group, a sanction has been placed upon the local or state educational agency. Through the sanctioning process the national association has informed its membership that conditions in the district or state under consideration have proved to be particularly antagonistic as teachers have attempted to make their voices heard.

THE DEVELOPING PROCESS

Although much of the process by which the bargaining act is undertaken is governed by law, much of the process will simply evolve as a modification of the labor management bargaining model. If bargaining is to take place, an initiating step is usually the organizing of eligible membership into a unit empowered to represent the total group. In many cases, this determination is made as a result of an election which may pit several competing organizing bodies against each other. As a rule, boards of education are not required to bargain with more than one unit and both groups seem to prefer that a single organization be chosen by the teachers to represent their particular organization. Once it is established who shall represent the teachers in the bargaining process, some operational guidelines are normally determined. The first order of business between the bargaining parties is to determine representation. Obviously, a teaching staff of 1,000 teachers cannot all be chosen as the bargainers. Similarly, boards of education have, therefore, often turned to members of their executive staff of administrators and to legal counselors to serve as their representatives at the bargaining table. After the bargainers have been determined, it is logical to take the next sequential step to establish an agenda of meetings to show the location and times of bargaining sessions.

At the first of these bargaining meetings, ground rules must be established concerning the items which are to be considered as legitimate for negotiation. In some cases, state law makes this step unnecessary for statutes may be in existence which instruct the employer and the employee as to the legitimate items to be bargained. Most often disagreement comes over a definition of the common labor term, "conditions of employment." In some states, rulings by state labor mediation boards and by the courts may have established a working definition of conditions of employment. In other states where such specific instructions are missing, the bargainers will be required in their early sessions to establish a discussion agenda. The agenda becomes quite important in the determination of the final contract, and professional negotiators recognize that, regardless of how tempting, it is usually wise to stay with the agreed-upon topics and to resist the temptation to introduce new items for negotiations particularly late in the negotiating process. The introduction of new topics to an agenda is sometimes interpreted as bad faith in establishing the original docket.

Also, early in the process, procedural rules must be established. Just as organizations have bylaws governing the manner in which they shall be governed, so should bargaining units have an understanding about the methods in which the two parties may get their wishes and desires before the other and about how they shall engage in resolving the differences. One of the major items of a final contract is provision for resolving differences. Such rules for resolution must be well known and accepted by both groups in order that stalemates can be avoided.

After all of the above ground rules have been determined, both of the bargaining bodies are free, under rules previously established, to present their requests for changes in contract before the bargainers representing the other group. There may be a simultaneous exchange of requests, in which case the bargaining process is likely to be instituted through agreement upon items of relatively minor conflict. Normal bargaining procedures result in delaying resolution of the greatest conflict until rather late in the process.

PATTERNS OF NEGOTIATIONS

Many patterns of negotiations have emerged. However, it is quite clear that neither the board of education nor the organization representing the teachers of the system should attempt to influence the choice of negotiators for the other group. Each must be free to elect, select, or appoint specific individuals to the bargaining team. The ground rules may spell out the number of negotiators to represent each of the groups, but it should not attempt to determine the method for selecting the representatives. Such should remain an individual prerogative of the board of education and the teachers' organization.

In larger school districts, boards of education have seen fit to employ professional negotiators to represent their interests at the bargaining table. In some cases, this has been a team of individuals; in others, negotiators have been chosen on an ad hoc basis to lead the board's team, which may be composed of other administrators or board members within the system. Assistant superintendents in charge of personnel have often been included in the teams representing boards of education. Teachers' organizations have normally found their negotiators within their own organization or have received assistance from the state and national units of the organization representing the teacher's group.

In only the smallest school districts have boards of education themselves seen fit to engage in the negotiating process. Lawyers have often been employed by both boards of education and groups of teachers to participate in the bargaining process. While legal aid has proven invaluable in the development of final contracts and in explaining the legal requirements of the bargaining act, lawyers have not brought an educational expertise to the table nor have they represented the concern for accomplishing educational goals and objectives that the other bargainers bring to the negotiating sessions.

When boards of education have elected to serve as their own bargaining unit in negotiating sessions with teachers, they have often been embarrassed by their inability to retreat from a position which might have been hastily taken. Bargainers who represent the teachers can make agreements in a negotiating session and have the agreements reversed by their constituency, who may refuse to ratify the negotiated contract. When such a reversal of the position taken by the teachers' negotiators takes place, there is no reflection on the part of the negotiators concerning the good faith which they showed in the bargaining process. However, should a board of education, meeting as a whole, in a negotiating session agree to the resolution of a conflict, their recourse is not so simple. They have no superordinate body to ratify the contract. As a result, a change in thinking which resulted in a reversal of the position taken could be interpreted as not bargaining in good faith. It is precisely for this reason that boards of corporations have remained aloof from the bargaining process between labor and management. When management representatives who bargain at the table in good faith return to the corporation board for approval, the board can consider the conflict resolutions away from the glaring lights of the bargaining table. Thus, by not serving as a whole, the board's position remains similar to that enjoyed by the teachers at large, who retain the right to ratify or accept the conditions negotiated in the bargaining process.

Negotiations and Systematic Changes

The labor-management bargaining model so often emulated by teachers and boards of education generally accepts that the persons in the baragining session are antagonists. Acceptance of the adversary roles is an almost sure guarantee that inner system turmoil will be increased. Only in those systems where bargaining has been accomplished under an aura of mutual respect have boards of education and teaching groups managed to survive the negotiating process without irreparable scars. Those districts have largely been capable of recognizing the differences between fundamental roles to be played by educational systems and the lesser roles which complement them. When major goals related to the education of student populations have superseded both the teachers' desires to accomplish economic goals and the community's desire to keep the cost of education at the lowest possible level, then negotiations have proceeded in a fashion which has retained the respect of both parties, with each recognizing the unique contributions the other continually makes toward the accomplishment of systemic goals.

To the contrary, those systems which have permitted relations between boards of education and teachers to deteriorate long before the institution of negotiations have done nothing except solidify the schism existing between boards and faculties. No hope exists of improving such situations so long as the basic goals of the two bargaining units are basically in conflict with each other—increased salaries and improved working conditions which are expensive to institute versus low cost and no tax increases for the community.

Much concern has been expressed and much ink expended in books and journals directed at superintendents about the role they should play in the negotiating process. It is suggested here that the most appropriate role for the superintendent takes place long before negotiations become a reality within a local district. His most important role is to establish a history of respected working relationships between boards and faculties which can serve as a basis for mutual trust and understanding when the negotiating process comes to his community. This role requires that he provide for extensive interaction between his board and his faculty and that he seek every opportunity to place each in a good light with the other. Boards and faculties which work together to solve mutual problems are likely to develop working relationships which can be carried forward in the same fashion under the guise and title of negotiations.

After negotiations come to his community, the role of the superintendent of schools has not yet been clearly defined. In some communities the superintendent has served as the board's negotiator in representing the interests of the board and the community in sessions with the teacher representatives. In other cases, the superintendent has attempted to remain aloof from the negotiating process and has served as an adivsor to both sides. While this role may be sought by those superintendents not wishing to "get involved," they are likely to be suspect by the teachers group, regardless of their attempts to remain as the "professional neutrals." In still other communities, the superintendent has attempted to play the role of arbitrator by participating in negotiating sessions and by attempting to help both sides with the resolution of conflict.

Perhaps it is too early to establish modal patterns for the roles of superintendents within negotiating procedures. Indeed, even after a long period of experience, no single role may emerge. Several patterns may still be accepted. It may be that the superintendent becomes the source of perspective needed by both negotiating parties; he may serve to stimulate discussion around the most appropriate means for accomplishing the goals of the enterprise. Such a role would require that the superintendent assist both boards of education, who are attempting to save money, and teachers, who are attempting to get increases in salaries, to remember that the reason for the systems initiation and continuance revolves around neither of the two demands represented by the opposing sides, but rather the system exists for the accomplishing of other goals against which both kinds of demands must continually be weighed.

The negotiating process has some very distinct potential impacts upon the systemic environment. The negotiating process is likely to disturb both the political and the economic environments of the system. When the disturbance is too great, a reaction can be expected to be precipitated. One such political and economic reaction which a community may take is a refusal to fund an overaggressive program which teachers have succeeded in pressuring through the negotiating process. Because teachers are unable to negotiate directly with persons who hold the power to finance public education, such a danger is indeed a reality. As a result, negotiations may move from the local to the state level. It is distinctly possible that, should communities refuse to finance negotiated contracts at the local level, teachers' organizations may move to the state level for the negotiation of improved state financing. With representative government normally operating at the state level, teachers' organizations may be capable of bypassing a referendum of all people and may succeed in improving the financial lot through increased state appropriations to local school districts.

No single factor will change the operating characteristics of American public school systems during the coming decades more than the outcomes of professional negotiations across the entire United States. Teachers' organizations have become restive and in many cases are seeking redress for perceived injustices at the hands of penurious boards of education. When such a perception exists, organized action can be expected. The degree to which the professional teacher, the professional administrator, and the lay boards of education can open communication lines built upon mutual respect will be reflected in the amount of harmony or conflict with which the system must wrestle in the years to come.

Problems and Issues

1. *How shall teachers be paid?* To many professionals, who earn their livelihood by the setting of fees, salary questions refer only to the size of the fees rather than to the manner in which they are determined. To the teacher, however, who serves as an employee within a local school system, a different type of financial relationship exists. Over a period of several hundred years the relationship has developed a great deal of inertia as communities have determined how and how much to pay their teachers, and teachers have generally accepted the manner and amount of payment or else they moved on to seek a better-paying position.

However, no longer are teachers automatically accepting community pronouncements concerning their financial worth. They have become more and more restive in seeking patterns of remuneration more reflective of their own concept of professionalism. Perhaps more than any other single factor, teachers have sought objectivism. They have wished to remain free of the subjective judgments of supervisors and employers. They have permitted the manner of their payment to be subjectively arrived at but not the amounts. Given the various assumptions underlying the typical teacher's salary program, how should starting salaries be determined?—How should increments paid for years of longevity or changes in academic backgrounds be determined?—Should differentiations exist among job titles?—How should those amounts be determined?—Under what conditions could merit salary programs be more universally applied?

2. *By what means should teachers advance professionalism?* The process of negotiating professionalism is a new phenomenon. Teachers have sought attainment of their professional perceptions through means designed to be more effective than the historical "sit-and-wait" philosophy, which provided only for evolutionary changes at a period in history when revolution among the teaching profession was being sought.

It has been suggested that the manner in which teachers are employed makes them somewhat different from other professionals. That very difference also provides teachers with the opportunities to apply unique kinds of pressures to seek their professional ends. The demand for tenure has been one such pressure which other professional groups have not found it necessary to secure. Organizations of teachers have turned to the tactic of sanctions and have sought to promote professional negotiations as a legitimate means whereby teachers would seek to bring change to their operating system.

In a few states, teachers have attempted to advance this professional status through the enactment of professional practices acts. These pieces of legislation have attempted to describe what constitutes professional status among the teaching corps. The relationship of license to behavior is also enumerated. Thus the teachers operating under professional practices acts have an additional tool for "policing" the professional activities of their peers. In advancing professional status, what is the role of tenure?—Is the need for the protection of tenure a function of the teacher personality?—Are sanctions and negotiations "professional"?—How should the profession be "policed"?

3. *How can a professional climate be retained in the presence of the antagonistic pressures of the bargaining table?* Those engaged in negotiations recognize the antagonism which can arise at the bargaining table. When the employees' representative says, "May I have—?", and the representative of the employer says, "Yes, you may," no bargaining is required. Bargaining is required only at the point when the employer says, "No." The spirit of bargaining stems only from antagonistic positions.

There may be a very real tendency on the part of both bargainers to respond with an automatic "No" to requests during the period from one contract to the next. The automatic "No" is used by many bargainers to improve their bargaining position at the time of the next contract talks. When bargaining is in effect within a local system, can anything other than differences be bargained?—What impact does the prebargaining climate have upon the negotiations? —Should the climate determine the nature of the bargaining representatives?—Is the bargaining process necessary for professionalism or is it antithetical?

Selected References

Allen, Roy, and John Schmid, eds. *Collective Negotiations and Educational Administration.* Fayetteville, Ark.: University of Arkansas and U.C.E.A., 1966.

American Association of School Administrator. *School Administrators View Professional Negotiations.* Washington, D.C.: AASA, 1966.

Lieberman, Myron, and Michael Moskow. *Collective Negotiations for Teachers.* Chicago: Rand, McNally, 1966.

Ohm, R. E., and O. D. Johns, eds. *Negotiations in the Schools.* Norman, Okla.: University of Oklahoma, 1965.

Steffenson, James. *Teachers Negotiate with their School Boards.* Washington, D.C.: United States Office of Education, 1964.

Stinnett, T. M., Jack Kleinmann, and Martha Ware. *Professional Negotiation in Public Education.* New York: Macmillan, 1966.

chapter 16

■ *Financing School Systems*

Today's educational programs have gone far beyond the stage of having a teacher seated at one end of the log with his student at the other end. Community expectations and educational goals accepted by professionals as appropriate to the direction of their enterprise have increased in complexity. With each new increase has come altered demands for new facilities, more and better-trained teachers, improved learning environments, increasingly complex educational media, and other physical requirements —all of which have contributed to making American public education an expensive capital investment.

In many cases, verbalization of desirable goals has proven to be far easier than the financing of them. As an example, both society and the profession expect that every child shall be taught to read, to write, and to make simple arithmetic computations. Such a simple-sounding goal for so many millions of people has required that American public schools involve more persons than any other single enterprise. The teachers required to accomplish this goal and the materials and facilities required to supplement their instruction place continuous strain upon tax resources. Acceptance of lesser goals would undoubtedly involve a simultaneous reduction in the amount of resources required to finance their accomplishment. However, society has generally preferred pursuit of the higher goal even at greater financial expense.

Variations in goal acceptance by communities is reflected in variations in their willingness to support specific educational programs. Those communities which accept low-level goals tend to provide low-level support; those that accept high-level goals tend to provide high-level support. The preceding generalization is sometimes untrue in districts that, for one reason or another, find themselves without the financial resources adequate to finance their educational expectations. In such communities, one normally can find that the community has levied taxes for educational purposes far out of proportion to their neighboring districts. Differentiation in the effort which such districts put forth is certainly evidence of a differentiation in their desire to accomplish the high-level goals they set for their public schools.

The responsibility for collecting the financial resources required of a public school system is legally vested with the board of education. As a matter of operational procedure, boards of education normally delegate to the superintendent of schools the responsibility for establishing financial need, for developing an educational budget, and for supervising the financial affairs of the system after the resources have been gathered. In many school districts, the board of education retains close supervision over the manner in which resources are obtained. Other agents within the total process include the community of taxpayers, the employees within the school districts, the state legislative and educational authorities, and the federal government. The roles of each are discussed later in the chapter.

Financial Strategy

LOCAL STRATEGY

At the local level the financial strategy of a school system is relatively simple. The school system is concerned with locating and collecting sufficient financial resources to permit it to move forward toward goal accomplishment. This strategy includes the development of a plan to enlist the assistance of those agents external to the system who have the capacity to make the financial plan a reality. Normally, the agents are school district taxpayers. Taxpayers, through their behaviors in annual tax referendums are capable of transposing educational and financial plans into facts or fancies. In school districts dependent upon agents other than the voting taxpayer, allocation boards, boards of alderman, city councils, and like agencies may have a role in determining the success of the local district in accomplishing its financial objectives. In every case, agents within the school system, normally the board of education and the superintendent of schools, accept responsibility for informing the external agents about educational plans and financial requirements and, when necessary, for persuading those agents to lend support to the financial needs of the system.

Developmental plans for local districts must include both short- and long-range fiscal requirements. Knowledge of immediate plans for retaining or for changing existing educational programs requires that annual revenues be provided to meet the expenses thus incurred. Because educational goals are seldom conceived on an annual basis, long-range planning must also be laid to insure that resources will be available at the time a need becomes apparent. When such needs are unlikely to be met from local sources, the local strategy must include a plan for securing the additional funds from nonlocal sources. It is on this basis that much educational lobbying is done in state legislatures across the country.

Another element within a long-range fiscal plan developed by a local school district is that of district expansion. At a time in history when a general population expansion is apparent, local school districts across the land are concerned with their capacity to develop facilities and to staff programs sufficient to meet the needs of expanding populations. Districts with a tax base that is increasing at a rate slower than student enrollments must become concerned with improved strategies for securing educational funds from nonlocal sources.

Figure 16-1 indicates that financial planning involves a consideration of local goals, resources, and needs as well as external resources. The output of the planning process is a local financial strategy designed to make local fiscal requirements a reality.

STATE STRATEGY

Although states across the country have verbalized their acceptance of the principle that education is a function of the state, the states have not fully accepted the responsibility for financing edu-

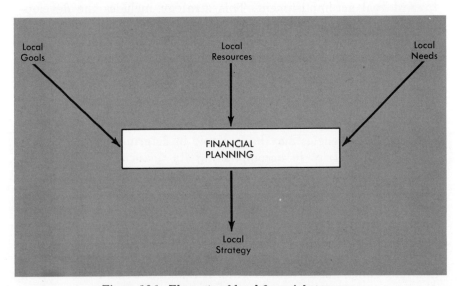

Figure 16-1. Elements of local financial strategy.

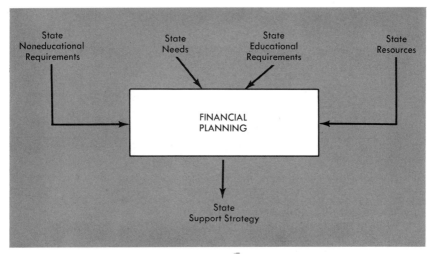

Figure 16-2. Elements of state financial strategy.

cational programs. As late as 1965, the average of state support was approximately 39 percent of local expenditures. Thus, local communities have been forced to raise approximately 60 percent of their needed income from sources other than state. In only fourteen of the fifty states did the state's revenue source supply as much as 50 percent of the total educational costs experienced by the local districts.[1]

The elements of a state support strategy are not too dissimilar from those used to develop a local financial plan. Figure 16-2 illustrates the four major elements considered by state agencies in developing their support strategies. These include state noneducational requirements, needs, educational requirements, and resources. The financial planning which results from a consideration of those four elements has as its output the state support strategy.

Even though a state spent all of its financial resources for eduction, few states would be capable of completely financing their public education with current revenues. In most states, the expenses incurred for education represent more than 50 percent of expenditures. Thus, states spend more than half of their revenue for education and yet supply only about 40 percent of the total money spent on education.

Development of the state support strategy must inevitably consider such noneducational requirements as highways, mental health institutions, recreational facilities, cost incurred in administering the affairs of state, and a host of other such expenses. Each of the noneducational expenses is reflective of programs of interest to people throughout the state. As a result, strong forces are at work

[1] *National NEA Research Bulletin.* XLIV (February 1966), p. 13.

to insure that the state develops an equitable spending plan based upon the needs of noneducational as well as educational agencies.

A second element in the state support strategy is a consideration of the needs of the state. Assessments by state boards of education and state superintendents of public instruction focus attention upon elements of the state's educational program which are in need of development or revision. Changes in manpower requirements, as an example, often result in the institution of new statewide educational programs. Likewise, demographic and sociological information often provide stimuli to the development of stated needs requiring educational attention. The stimulation of new programs is often accomplished through financial incentives provided through special legislation and funded from the state treasury.

The third element in the state support strategy is concerned with the diversity of educational needs which the state is required to meet. States supply support in various forms to educational agencies other than public school systems. In addition, various kinds of interests and noneducational needs within public school systems have been met by specified appropriations from the state legislature. Examples of some of a state's other educational considerations are aid to institutions of higher education, aid to county boards of education and intermediate school districts, aid to specialized vocational education programs, aid for the transportation of school pupils, and subsidization of school lunch programs. Each of the above programs requires that finances be allocated to their support and each of the allocations diminishes the funds available for the support of the general educational programs within public school systems.

The final element considered in the determination of the state support strategy is concerned with state financial resources. In the consideration of statewide resources, financial planning inevitably involves consideration of (1) the source of revenues available, and (2) the manner of revenue distribution.

The majority of monies available at state levels for the support of public education come from income taxes and taxes on the sale of goods and services. The most serious problems have arisen in states where statewide obligations and the subsequent requests for funds have risen at a rate faster than the capacity of the existing tax structure to provide the required funds. Such states have often resorted to supplementing the revenues from existing tax sources with temporary or "nuisance" taxes.

When financial resources come from a patchwork taxing program, fiscal reform is a difficult procedure to accomplish and as a result support for public education tends to be dependent upon a multitude of differing tax sources. The regressive and progressive characteristics of sales and income taxes are well known by the political parties, and fiscal reformation inevitably takes on partisan political overtones. Thus it is within this political framework that the state support strategy must be developed.

In considering statewide financial resources in the process of financial planning, consideration is given to the distribution of funds as well as to the source of funds. The manner in which funds are distributed among the various school systems of the state is reflective of the educational and political philosophy of the state. One educational-political concept which has been accepted in many states is that of equalization.

The equalization of educational opportunities through financial incentives has several dimensions. The first dimension is reflected in differentiated educational programs, supported by the state, that are designed to provide appropriate experiences to children whose backgrounds and capacities deviate grossly from that of the general population. States have attempted to equalize the educational opportunities of these children through the provision of "stimulation funds" to encourage school districts to adopt specialized educational programs to meet their needs. Thus the equalization is attempted on a compensatory basis for atypical children of many kinds.

A second kind of equalization attempts to make the tax burden borne by citizens of the state more equitable. In addition to equalizing the valuations on which local property taxes are assessed, the state concerns itself with equalizing, at least to some degree, the minimum funds available for the support of educational programs of all children within the state. Thus provisions are made within the state support strategy for supplying additional funds to those school districts which are deprived of adequate resources because of unfortunate local conditions. Formulas by which states attempt to equalize the amount of money available to support educational programs vary greatly from state to state. In most cases the distribution formulas give consideration to local wealth, the rate at which local wealth is assessed, and the actual dollars being raised within the local community for the support of public education.

Distribution formulas inevitably require additional taxes to be levied within wealthy school districts for subsequent distribution to the poor districts. More politically palatable state distribution formulas often show "flat grants" to local school districts made on the basis of the number of children being educated within that district and without regard for the capacity of that district to support public education. Thus, state support systems often show a flat grant and an equalization formula. Changes in the equalization formula are often accompanied by changes in the flat grants in order that all school districts will receive some benefit from the distribution of additional revenues. When only the equalization portion of state aid programs is revised, political support is often lacking from those geographic areas within the state that would have to provide the revenues to poorer districts. Thus, the concept of equalization must be considered as both educational and political.

The Budget Process

To the layman concerned with making ends meet, the term *budget* normally connotes the idea of a spending plan. Many unenlightened school boards and superintendents also conceive the educational budget in these terms. In a conservative district, where a board of education is committed to saving the taxpayers money, practical operation consists of establishing the income to be derived from current revenue sources at current rates of taxation, and then subdividing that revenue among the various subsystems requiring financial assistance. The overriding consideration in such districts is not what educational plan is to be financed but rather how to divide the money currently at hand. In those districts, the budget is indeed a spending plan.

In more enlightened school districts, the budget serves a far different purpose. It is, in fact, the document which translates educational plans and educational programs into monetary terms. The budget will express those program commitments recommended by professional staffs and approved by boards of education as requisite to the accomplishment of long-range goals. Budgets which reiterate the educational goals of a school district and express the educational plans and programs for their accomplishment are capable then of directing attention to the immediate, annual objectives to be financed during a future period. In this manner, educational expenditures carry an educational justification.

The budget document also serves the chief executive officer of the educational system as he attempts to execute the policy decisions of his governing board. It provides the same general guidelines that adopted school board policy provides and should permit latitude in choice of expenditures. The annual educational plan cannot be static, and as a result the spending plan must similarly have some flexibility to accommodate extemporaneous and emergency variations within the educational plan. Thus, the budget is conceived as a flexible document offering general guidelines to the financing of educational programs.

The budget process consists of three distinct steps: (1) budget preparation, (2) discussion and approval, and (3) budget management. The first of the sequential steps has its genesis in curriculum processes. No document designed to do what the budget will do would be complete without an assessment of both long-range and short-range educational plans needing financing. Program determination is, therefore, the first step in budget preparation (Figure 16-3).

Figure 16-3. The budget process.

Preparation	Program Determination Cost Translation Cost Evaluation
Approval	Discussion Formal Action
Management	Acquisition Utilization

PROGRAM DETERMINATION

The determination of educational programs to be financed on both short- and long-range bases is not essentially a financial planning activity but rather it is the end-product of curriculum evaluation. Program determination, as the first step in budget preparation must utilize the outputs of curriculum evaluation as its primary documents. Often, however, the curriculum documents in and of themselves are insufficient to meet the various requirements of budget preparation. Curricular evaluations are likely to be couched in terms of student learning and student activities; they are likely to be limited to an assessment of the degree to which the activity has succeeded in meeting the educational goals and objectives set for it. Later in the budget preparation process, it will be noted that the curricular activities, to serve as complete budget preparation documents, need translation into financial terms.

However, during the initial stages of budget preparation, program determination must be based primarily upon the educational values of the programs under consideration rather than their financial implications. Thus, program determination consists of assessing each and every curricular program offered throughout the school system to determine which are to be continued, which are to be revised, and which are to be abolished. As an actuality, evaluation of curricular programs for budgetary purposes is likely to be focussed upon new programs, experimental programs, and those programs receiving support for major revisions. As a matter of fact, those curricular activities which have proven over long periods of time to be adequate and goal-producing are likely to receive only a perfunctory examination as far as the budget process is concerned. Programs which will carry new or expanded price tags are likely to be those which receive the greatest scrutiny, from both a curricular and financial standpoint, during the period of budget preparation.

In the early stages of budget preparation, the main concern is with the selection of programs rather than the cost of the programs. Following an examination and an assessment of the various educational programs to be offered during the upcoming budget period, three tasks, in the program determination process, remain. First, the priority order of the various educational programs must be established. It seems important to initially determine the priority on the basis of educational potential and accomplishment rather than on financial costs. There are programs which school districts obviously cannot afford to have; but on the other hand, there also may be programs so educationally potent that school districts can ill-afford not to have them. It is precisely these latter programs for which the development of priorities is so important.

Following the determination of priorities for various educational programs, it is essential that consideration be given to both the sequence and the timing of their introduction. Development of sequence and timing plans are often more related to the development of long-range budgets than they are to those of the annual budget. Nevertheless, plans must be made for introducing the second stage and third stage when second and third stages are appropriate to programs being introduced in sequential order.

Finally, timing is also appropriate to consider. There may be those programs which school districts must have, as a part of long-range development plans, but which may legitimately be delayed. Legitimacy may be related to the outcomes of experimental and pilot programs or to the introduction of intermediate programs within a sequence.

Cost Translation

Once a determination has been made of the educational program to be financed, that program must be translated into financial terms. Such is the function of the cost translation process. Cost accounting procedures can be used to determine the actual cost of programs previously introduced. Such cost accounted figures can also serve as legitimate bases for generalizing about the potential costs of new and related programs. The history of program costs is likely to be the most important single source of information upon which projections can be made of the costs of other educational programs. In estimating new program costs, four financial projections are normally made: personnel requirements, equipment and supplies, facilities, and operational overhead.

Projection of personnel requirements is accomplished by assessing both the quality and quantity of persons required to accomplish the educational program. Quantity questions, in terms of how much manpower is required, are normally much easier to answer than the quality questions. However, the quality questions must be asked and answered because of their financial implications. If a program requires experienced teachers, the cost will be different from that of a program which may employ inexperienced teachers. If persons with specialized training are required, such as television engineers or laboratory technicians, the level of skill sought in these persons will be reflected in monetary terms. Once the quality and quantity questions have been answered and the "going rate" determined, personnel requirements can be translated into monetary costs.

Equipment and supplies required for new programs must be determined. When similar equipment and supplies have been purchased for other programs, cost estimates can be made quite accurately. When no similar materials have been purchased, quotations and cost estimates are received from suppliers in order that reasonable determinations can be made. For estimation purposes, the long-term relationships which have developed between business manager and school suppliers serve to make the estimation of equipment and supplies a relatively rapid and accurate process.

In those few cases where changes in educational program require changes in facilities, additional cost determinations must be made. If facilities are to be altered, bids and quotations are normally received. When new facilities are required, sketches and drawings may be required from architects and estimates may be received from building contractors. When the expenditures are large in size, a separate process for the securing of bonds may be required.

The last item normally involved in the translation process is operational overhead. Programs being housed in school facilities require that the classroom or other learning environment be heated, lighted, cleaned, repaired, and insured. Prorated costs based upon educational space are not difficult to obtain in those school districts where adequate records are maintained.

COST EVALUATION

The final step in budget preparation is cost evaluation. Once figures have been received from the translation process, a crucial and often painful assessment must be made of the educational value of existing or projected curricular programs in relation to their estimated costs. In a few favored school districts, the cost implications of educational programs are hardly given a second thought. However, in most districts economic reality requires that the financial implications of expanded educational programs be given serious examination.

One of the major kinds of evaluations normally undertaken involves the comparison of one program against another. If the best educational programs carried the smallest price tags, the problem would indeed be quite simple. The problem gets compounded when better educational programs carry higher financial costs. In such a circumstance the evaluation of one program against the other must consider the educational priorities assigned to programs in the program determination process as well as the sequence recommended at that time.

A second phase of program cost evaluation involves relating revenues to program costs. The impact of the introduction of a new curricular program on the financial resources of the district must be assessed. Consideration is normally given to current revenues as well as to any expected changes. Both local and outside sources of revenues must be considered in evaluating the relevance of a program to the financial capacity of the district to support it. The evaluation process also is concerned with assessing the willingness of a community to extend itself financially for a program of great educational merit.

When a new program of high merit is proposed and the evaluation process discloses the degree of strain it will place on the resources of the system, a final kind of evaluation must take place. Past programs must be analyzed to determine the desirability of abolishing or revising them to release their resources for the new program. Such an analysis must inevitably be made in dollar terms as well as goal accomplishment terms. High cost programs found to be contributing little to goal accomplishment are prime targets for abolishment or revision as the administrator seeks new ways of financing potentially good educational programs.

Budget Approval

The process of approving the budget document is one involving discussion and final action. It is the responsibility of the board of education to study the budget document as developed and presented by its executive officer and, in most states, to provide the means for the general public to examine the proposed educational and spending plan. The board must rely heavily upon the recommendations, particularly educational recommendations, made by the superintendent of schools, the heads of various programs, and the various operations chiefs.

From these persons, boards of education become acquainted with the rationale for the recommendation of various educational programs and for the various changes appearing in the financial spending plan. Program heads, responsible for developing educational plans, are likely to be good sources of information about the goal expectations held for proposed programs and the adequacy of existing programs, as recommended for continuation in the budget, for goal accomplishment. Operations chiefs, such as cafeteria managers, heads of transportation systems, and the directors of building maintenance are likely to be excellent sources for assessing the adequacy of prior budget allocations to meet the operational needs of the system.

Program heads, operation chiefs, the superintendent, and other administrators are also responsible for evaluating the effectiveness of previous budgetary decisions. In the area of personnel, as an example, the superintendent of schools must be ready to discuss the success of new employees. The quantity and quality of educational and professional personnel employed to operate the school system must be evaluated. Similarly, the impact of introduced programs upon student personnel can be assessed by program heads. Operations chiefs need to be ready with recommendations concerning changes in supplies and equipment and in the procurement of material.

The final adoption process varies from state to state and from district to district within states. In many states the board of education may, in and of itself, approve the budget, revise it, and ultimately adopt it without the necessity of any formal action by the community at large. In other states, formalized budget hearings must be announced and held to satisfy the conditions of the laws operating within those states. In still other states, the budget is presented at a meeting open to the general public with adoption coming as a result of formal action taken by all persons attending the meeting who are of legal voting age. As indicated earlier, should a budget require the securing of additional local resources, most states should make provisions for the voting public to pass upon any new taxing proposal. Regardless of the state requirements, it seems politic for local boards of education to announce budget discussions, to hold discussions concerning the budget in open meetings of the board, and to make adoption of the budget a formal action at such an open meeting.

Budget Management

ACQUISITION

In the process of translating educational programs into monetary costs, the cost and sources of various materials, supplies, equipment, and facilities were identified. Persons responsible for heading approved educational programs make normal requests through a business office, indicating their desire that particular kinds of material be obtained. When the cost is quite large, business offices may, as a matter of fact or as a matter of legal requirement, secure bids from suppliers to determine the cost–quality relationships available. Operations chiefs are also responsible for ordering their needed materials in time for delivery prior to the crisis point. The process normally includes the submission of a requisition which serves as the initiating document to the business office. Following requisition submission, specification development, and the obtaining of bids, when required, the responsible business official prepares purchase orders for submission to suppliers. Purchase orders serve as requests for delivery of specific materials at a given cost and guarantee payment when delivery is made of merchandise meeting the specifications outlined on the purchase order document. Upon delivery and receipt of bills, the business manager is responsible for payment and for recording the purchase in accounts as required by law. Bills as paid normally constitute a monthly item on a board of education meeting agenda.

While the business manager is largely responsible for the acquisition of various kinds of materials, supplies, and equipment, the superintendent of schools is normally responsible for obtaining professional personnel required by program changes. Procedures utilized in the procurement of professional personnel have been outlined in Chapter 11. The procurement of nonprofessional personnel may be a responsibility of the superintendent and/or various program and operations chiefs. In many school districts, the business manager is responsible for the employment and ultimate supervision of nonprofessional personnel. Transportation chiefs, cafeteria heads, and maintenance directors are commonly involved in nonprofessional procurement.

As indicated earlier, the budget document is not conceived strictly as a spending plan. As a result, many items required on a day-to-day operational basis do not have specific reference within the budget document. It is the responsibility of the superintendent of schools to make appropriate decisions concerning the desirability of securing nonbudgeted items. His decisions are subject to review by his board of education; only the most mechanistic and legalistic superintendent would consider his budget document as the exact and final word on all purchases to be made within his school system.

UTILIZATION

The acquisition of both material and personnel is not the only task to be accomplished in budget management. Feedback systems must be developed which determine the ultimate effectiveness of personnel and material in accomplishing those program elements for which they were designed and secured. Various kinds of quality checks are designed to evaluate their effectiveness. For nonpersonnel items, the use of an annual inventory is a common procedure. Inventory records provide useful information about the life of products and about the manner of their utilization. Subjective evaluations are also made concerning the effectiveness of material to contribute to goal accomplishment.

The utilization of human resources is a more difficult problem. However, with 70–80 percent of the normal school budget assigned to personnel costs, it seems imperative that the effectiveness of personnel contributions to goal accomplishment also be measured. Reference is again made to Chapter 11.

A summary of the responsibilities which various persons hold in the budget process follows:

Responsible Agents	*Tasks*
Professional Staff	1. Program Determination
	2. Utilization Effectiveness
	3. Cost Evaluation
Superintendent	1. Document Preparation
	2. Acquisition of Professional Personnel
	3. Cost Evaluation
	4. Program Determination
Business Staff	1. Cost Translation
	2. Acquisition
	3. Utilization Records
Board of Education	1. Discussion
	2. Approval
	3. Cost Evaluation

Problems and Issues

1. *How can a purchased item best be evaluated to determine its comparative curricular effectiveness (textbooks, for example)?* In a manufacturing system a comparison of the introduction of a particular new machine or new configuration of men and equipment can be evaluated rather easily. Goals for such a system would normally involve turning out a product at a faster rate, at lower cost, or of better quality. Each of the three desired ends can be objectively determined by mathematical and experimental means. Such is not the case in a system such as education where the ends are not objectively determined.

The education profession has been conditioned to experimentation as a means of satisfactorily answering questions of comparative effectiveness. One method versus another serves as the basis for much experimentation. Experimentation, however, cannot be accomplished for all of the multitude of items purchased by a school system during any given year. Classes and their needs change, and the physical means for comparison are normally missing; for example, frequently only one set of textbooks may be purchased rather than two different sets. In view of the problems involved in testing effectiveness, how should it be determined which products to test?—Who should determine the testing procedure?—Who should perform the tests?—How can effectiveness be related to systemic goals?—How should costs be related to effectiveness?

2. *On what bases should equalization be accomplished?* At various times, many kinds of equalization have been proposed—federal, state, county. In each case, proponents and opponents have soon been identified, usually on the basis of the impact of equalization upon their particular system. In those districts profiting from an increase in resources via the equalization process, support has usually been vigorous. In districts whose resources would be siphoned away to provide for the less fortunate, support has usually not been overwhelming.

The manner and impact of equalization have also been a concern to school systems. When an equalization type of aid has been proposed for states not complying with federal statutes, normally civil rights, resistance has come from many quarters. When increased funds made available through equalization processes have been used to reduce local tax rates rather than to increase the money available for supporting the system, those supplying the funds have been particularly upset to find their own tax efforts are already greater than that of those who have done the reducing.

Yet another controversy arises over the distribution of state funds. In some states, monies collected through an income tax are distributed to local communities. Controversy arises over whether the money should be distributed on the basis of where the wage-earner lives or on the basis of where the wages are earned. In metropolitan areas with the surrounding suburbs, this issue is exceedingly important because of the large amounts of money earned in the central city and the large number of wage-earners who live in the suburbs. Given the large number of problems surrounding the equalization issue, how should equalization be accomplished?—What political issues are involved?—What economic issues?—What ethical issues?

3. *What role should teachers play in encouraging financial support from their local community?* Teachers have not been excited about the prospect of improving the financial resources available to their system through participation in local fund-raising

activities. In many cases, teachers have become concerned only with financial support when more dollars were needed to finance their own salary program. Such a vested interest often led to bad relations between the community and the professional teacher.

On the other hand, the advent of negotiations and collective bargaining often has resulted in the teacher's refusal to participate further in fund-raising activities. In the process of negotiating contracts, many teachers' groups have left their boards of education with the problem of rallying financial support without the aid of the teaching corps. Given their role within the system, what impact might teachers have in fund-raising activities?—How actively should they support tax rate and bond proposals?—Should their role be different when resources are being required for salary and when required for other financial obligations?

Selected References

Barr, W. Monfort. *American Public School Finance.* New York: American Book Co., 1960.

Blum, Virgil. *Freedom in Education-Federal Aid for All Children.* Garden City, N.Y.: Doubleday and Co., 1965.

Committee for Economic Development. *Paying for Better Public Schools.* New York: The Committee, 1959.

Corbally, John E., Jr. *School Finance.* Boston: Allyn and Bacon, 1962.

Freeman, Roger. *School Needs in the Decade Ahead.* Washington, D.C.: Institute for Social Science Research, 1958.

Freeman, Roger. *Taxes for the Schools.* Washington, D.C.: Institute for Social Science Research, 1960.

Johns, Roe, and Edgar Morphet. *Financing the Public Schools.* Englewood Cliffs, N.J.: Prentice-Hall, 1960.

Jones, Howard. *Financing Public Elementary and Secondary Education.* New York: Center for Applied Research in Education, 1966.

Mort, Paul, and Walter Reusser. *Public School Finance.* N.Y.: McGraw-Hill Book Co., 1951.

Roe, William. *School Business Management.* New York: McGraw-Hill Book Co., 1961.

chapter 17

■ Planning the School Plant

Although the end product may vary considerably from other structures, the process of planning an educational facility differs little from that used with facilities that house other kinds of activities. A well-planned building, regardless of its function, is a spatial expression of a conceptualization about the most appropriate housing for its required activities. Differences in building reflect differences in functions. Thus, space utilization within a hospital or a hotel or a school building varies one from the other on the basis of the needs being served.

The planning of most educational space is concerned with the activities conducted by personnel utilizing that space. So it is in the hotel and hospital analogy. No operational system designed to aid a hotel to function efficiently would be complete if the hotel consisted only of rooms to house and refresh the traveler. Laundries, eating facilities, and business space are only three of the tangential activities of a hotel system. In the hospital analogy the operating rooms and patient care centers must be supplemented by such spaces as business offices, food preparation centers, and housing for emergency vehicles. In all cases, concern is exhibited for the kinds of tasks which must be undertaken by persons in the conduct of their role as system components. The composite of roles and activities to be housed serve as the master plan for constructing appropriate space.

Thus, the planning of an educational structure must take into account the various kinds of educational and noneducational activities engaged in by the personnel of the system in pursuit of systemic goals. It would obviously be expected that educational facilities would consist of large numbers of spaces to be devoted to instruction. However, there are other components of the system besides teachers and students. As a result, educational facilities contain such "noneducational space" as offices, bus garages, cafeterias, and boiler rooms. Planners of educational facilities must be concerned, therefore, not only with the space to be used in pursuit of primary goals but they must also concern themselves with adequately housing those auxiliary services.

Many features of current school designs are the result of curricular changes. For example, changes in philosophy about the most appropriate kinds of language instruction have resulted in language laboratories. Science laboratories at the secondary level and gymnasiums at the elementary level are two other examples of special facilities which have resulted from changes in thinking about what constitutes appropriate educational programs.

Establishing Need for Educational Facilities

The stimulation to construct new buildings may proceed from the deterioration of existing ones. After a period of 50 to 100 years even the best-constructed school building is likely to be deteriorating, not only in its capacity to house new educational programs but also in a very physical sense. Some buildings simply "wear out."

The necessity to construct a new facility may also come from curricular requirements. Should a school district or a state agency elect to make changes in the educational requirements imposed upon children, the impositions may carry demands for new kinds of educational space. As an example, a statewide requirement that physical education or art should be taught daily to all elementary school pupils would result in the construction of large numbers of gymnasiums and special art rooms. Because of the rapid changes in both elementary and secondary school curriculums, following World War II, additional attention has been paid by school plant planners to the inclusion of "flexible space." Observation of new spatial requirements resulting from the introduction of new curricular elements, has been followed by attempts on the part of planners to include spaces in buildings capable of adaptation from one curricular use to another. The success of the designer in creating flexible space will largely determine the number of years which the facility can adequately house its educational activities.

The consolidation process during the past decade is another factor in the need for new facilities. When four small school districts, each with its own high school, are consolidated, it is unlikely that any one of the four buildings will be capable of housing the influx of new students coming from the other three. As a result, the consolidation process is often followed by the construction of school buildings. Annexations and reorganizations of other kinds are also stimulators to the construction of new facilities.

Changes in land use, particularly in metropolitan areas, may also have impact on the necessity to provide additional schools. When land usage and the related zoning are changed from single-family dwelling units to apartment buildings or other types of multiple housing, the number of persons to be served within a given area is likely to increase. Similarly, changes of land use from agriculture to family dwellings also creates an influx of new persons, who must be housed within the school system.

Additional pressures for the construction of new facilities may come from patterns of migration. For example, recent population shifts from the south to the northern city have had large consequences for the planners of facilities in those metropolitan areas receiving the brunt of the migration. The different ethnic, religious, or racial characteristics of the migrants have been reflected in family size and in the number of school children for which accommodations must be made.

The growth rate of the general population is yet another factor which has impact upon the facilities plans of educational system. Wartime, postwar, and depression periods and periods of high or low employment have all influenced the size of families in the United States. The rate at which families have children is ultimately reflected in the school building requirements faced by systems within affected areas.

QUANTIFICATION OF NEED

One of the more vexing problems facing executive officers of the school boards is the preparation of recommendations for the construction of new facilities. Recommendations are inevitably based upon estimations of the need to replace, to renovate, or to construct new facilities, and estimations in districts where school populations are rapidly changing are subject to so much error that the estimates are hazardous indeed. The committed school board that desires to have adequate educational facilities available for students must start the planning process a long time prior to the anticipated population changes.

In an effort to reduce the hazards involved in the school plant planning process, several methods of estimating future school enrollments have been developed. Of these methods, the simplest is to chart the past enrollment histories of the district and to extend the scope of the graph forward to future years. Obviously this estimation method offers no opportunity to incorporate knowledge of such hard data as changes in the rate of in-migration, changes in the birth rate, or changes in the percentage of the total population attending parochial or private schools. Secondarily, few educational administrators, charged with developing future enrollment projections, would find it easy to mathematically determine the slope of the projection. A mathematical error of only a few degrees can mean an educational error for many children.

A second method used to estimate the future enrollments involves the determination of a pupil/population ratio. The number of students is divided by the population of the school district. The administrator can then take projections of population, and by applying the pupil/population ratio to the projected population can determine an estimate of future student enrollments. Such a technique is predicated upon the assumption that the number of pupils from a given population will remain constant in future years, and that the population forecasts are accurate. Changes in the ethnic or religious makeup of a community and changes in the birth rate could upset such a ratio.

A third method commonly used for estimation purposes is based upon the percentage of students surviving a particular academic milestone. With this method, projections for elementary schools, for example, can be prepared by recording the percentage change in enrollments over a past period in history, converting that percentage change into an average rate of change, and applying the average change in an annual fashion to current enrollments. In mathematical terms, this method differs little from a slope extension, except that it does help the mathematically unsophisticated administrator to place the elements of the projection into rather simple mathematical formulas.

Another method used to estimate enrollments derives from the determination of a ratio of pupils to home units. From annual census data, the number of homes within a district is established and by dividing the number by the school enrollments, a ratio of children attending public schools from each home can be determined. Information is then sought on the number of new homes projected within the district over a given period of time and the ratio applied to that figure. The obvious disadvantage of this method of projection is the difficulty in getting sufficient data about potential new homes or apartments to be constructed. The critical assumption is that the ratio of children/home will be fairly constant.

Each of the four common methods of projecting school enrollments leaves much to be desired. Each requires that some subjective judgments, some educated guesses, and some basic assumptions be made concerning the input data. The "kind of community" being served by a school system and the changes taking place therein will largely determine the adequacy of a given formula to accurately project the number of children to be housed within the district. The application of the various formulas to historical data has provided administrators with the opportunity to determine which method is most accurate for projecting future enrollments within the type of community served by their district. History proves to be a powerful ally in the projection process.

The Planning Process

The process of converting an established need into a physical structure capable of housing an educational program is an exceedingly complex process. It involves utilizing the time and talents of professional educators, boards of education, architects, contractors and other persons allied with the building trades. Figure 17-1 outlines the various kinds of activities engaged in during the school plant planning process. For the sake of convenience in studying the process, a distinction has been made between those operations carried on within the educational system and those conducted by agents or agencies outside of the control of the system.

INTERNAL OPERATIONS

The launching of school building plans is normally accomplished by studying the space requirements of the system. The processes alluded to in the discussion on determination of need is appropriate at this early stage in the process. The study activities also involve an assessment of the capacity of the school system to finance a school building program. If bonds are required in the financing process, then the system's position within constitutional limits must also be analyzed. The study process normally culminates in a decision about the desirability to construct specific kinds of educational space.

Once the decision has been reached to proceed with the planning and construction of a new educational facility, appropriate administrative officers are charged with developing appropriate strategies. One element is a time table for accomplishing the various tasks. The superintendent is concerned with determining the points at which (1) architects should be employed, (2) bids and estimates received, (3) bonds secured, (4) contracts let, and (5) the building occupied. It is his responsibility to program the various elements of this strategy so that the building will be ready for occupancy at the appropriate time. He is in charge of rallying resources in and out of the system to the accomplishment of the task.

Not only must a strategy be developed, but the professional staff should engage in developing educational specifications. An architect is employed to convert the educational plans of the school district into educational space. Without discussions between educator and architect, the school district will receive only the types of educa-

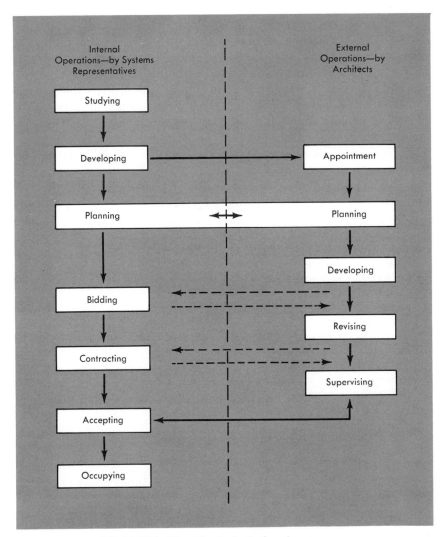

Figure 17-1. The school plant planning process.

tional space as conceived by the architect as appropriate to serving the ends of the district. Educational specifications serve as the initiating document to a lengthy dialogue between educator and architect as the latter engages in his part of the planning process.

Educational specifications must inform the architect about the kinds, number, and amount of spaces required and the kinds of activities to be housed within them. Normally the specifications will include a brief statement of the purpose of the educational program to be housed, the activities to be engaged in during the pursuit of that program, and information concerning special requirements which might be overlooked by a noneducator.

In many school districts, the development of educational specifications serves as the first step in a rather extensive review of curricular offerings. No specifications are complete without an evaluation of the kinds of experiences being planned for children. Normal ongoing curricular evaluations are helpful in the process of preparing educational specifications, but they are usually incomplete in terms of defining relationships between activities and spaces which house them.

Following is one page of a set of educational specifications prepared for the Bloomfield Hills, Mich., School District.[1]

Language Arts

General Remarks:
The language arts program is basically college preparatory in nature. Emphasis is placed on grammar, spoken and written composition, etc. Research is an important part of the program. Provide for excellent ventilation, lighting and sound control. Chalkboard and tackboard in this room should be interchangeable.

Activities:
Viewing slides, films.
Listening to recordings or broadcasts.
Recording voices of individual or groups of pupils.
Writing or drawing at desks or tables.
Writing or drawing at chalkboard.
Teacher-pupil conferences.
Displaying pupil's projects.
Debate.
Panel discussions.

Teaching-Learning Spaces	*Sq. Ft.*	*Remarks*
4	800	

Locate in house.† Direct access to building corridor. Convenient access to other language arts rooms, library, large group instruction space, seminar rooms, little theater, speech and drama area, language laboratory.

Provide space for: 25 students at study-top desks, project center with 30″ × 60″ table and 6 chairs, teacher's desk and chair, movable platform 6″ high and 15′ line × 80″.

Provide: 30 lineal feet of chalkboard and 8 lineal ft. of tackboard for each teaching-learning space, means for hanging pictures, storage for: (a) teachers' personal clothing

[1] Richard L. Featherstone and Donald J. Leu, *Educational Specifications for the New Bloomfield Hills Senior High School.* Unpublished material, June 1965, p. 28.
† Refers to manner of school organization in Bloomfield Hills.

and professional books (30 volumes) (b)
300 volumes resource books (locked-adjust-
able shelving), (c) wall display area. Light
control to "dim out" room, four file drawers
(legal size).

As indicated, similar information must be prepared for noneducational space. Below is a sample of information to the architect,
from the same report, designed to aid him in the process of planning transportation and parking facilities.[2]

It is anticipated that approximately thirty per cent of the pupils may
drive private automobiles to school. In addition, some provision shall be
made for large crowds in attendance at cultural and competitive events.
Further, some sixty per cent of the pupils will be bussed to school (at the
opening of the building as high as ninety per cent may be bussed). The
Board requests that the architects obtain the help of the proper officials
(city, county and state) in the planning of ingress and egress from the
parking areas to and from the appropriate city, county and state roads.
Further, that:
1. Faculty parking be separate from student parking.
2. School bus and auto entrances be separated.
3. The large parking area be designed to service multiple programs,
   including driver training and school bus parking.
4. Temporary tennis courts constitute a part of the parking lot (4
   units).

The developing portion of the process also includes the employment of an architect to work with the board of education in planning the required facilities. Conversations are conducted with other
school officials, with the architect, and visits are normally made to
school buildings planned by the architects being considered. When
the board of education reaches agreement about the capacity of an
architect to serve its ends, contractual documents are prepared and
the architect employed.

Planning is the first stage of the total process which involves
both internal and external operations. For the board of education,
the major planning item remaining for their attention is the financing of land acquisition and construction costs. Because the process
of obtaining money by bonding is long and cumbersome, the
strategy developed in earlier stages will have financial planning as
a high priority item. The process of getting financial support is a
function of the board of education, but they are ill-equipped to
make judgments about the specific quantity of monies required to
accomplish their tasks. As a result, the architect's planning process
begins with a study of the educational specifications and the pro-

[2] *Ibid.,* p. 23.

duction of preliminary sketches and drawings which attempt to conceptualize the kinds of spaces required to house the activities alluded to in the specifications. (In many cases, architects are employed only after preliminary sketches have been received from several competing firms.) The production of preliminary drawings involves the development of plans showing the relationship of one space to another, the size of the facility required, and special features which might be of consequence in the process of estimating costs. Cost may be estimated in a number of ways: a board may rely upon cost estimates made by the architect; the architect may submit preliminary drawings to contractors for the receipt of estimates; or the preliminary sketches may be compared with recent school buildings constructed in the area.

With preliminary sketches and cost estimates in hand, the board of education can proceed with developing plans for financing the project. In accordance with the laws of the state, the board of education will place before the people a proposal for the membership of the district to bond itself for the purpose of raising monies to construct an educational facility similar to that represented in the sketches. Following approval by qualified voters, and upon the sale of bonds to interested financial houses, the board is free to proceed with the construction process.

The heart of the joint-planning portion of the process is the educational specifications. They serve as the core of conversations between the school system and the architect. Analysis of preliminary sketches is done on the basis of the degree to which the architect accomplished the most appropriate housing of educational activities and the degree to which he was capable of reflecting spatial relationships sought by the school system. During the preparation of his preliminary drawings, the architect makes continual reference to the specifications and seeks to design a structure which provides the fewest number of conflicts between the various features requested.

Following the joint-planning conferences, the preparation of preliminary drawings, the receipt of estimates, and the securing of financial support, the architect is commissioned to prepare working drawings. As he develops the plans, he receives specialized help from others external to the system. The architect receives aid from various mechanical engineers who assist him in the planning of heating, plumbing, and electrical subsystems. The outputs of these developmental activities are sets of drawings capable of guiding contractors and a set of building specifications which outline in detail the kind and quality of materials to be used in the construction of the building. The drawings are necessary not only for the construction stage but also for the bidding stage.

Bidding is initiated by contractors upon receipt of plans and specifications from the architect. The architect serves as an advisor to the board as it seeks to determine which contractors are to be invited to participate in the bidding process. Advertisement of the board's desire to secure bids is a normal legal requirement. A contractor's capacity to comply with drawings and specifications and to complete buildings on or before deadline dates and his financial responsibility are factors considered by the architects in making recommendations. Except in rather unusual circumstances, boards of education are normally committed to award the contract to the lowest of the responsible bidders.

If bids are received in amounts larger than the financial resources which have been raised to cover expenses, the board of education faces a crisis of no small magnitude. Revisions are obviously in order. These are undertaken in conference with the architect. When bids are only slightly more than the bonds available, revisions can often be made in the specifications which lower the quality of material, while retaining safety features, which seem relatively unrelated to educational programs. As an example, schools planning ceramic tile in a gymnasium might find a painted cinder-block wall adequate for their educational purpose at quite a savings in cost. On the other hand, when bids are well over the amounts of money available rather major revisions are often required. Actual portions of the buildings as planned may have to be abolished, with the result that decisions concerning the priority values are made. It should be noted that in many states major revisions in plans as submitted to contractors require that the bidding process be initiated a second time, based upon revised drawings and specifications.

If sufficient monies were available to meet the bids, or if the revising process has been completed, boards of education enter into contracts for the construction of the facility. Contracting with a construction firm requires formal action on the part of the board of education, with such action taking place in an open meeting. The contract enumerates the responsibilities of the board of education, the architect, and the builder as each plays his respective role during the construction stage. Penalties for late completion and bonuses for early completion are sometimes features of the contracts.

Throughout the period of construction the architect supervises. Most contracts make the architect largely responsible for insuring that the plans and construction specifications are adhered to in every detail. A representative of the architect's office should be at the site during every phase of construction. In some systems, largely those far removed from the architect's headquarters, school systems employ a "clerk-of-the-works" to represent them and their interest in securing a structure which measures up to contractual expectations.

When the building is completed, the architect normally certifies that the contractor has fulfilled his responsibilities. The board of education or its representative then makes a final inspection of the structure before releasing final payment to the contractor. Final payment may be delayed until the facility has been fully tested in use. When the board of education, as owner, is satisfied that all contractual conditions have been met, it accepts the building and prepares it for occupancy.

Long before a building is occupied, large amounts of planning must be devoted to equipping the structure to serve educational goals. Orders for desks and chairs, typewriters and pencil sharpeners, erasers and chalk, and the other equipment and supplies must be made. Because of the magnitude of the order, much of the equipment required is also submitted for bidding to various suppliers. Occupying only follows after the building has been equipped and inspected by the appropriate governmental units. The inspection process may consist of local personnel, such as fire marshall, or state officials from a state school building office. In many places, formal permission from an appropriate political unit may be required prior to occupancy.

Role and Interaction Analysis

Compared with many of the tasks in which educators engage, the construction of a new school building often proves to be a very satisfying activity. When the new building is completed and occupied, the participants can point with pride to the end product of their labors. Many of their own responsibilities result in end products which are not physically available for viewing. So many teaching activities never reach the point of conclusion, and satisfying psychological closure is not enjoyed. However, each of the participants in the process of planning and constructing educational facilities must find satisfaction at various points in the process. Respective tasks end at various stages of the process, and perhaps only the superintendent is involved from the beginning to the end.

Although no two school buildings are built in exactly the same way because of differences in legal requirements and professional operating styles, some rather generally well-accepted roles have been established for planners (Table 17-1).

Although the success of the building venture will depend upon many things, the capacity of participants to communicate their

Table 17-1. Role Analysis by Major Tasks

Board of Education	Acts upon need.
	Employs architect.
	Authorizes bond referendum.
	Sells bonds (through agents).
	Solicits bids.
	Contracts for construction.
	Accepts building.
Superintendent	Foresees Need.
	Reports on need.
	Solicits educational specifications from professionals.
	Participates in joint planning conferences.
	Prepares progress reports for board.
	Recommends acceptance.
Business Manager	Secures equipment and supplies.
	Prepares financial reports for board.
Curriculum Coordinator and Professional Staff	Converts current and planned programs into educational specifications.
	Engages in joint planning with architect.
Architect	Participates in joint planning.
	Prepares preliminary sketches and construction specifications.
	Directs revision process.
	Recommends acceptance.
	Supervises construction.

ideas to others effectively is one of the most crucial. Throughout the planning process, some rather continuous interactions must take place. Among the more important are interactions illustrated in Figure 17-2, which indicates the kinds of interactions that impinge upon the success of the venture.

Problems and Issues

1. *How important is it for teachers to participate in school plant planning?* Teachers are not experts in school buildings. At no place in the typical teacher preparation program is consideration given to school architecture. It is only through experience that teachers come to know the capacity of a particular architectural feature to promote or to inhibit the learning process. Other members of the school system are not likely to have much more background and experience than the teacher. The board of education may or may not have built other buildings, and the superintendent of schools may or may not have had college training in school plant planning

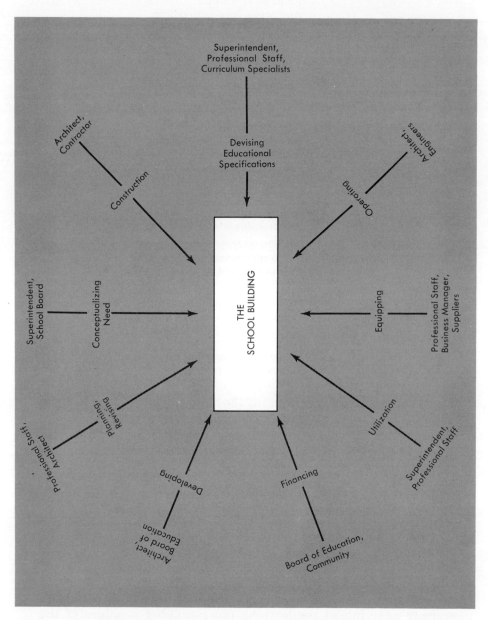

Figure 17-2. Major interactions in the building process.

or experience in the building process. The architect, on the other hand, has the needed expertise in the school plant planning process.

The life of a school building is quite long, usually longer than the tenure of any teacher likely to be housed in it. The teacher turnover rate also dictates that many, many persons will utilize the various areas of a school building from its inception to its destruction.

Boards of education and large school systems, in an effort to save tax dollars, often have reproduced a "good" building in many places throughout their district. The reproduction of a design saves much of the planning costs and often facilitates construction time. All of the above mitigate against teacher participation in the planning of a particular school facility. At what expense is such participation sacrificed?—What particular expertise do teachers bring to the planning process?—How can differences in teachers' methods be accommodated within a single building?—What shall determine the extent of participation?—How can effectiveness of participation be improved?

2. *What architectural elements contribute to making space "flexible"?* Changes in student populations often dictate that changes be made in the manner in which a school building is utilized. A classroom used for social studies in one year may be used for mathematics or English in subsequent years. Changes in the subjects which students elect to take at the secondary level are reflected in the number of rooms required for the various departmental areas. As the requirements change, so must the building utilization change. In addition to changes in room utilization occasioned by changes in the curricular use of the room, changes are also dictated by the instructor's method. Methods may change as a part of the normal evolutionary procedures or they may change as the result of changing faculty.

Those school systems having large evening programs may find that spaces adequate for instructing young people during the day may be inadequate for housing a different curricular program for adults during the evening hours. Somewhat the same problem may exist during summer months when the kinds of curricular offerings may vary from those of the academic year. As the concept of educational practice changes from hour to hour, from day to day, from year to year, how shall the different changes be accommodated?—On what basis can effective planning be made?—By whom?—What elements need to be variable?—Size?—Shape?—Accoustical treatment?—Heating and ventilating?—Special features?

3. *What kinds of educational space need to be located in close proximity to each other?* An elementary school building is often

composed of classrooms. special educational spaces, for art, music and physical education, a library or instructional resources area, and such noninstructional space as cafeterias and washrooms. Educational spaces within a secondary school include not only classrooms and libraries but laboratories for science, industrial arts, home economics, and so on, as well as other special spaces to house music, art, speech, journalism, and the like. Given the various kinds of spaces which are specifically designed to house educational activities at specific grade levels or for specific subject treatments, an almost infinite number of configurations is possible. When the building is completed, rooms will be adjacent to one another. On what basis shall the decision about the relationship of one educational space to another be made?—What is the relationship between various curricular areas and libraries?—How do "noisy" subjects relate to the quieter ones?—What various support functions should be considered in arranging educational spaces?—What impact does a "core curriculum," or team teaching, or individualized instruction have upon the relationship of one curricular space to another?—How might community use affect the arrangement of space?—What relationship might exist between educational and noneducational spaces?

Selected References

American Association of School Administrators. *Planning America's School Buildings*. Washington, D.C.: A.A.S.A., 1960.

Engelhardt, N. L., N. L. Engelhardt, Jr., and Stanton Leggett. *Planning Secondary School Buildings*. New York: Reinhold Publishing Corp., 1949.

Leu, Donald. *Planning Educational Facilities*. New York: Center for Applied Research in Education, 1965.

MacConnell, James. *Planning School Buildings*. Englewood Cliffs, N.J.: Prentice-Hall, Inc., 1957.

McQuade, Walter. *Schoolhouse*. New York: Simon and Shuster, 1958.

National Council on Schoolhouse Construction. *Guide for Planning School Plants*. East Lansing, Mich.: N.C.S.C. and Michigan State University, 1958.

Schools for the New Needs. F. W. Dodge Corporation, 1956.

Strevell, Wallace and Arvid Burke. *Administration of the School Building Program*. New York: McGraw-Hill Book Co., 1959.

Index